SOMERSET CRICKETERS 1919 – 1939

Also Available:
SOMERSET CRICKETERS 1882-1914

"Prepare to be surprised and enchanted at every turn of the page"
Vic Marks (Somerset & England)

"A monumental labour of love, this book transforms our knowledge
and understanding of the early years of Somerset CCC"
David Wood (Curator, Somerset Cricket Museum)

"There are gems ... to be found on every page.
This book is not just for Somerset aficionados but an
important addition to any cricket historian's library"
Roger Heavens (*The Cricket Statistician*)

"Pieces together a compelling story"
Somerset County Gazette

SOMERSET CRICKETERS 1919 – 1939

STEPHEN HILL & BARRY PHILLIPS

HALSGROVE

First published in Great Britain in 2017

Copyright © Stephen Hill 2017

British Library Cataloguing-in-Publication Data
A CIP record for this title is available from the British Library

ISBN 978 0 85704 306 1

HALSGROVE
Halsgrove House,
Ryelands Industrial Estate,
Bagley Road, Wellington, Somerset TA21 9PZ
Tel: 01823 653777   Fax: 01823 216796
email: sales@halsgrove.com

Part of the Halsgrove group of companies
Information on all Halsgrove titles is available at: www.halsgrove.com

Printed and bound by Parksons Graphics, India

Contents

Among the men who made their debut in the inter-war years, Somerset's England internationals Harold Gimblett (left) and Arthur Wellard (right) were arguably the greatest crowd-pleasers, with their fearless brand of cricket.

Foreword & Acknowledgements

I still recall the moment when I was introduced as a young boy to Somerset and England cricketer Harold Gimblett. As far as I'm concerned, he was a shy, elderly man with a kindly smile, shorter than you might have expected but with a tremendous pair of shoulders on him. I can't relate to any of those revelations about his having been a tortured soul, but only because I never saw that side of him. What I *do* recall very vividly is the moment he first shook my hand. Those hands seemed enormous. His right hand enveloped mine. I should have been more starstruck but my hero at the time was Brian Roe. Brian would have been the first to admit that, unlike Harold Gimblett, his place is in the margins of Somerset's cricketing folklore. It's of course only natural that schoolboys should be engrossed in the present with little thought of the future and no great appetite for the past. But that handshake stirred something. I went away and swotted up on Harold's exploits, which were of course prodigious. For a while I wanted to be Harold Gimblett when I batted on the village green. The handshake had proved a catalyst that introduced me to a whole new world. History helps us to understand the present. I used to be bewildered by the fact that the Championship had proved so elusive to Somerset. Only after immersing myself in the club's history did I understand why this should have been so. But as Raymond Robertson-Glasgow, a man who appears in this book, put it:

> In the long view, it is not the arithmetical performances of this or that player, not merely the times of success and failure that strike the historian of Somerset cricket. It is rather the spirit – the spirit which win or lose has always been a happy compound of humour and independence.

The men who appeared in *Somerset Cricketers 1882-1914* were a varied and interesting bunch. When we first embarked on this volume, my co-author Barry Phillips and I feared that the lives of the 124 who made their debuts between the two World Wars might prove less engrossing than those of their forbears. We were wrong. We got to 'meet' all manner of men. Somerset cricket has thrown up any number of remarkable, larger than life characters. We hope that when introduced to them you might feel that they have reached out in a metaphorical sense and shaken your hand, inviting you to explore further the history of this fascinating club. As with this book's companion volume, which included every first-class debutant prior to the First World War, we have included an illustrated biography of each player in order of their debut appearance.

Barry and I have once again been hugely dependent on the help of others. A project such as this is a communal effort involving a cast of hundreds. Many people have helped us in our quest to outline the lives of every inter-war cricketer. We'd like to thank the following in particular and offer our apologies if we've forgotten to name anyone owing to the sheer volume of those who've joined us on our journey:

Frances Allsop, Allison Barnes, Tom Bass, Simon Bennett, Antony Berry, Michael Bevington, Louise Brook, Mike Burnaby, Ray Burrough, Stephen Chalke, Martin Chapman, Judy Chetwood, Maurice Chidgey, Jo Conachie, Jackie Cook, Jean Cowley, Guinea Dodgson, Jason Dors, Bill Draper, James Draper, Richard Draper, Heather Dunn, Elizabeth Ennion-Smith, Ivor Ewens, Ted Ewens, Garry Falck, Neil Falck, Suzanne Foster, Stewart Gillies, Ian Golding, Robin Gomm, Kelly Gorry, Rev. Arthur Hack, Jenny Hartree, Rachel Hassall, Kathy Hatt, Peter Henderson, John Hill, Joshua Hill, Phil Hill, John Hobson, Clare Hopkins, Georgina Hughes, Dr Lucy Hughes, Ben Ingle, Richard Isbell, Sue Jenkins, Steve Jennings, Danielle Joyce, Natalie Kent, Frances Killick, Hertford King, Robin Knight, Dr Charles Knighton, David Lambden, Graham Law, Sue Leach, Ian Leonard, Margaret Lewis, Grainne Lenehan, Ann Lovell, Mike Lovell, Neil Lovell, Diana Lumsden, Ruth McCann, Trevor McCann, Roger Mann, Frances Menges, Frances Middlestorb, Richard Miller, Catherine Mortimer, Sibusiso Msawoni, Michael Nicholson, Shirley Oatway, Owen Parnell, Richard Pelham, Dr Tony Reeve, Ed Richardson, Michael Riorden, Hugh Rowdon, Neil Rowdon, Jerry Rudman, Clare Russell, Anna Sanders, David J. Smith, Frances South-combe, Peter Southcombe, Paul Stephens, Colin Strachan, Jennifer Thorp, Ron Tred-gett, David Trevis, Kaylee Tudball, Stuart Tudball, Jodie Walker, Keith Walmsley, Eleanor Ward, Ian MacDonald Watson, Robert MacDonald Watson, Tom Webb, Thea Wells-Cole, Caroline Whitlock, John Williamson, David Wood, Geoff Woodcock, Julia Woolcott, Peter Wynne-Thomas.

We also wish to acknowledge the institutions that many of the above-named repre-sent, including all the schools, university colleges, clubs and businesses that helped us. Some are accredited alongside images. In addition to these, we would also wish to thank: Bristol Record Office, British Library, Camden Registrar's Office, Frome Museum, Imperial War Museum, Petersfield Bookshop, Somerset Cricket Museum, Somerset Heritage Centre and Watchet Library.

Finally, thanks to Halsgrove Publishing for believing in the project and to our longsuffering wives – Kate and Wendy – for tolerating our immersion in the under-taking to the point of obsession.

STEPHEN HILL

1919

"... things turned out far better than even the most sanguine supporters of the club could have expected."

Wisden (1920)

Championship Position: 5= of 15

Prior to the First World War, Somerset cricket had limped along, sometimes threatened with collapse. The summer of 1892 apart, they had been mired in cricketing mediocrity, bursting bubbles and puncturing pride with the occasional giant-killing deed, stirred into their finest performances against the might of Surrey or Yorkshire. But first-class cricket had survived in the county. By 1914, they had been in the doldrums for a number of years and the future for the club and indeed for the country as a whole had appeared bleak.

Fourteen former Somerset players died as a result of the First World War. *Wisden* observed in its preview of the 1919 season that 'Somerset will take part in the Championship, but the immediate outlook is not very hopeful, as it may be a hard matter to get together a team of adequate strength'. As it happened Somerset would surprise everyone, themselves included.

Having begun the First World War with a deficit of more than £600, they were able to announce a bank balance of £93 by the start of the 1919 season. This remarkable turnaround resulted from the generosity of the many supporters who had agreed to continue paying their membership subscriptions despite there being no cricket to watch. Given Somerset's dire performances in the pre-war years, some may have regarded this as a merciful release.

Inevitably, there was a makeshift quality to the season. It was agreed that all matches would be two-day affairs, ending at 7.30 pm if necessary. Worcestershire felt unable to compete and Somerset settled for the minimum requirement of twelve fixtures. Matches were played, home and away, against six teams within reasonable geographical reach. As a result, the only strong county side Somerset were required to compete with were Surrey (who beat them home and away). The Championship position of 5= therefore flattered them, although, with an unbeaten run sandwiched between three defeats, the *Western Gazette* was able to state that 'this record reflects great credit on a plucky side rather than a great one'.

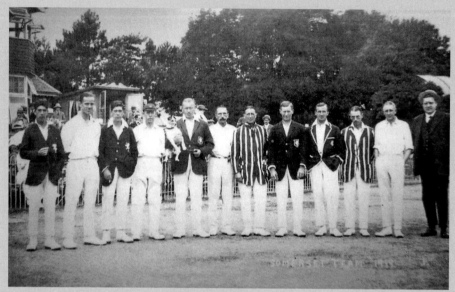

The Somerset XI who played Hampshire at Dean Park, Bournemouth, in 1919: the entire team had made their debuts prior to the First World War but their combined experience counted for little as they were bowled out cheaply in their second innings on a deteriorating wicket.

LEFT TO RIGHT: A.E.S. Rippon, J. Bridges, A. D. E. Rippon, H. Chidgey, E. S. M. Poyntz, E. Robson, J. Daniell, J. C. White, N. Hardy, J. C. W. MacBryan. L. C. Braund, G. S. McAulay (Scorer).

There had been some scrambling around at the outset to find a captain. Club secretary Reginald Brooks-King – a Taunton estate agent who had played Minor Counties cricket and had won an Olympic silver medal at archery – mooted the idea of Ernie Robson as captain. The notion of a professional leading a side that included amateurs had the traditionalists up in arms, and so Jack White stepped into the breach until the return of John Daniell.

In light of the neglect that pitches had suffered for four years and given the need for haste and risk-taking in engineering two-day results, it is unsurprising that the batsmen fared appallingly. It was left to the bowlers – Jack White in particular, supported by the dependable Ernie Robson – to carry the day.

In this most extraordinary of seasons, Somerset's first home fixture – against Sussex in May – became the most talked-about of matches. Somerset had eked out a first innings lead of one run. Sussex had edged past Somerset's second innings total by the same margin. The scores were tied with one Sussex wicket remaining. There was a pregnant pause. Sussex had already informed their opponents that H. J. Heygate, still suffering terribly from his war wounds, would take no further part in the game. And yet, there he was, emerging from the pavilion, dressed in his civvies (some reports suggest a blue lounge suit), hobbling towards the wicket. Progress was painful and slow. He was timed out and the umpire removed the stumps. The most controversial of ties. To be fair to Jack White, he offered to continue. In the best spirit of the game, his opposite number, H. L. Wilson, agreed to abide by the umpire's decision. None of which stopped the press from having a field day.

Among the season's debutants, Ulick Considine would prove a useful batsman and a brilliant fielder until a rugby injury on England duty hampered his mobility. Philip Foy – an excellent pace bowler – was only with the county fleetingly.

All in all, it was a satisfactory season. As Ron Roberts put it in *Sixty Years of Somerset Cricket*, 'Somerset were set on their feet again'.

228
Laurence Henry Key
16 May 1919 v. Surrey, Kennington Oval

The first newcomer to the side after the First World War and Somerset's 228th debutant, Laurence Key was born on 5 May 1895 in the city of Lincoln, the eldest child of a post office clerk, Henry Swinton Key, and his wife, Sarah. The family moved to Somerset when Henry was offered the role of Post Office Superintendent at Rowbarton, Taunton. Laurence was sent to Taunton School where he played cricket and football alongside the Marshall brothers, Leslie and Alan, both of whom played for Somerset on an occasional basis. Another recent member of the school team was Jack White, whose contribution to Somerset's fortunes was more significant. Like White, Key was a slow left-arm bowler who benefitted from the coaching skills of Somerset and England cricketer, Edwin 'Teddy' Tyler.

On leaving school Laurence worked as an articled clerk for A.C. Mole & Co., a firm of accountants at Billetfield, Taunton. He remained there until he was mobilised in March 1916, serving in France – first as a private then later as a lance corporal – with the 15th London Regiment. He was discharged at the end of 1918 suffering from the debilitating effects of trench fever.

On returning to civilian life he worked as an accountant for an auctioneer and became actively involved with Taunton CC, also playing eight times for Somerset between 1919 and 1922. Ever in the shadow of Jack White, he was only granted one over until his final match, at Leicestershire in 1922 when, in White's absence, he took 2 for 50. His batting average was 8.00 with a highest score of 30. In 1926 he was married at the Register Office in Wandsworth to Rose Mary Louise Crosley, a divorcee, born Budd, the daughter of a mining engineer. They had no children and their marriage would end in 1940 with Key claiming that he had just discovered that Rose had been deemed guilty of desertion at the time of her divorce from her first husband, in South Africa. By early 1939 Laurence had separated from Rose and moved into his parents' home in Elm Grove, Taunton. He would continue to live there after his mother and father had died.

Although still referring to himself as an accountant and auctioneer, he had by this time taken ownership of a tobacconist's shop on Bridge Street, Taunton, a short walk from his home. Judging by local newspaper reports, he suffered regular break-ins that must have tried his patience and that of his insurers. He had won a national prize for his window display in 1938, being praised by the local newspaper as a 'clever window dresser' in a week when news was clearly in short supply. Laurence was married for a second time in 1945. His new bride was Jessie Florence Brant, a civil servant and a spinster in her late forties.

In his spare time, he delivered humorous monologues and was a member of the Magic Circle, performing regularly at children's parties. One newspaper report informs us that 'Mr Laurence Key, in his usual clever and entertaining way, interested the children in his mystery tricks, and these were much enjoyed'. A pity, then, that, Taunton's popular prestidigitator had been unable to deploy any sleight of hand to help him rise above mundane predictability in his eight matches for Somerset. Amateurs such as Laurence Key must sometimes have wondered about the appeal of turning out for a three-day Championship game, knowing that their involvement with bat and ball would be limited. Perhaps he had spent those hours in the field mulling over his humorous monologues and used his time in the pavilion honing his skills as a magician. There is certainly evidence for the latter. A report in the *Taunton Courier* by H. J. Channon informs us

Magician L. H. Key, with and without spectacles: now you see them, now you don't.

that 'we were playing for Somerset Club and Ground. In the dressing room Laurence was entertaining us with some of his conjuring tricks, with Sam Woods looking on. Sam's willpower to beat everybody at everything was terrific. He turned to Laurence and said that he had a trick up his sleeve that would mystify the best of conjurors.' The report then goes on to explain that Somerset legend Sam Woods took off his coat and 'proceeded to rub with his mighty hands a spot on the wall', informing the onlookers that the friction would enable him to suspend the coat 'and behold, it was so'. Something approaching a miracle. There had been plenty of near-miracles during Sam's days as a player. The same could not be claimed for Laurence Key.

In later life he ran the Pyrland Stores in Cheddon Fitzpaine, Taunton. He died in Taunton on 18 April 1971 at the age of seventy-five. His second wife, Jessie, died the following year.

229
Wilfrid Noel Kempe
9 July 1919 v. Derbyshire, Derby

Wilfrid Noel Kempe

Known as Noel, he was the son of Wilfrid John Kempe, the proprietor of a school at Long Ashton, near Bristol. Wilfrid John had taken over the running of the school from his father and at one point the institution housed upwards of eighty boarders, producing a number of fine cricketers, including two Grace brothers, E.M and Fred.

Noel Kempe was born in Long Ashton on 10 October 1887. He had some sporting pedigree, in that his mother, Ellen North (née Richardson) was the daughter of the Rev. John Richardson, who had rowed in the 1843 and 1845 Varsity Boat Races, the latter being the first to be staged from Putney to Mortlake. One of Ellen's brothers – hence Noel's uncle – was the cricketer Alfred Graham Richardson, who played for Somerset in 1895 and also represented Gloucestershire.

Educated at The King's School, Canterbury, he played for three years in the cricket XI from 1905 to 1907 inclusive, keeping wicket and proving a competent batsman, with the school magazine, *The Cantuarian*, noting that 'his strokes are limited, [but] he is hard to get out as he plays very straight'. Noel won a Parker Exhibition to Corpus

W. N. Kempe at The King's School, Canterbury.

Christi, Cambridge. The college newsletter, *The Benedict*, makes jocular reference to his efforts on behalf the Corpus Christi football team, noting that 'when roused [he] plays with much dash and spirit; but otherwise he is inclined to be too ladylike – though we hear he is a misogynist. His tackling is good and he dribbles well.' His captaincy of the cricket XI is praised – 'a good captain with an encouraging word at the right moment' – and he was also President of the 'Gravediggers' Dramatic Society. It is to be hoped that his capacity for gentle encouragement rather than his misogyny or a propensity for dressing up and holding forth was what drew him to a career in the Church of England.

After graduating in 1910, he trained at the Cuddesdon Theological School in Oxfordshire and was ordained in 1912 by the Bishop of Southwell. Working as a curate at St James's church in Derby, he was a competent enough wicket-keeper to play for the Derbyshire Second XI in 1913. During the

First World War he acted as a temporary army chaplain, arriving in France in May 1915 and being awarded a 1914-1915 Star. He was then appointed to St Andrew's in Derby in 1918. While there he played as a wicket-keeper for Somerset in the away game at Derby that Somerset won at a canter. Batting at number eleven in the first innings, he made 9. With Somerset needing only two runs to win the game, Noel opened in the second innings, perhaps on the basis that he was already padded up, but did not face a ball. This was his only appearance, making him one in a long list of Somerset's one-match wonders. He is also one of eighteen clergymen to have played first-class cricket for the county.

Rev. Noel Kempe.

In 1922 he was appointed Chaplain of the Nautical School at Portishead, retaining the position for two years before returning to a more traditional role as Rector of Flax Bourton, not far from his birthplace. He played during the mid-1920s both for the Somerset Clergy and for the Somerset Stragglers side, for whom background was generally considered as important as ability. He remained an enthusiastic though not hugely successful club cricketer until the Second World War.

In 1932 he became the vicar of Yatton, where he remained for thirteen years. In 1936 he was accorded the status of Prebendary and was made a sub-deacon in Wells Cathedral. Then in 1945 he was appointed Rural Dean of Castle Cary. Finally he became Rector of Wraxall and Failand, to the west of Bristol, combining these duties with the role of Rural Dean of Portishead.

Noel Kempe was never married. He serves as an archetype of a well-connected clergyman who lived a comfortable life of quiet devotion, respected by his parishioners and indulging his passion for sport in his leisure time. He died on 17 October 1958 at Frenchay Hospital, to the north of Bristol, at the age of seventy-one.

230
Arthur Thomas Sanders
18 July 1919 v. Essex, Leyton

A. J. Sanders

Arthur Sanders was born on 21 December 1900 in Pimlico, Westminster. His father, Sir Robert Arthur Sanders was MP for Bridgwater and later Wells and was subsequently made a peer, becoming the 1st Baron Bayford in 1929. Arthur was educated

A. T. Sanders at Harrow School.

Arthur Sanders – whose military and first-class cricket careers were brief and wretched.

at Harrow for the final four years of his schooling and was the leading batsman in his final year, albeit with an average of 21.60 in a decidedly mediocre Harrow XI. His headmaster, Lionel Ford, wrote at the time that Arthur was 'full of brains and determination - good athlete, well known with the Blackmore Vale and the Devon & Somerset [Hunts]. A quite exceptional boy who was hard and apt to hit out rather wildly but under strong personal influence has now got himself well in hand'.

Arthur had not in fact sorted himself out in the way his headmaster had hoped or believed. On leaving Harrow he was initially rejected entry to Sandhurst on the basis of a hernia but after a number of conflicting doctors' reports he was admitted in January 1919. Reading between the lines, Sandhurst possibly had serious doubts about his suitability as officer material but paternal influence had won the day.

He graduated in July 1920 as a second lieutenant in the 3rd Battalion of the Grenadier Guards. A mere four months later, while stationed in the Tower of London, tragedy struck. On 22 November 1920, Arthur's batman – Guardsman Potter – entered the room at 7.00 am to rouse him ahead of the scheduled parade and found him lying on his bed with a coat over his face. At 8.10 am Potter went back again as Sanders had not emerged: he found him unconscious in his blood-soaked pyjamas with a revolver lying on the floor. Arthur Sanders was rushed to the London Hospital and then to the nearby Millbank Hospital for Officers, where he died later in the day. He had taken his own life at the age of only nineteen.

At the inquest, Sir Robert confirmed that, having enjoyed two days' hunting leave, his son had dined with him the preceding night and had confessed to a gambling debt of £200. Sir Robert had reiterated that Arthur's annual allowance was £500 (with the implication that he had no intention of increasing it to feed his son's gambling addiction), that he should pay what he could to the bookmaker and agree to pay the balance in instalments, coming to his father if he got into any trouble. Like many a gambler, Arthur had seriously understated the extent of his debt. It became apparent at the inquest that the £200 (which was in truth £250) was merely the amount due on 23 November of that year. He owed a total of £700 to moneylenders and had further betting debts of £900. In short, he was in an unholy mess. The coroner noted that 'young men often do foolish things' and that Arthur 'kept his trouble to himself like most Englishmen'. He also opined that Arthur had taken his life because of 'not wanting to distress his parents'. Out of the mouths of coroners sometimes spring the most extraordinarily crass proclamations. The verdict was one of suicide whilst of unsound mind. This ran counter to the original regimental report, which speculated, perhaps with a view to parental sensibilities, that the death may have resulted from an accident.

The preceding summer, Arthur Sanders had played only one game for Somerset and, batting at number nine in the county's only innings, had not troubled the scorers. His first-class career was thus as shortlived and wretched as his military one.

231
Stanley George Ulick Considine
8 August 1919 v. Hampshire, Weston-super-Mare

Known as Ulick, his parents resided in Bilaspur in the Bihar Province, India, at the time of his birth on 11 August 1901. His father, William, was at the time an 'emigration agent'. On subsequent censuses, Ulick's place of birth is given as Darjeeling and he was certainly baptised there on 28 August, a little over a fortnight after his birth.

Ulick was brought up in Bath. Educated at Blundell's School in Devon, he was still a schoolboy of seventeen when he first played rugby for Bath in 1918. His brother Harold also played for the team. Appearing as a wing three-quarter or fly-half, he represented Somerset at rugby from 1919. Qualifying via his paternal line, he was a triallist for Ireland at Dublin in 1921, but having failed to be selected for the Irish, he was later able to represent England at the game. After a number of trials for the latter, he was finally chosen for the game against France in Paris on 13 April 1925. Appearing at left-wing, he suffered a major knee injury but was obliged to play on, unaware of just how serious the problem was. Indeed, his England debut would prove to be his final appearance as a rugby player and thereafter, when taking part in the

S. G. U. Considine – his England rugby career was cut short by injury.

more gentle sport of cricket, he wore specially designed knee strapping. Later the same year, on 5 August 1925, he was married to Gwladys Ethel James. Although the wedding of the rugby international made the front page news in the local press, the ceremony had remained a secret kept from most friends, colleagues and teammates. The couple had both wanted a studiedly quiet ceremony.

An amateur sportsman, Ulick practiced as a solicitor in Queen's Square, Bath. He remained a colourful and well-known member of Bath society and played in a total of eighty-nine first-class fixtures for Somerset, scoring nearly 3,000 runs as a right-handed batsman. *The Cricketer* informs us that 'his style is ungainly and he has a bad habit of stabbing at the off ball and of getting lbw' but concedes that he showed 'rare grit and no little skill'. He completed one century and sixteen half-centuries and could boast a respectable average of 21.33. In addition, he was reportedly an 'excellent cover point' who took forty-two catches, though his movements were of course more restricted after his injury.

During the Second World War he became a squadron leader in the RAF, but when he returned to civilian life his health went into serious decline. In short, he drank far too heavily for his own good. A GP, Dr Ernest James Boschi, had moved from Bruton with his wife and two children to join a practice on Pulteney Street in Bath in 1935. Gwladys Considine and Ernest Boschi would embark on an affair and by December 1947, they were both divorced from their partners. They were married at the Register Office in Bakewell. It appears that the son of Ulick and Gwladys, named John, continued to live with his mother.

Ulick Considine died less than three years later on 31 August 1950, at the age of forty-nine. Initial reports suggested that he had died as a result of a heart attack and had been found beside his bed. At his subsequent inquest, it became apparent that he had been found outside his flat in his pyjamas, having choked on his own vomit. The inquest recorded that he had 'died from shock following ingestion of gastric contents into the air passage following a rupture of a varicose vein in the top of the stomach following fatty degeneration of the liver due to alcoholism'. He was described by his doctor as an alcoholic who drank heavily over a period of years. It was also revealed that he had previously suffered a nervous breakdown. In a surprising twist – for motives that are unknown and could be anything from spite to generosity of spirit – he left his remaining estate to Rosemary Parker Boschi, former wife of Dr Ernest Boschi.

Ulick Considine had been a naturally gifted sportsman who might have achieved greater glories, but for a life-changing injury on his debut as an England rugby international. His decline and the nature of his death were anything but glorious.

232
Arthur Holland Dyer Gibbs
8 August 1919 v. Hampshire, Weston-super-Mare

Known as Holland Gibbs, he was involved – along with the bowler Jim Bridges – in what remained for many years a tenth-wicket partnership record of 143 against Essex at Weston-super-Mare in 1919. In his autobiography, Somerset stalwart Bill Andrews recounts that a sizeable number of the runs came from shots that had evaded the slips, that many catches were dropped and that the bowler to suffer most was Johnny Douglas who 'could stand it no longer when yet again the ball flew agonisingly near the slips who remained like statues in a crouching position as the ball went on its way to the boundary. He dashed down, sliced through the stationary slips and said: 'I'll fetch the bloody thing myself.'' It should be noted, however, that Bill Andrews, an entertaining raconteur, was not averse to embellishment.

Holland Gibbs was born on 15 April 1894 in Weston-super-Mare, the son of Arthur May Gibbs, a chartered accountant, and Amy (née

A. H. D. Gibbs – enjoyed a remarkable tenth-wicket stand with Jim Bridges.

Dyer). A talented club cricketer who kept wicket for Weston-super-Mare, he also generally batted at number three. When called up by Somerset, however, he batted as a tail-ender. Over the course of three matches in 1919 and 1920 he averaged 13.20 with the bat and effected six dismissals. In his celebrated record tenth-wicket stand, we are told – by sources more reliable than Bill Andrews – that the first fifty runs came in forty minutes and then, with the two batsmen throwing caution to the wind, the next fifty were racked up in eight minutes. Their efforts earned them both promotion up the order in the second innings, although the match ended in a tame draw.

As for his life beyond cricket, on leaving school, Holland became a draper's assistant working in Weston-super-Mare. By the time of his marriage in 1921 to Gladys Ada (née Workman), the daughter of an insurance broker from Cheltenham, he had established a career as a commercial salesman. A later record in the 1939 census confirms that Holland was still working as a travelling salesman for a shirt and tie manufacturer at the outbreak of the Second World War.

He died at the age of sixty-nine on 29 October 1963 at Uphill, Weston-super-Mare. He was survived by Gladys and their two sons.

233
Arthur Kenneth Gibson
29 August 1919 v. Australian Imperial Forces, Taunton

Arthur Gibson was born in Kensington on 19 May 1889. His father, George Robert Gibson, was a Glasgow-born gentleman farmer and his mother, Kate, a solicitor's daughter from Camberwell. After his early schooling at The Grange in Eastbourne, Arthur went on to the Britannia Royal Naval College in Dartmouth. He began his Royal Navy career as a midshipman on HMS *Bulwark*, becoming a sub-lieutenant in 1909 and a lieutenant (serving on HMS *Cumberland*) in October 1911. During the First World War he served as captain on a number of vessels. These included the destroyer HMS *Crane* (in 1915), the reconditioned torpedo boat *TB 1* in 1916, followed in quick succession by HMS *Acheron* and HMS *Rattlesnake*. In December 1918 he took control for a brief period of the destroyer HMS *Plover*.

In October 1918, he was married to Beatrice Mary Mason, a divorcee born Wynniatt. Arthur had previously been named as a co-respondent in Beatrice's divorce. Despite the fact that he and Beatrice were living together in Newhaven at the time of the divorce hearing, Arthur had the brass neck to deny the accusations. Unsurprisingly, the court found in favour of the husband, Hugh Mason. Beatrice and Arthur in fact had a son, born in 1917 before they were married, although he later adopted the name of Gibson.

As for his cricketing career, he appeared for The Navy on occasions between 1914 and 1924 and was 'granted leave from 10-27 July 1919 in order to represent HM Navy in various cricket matches'. His leave was clearly extended, given that he played for the combined Army and Navy XI against the Demobilised Officers on 26 August 1919 and immediately afterwards made his only appearance for Somerset, against the Australian Imperial Forces. Arthur Gibson's connection with Somerset was tenuous but there had been an agreement prior to the 1919 season that the normal rules of qualification would be suspended for a year for members of the military, many of whom were stationed away from their home county.

In a low-scoring game in which Somerset were easily beaten, Arthur top-scored with 22 in the first innings and was out for 5 in the second. The *Western Daily Press* gives an account of his performance, reporting that 'besides showing smartness in the field, his first innings showed him to be a batsman. His style induces confidence, and whilst he displayed a sound defence when occasion demanded, he can be aggressive and hits hard and true. He selects the right

A. K. Gibson of the Royal Navy – an officer but not always a gentleman.

ball to hit, and knows where to place it, but it was his cutting and driving that one noticed particularly.' In short, in difficult batting conditions he had demonstrated that he was by no means out of his depth and had acquitted himself well.

Arthur Gibson trained as a Physical Education instructor shortly thereafter and although he would enjoy a spell as commander of HMS *Heliotrope*, he invested much of his time between 1928 and 1938 in organising boxing tournaments for the forces and acting as a referee during bouts.

Early in 1935 local papers in Portsmouth reported that he had caused mayhem in a scene reminiscent of Laurel and Hardy when he knocked over a window cleaner who was pushing his cart, which shed its ladder, hitting a motorcyclist who careered into a cyclist, who in turn knocked over another cyclist. Meanwhile the motorcycle struck a pedestrian. More prosaically, Arthur had simply ground to a halt on impact with another car. The advent of mobile phones came almost eighty years too late to capture the scene of carnage. Like the upstanding officer he was, Arthur informed the police constable that: 'It was careless driving on my part and you can report it as such.' He was fined £5 and banned from driving for a month. Perhaps Arthur's mind had been elsewhere. He was placed on the retired list – at his own request – on his forty-sixth birthday that same year, listed as a commander with the rank of captain. The decision was sparked by an affair during what one might term a mid-life crisis.

In 1936, history repeated itself when another cuckolded husband named Hugh cited Arthur as a co-respondent in divorce proceedings on the not unreasonable grounds that he was living with the man's wife. In this case, Emily Bamford, a young woman little more than half Arthur's age, the wife of Hugh Bamford, was living with him in Liverpool. Again Arthur denied any wrongdoing but again no one believed him. And once more, his new partner was soon carrying his child. The recently retired officer was proving himself not much of a gentleman. Their joy proved all too fleeting when Emily died in April 1938, her death certificate indicating that she had died in the aftermath of a miscarriage or termination. Arthur, present at the death, fabricated the details on the certificate, claiming that Emily was his wife and that she was named Gibson. The entries were later corrected by the registrar. Yet again, Arthur had demonstrated an arrogant belief that he was above the law. His wife, Beatrice, had of course by then lost patience with him and left him to his own devices during the remainder of his retirement.

He died of a coronary thrombosis at the age of sixty on 28 January 1950 at the Royal Infirmary in Edinburgh.

234
Philip Arnold Foy
29 August 1919 v. Australian Imperial Forces, Taunton

Philip Foy was born in Axbridge on 16 October 1891 although his acquaintance with the small Somerset market town proved shortlived. His father, Arnold, spent much of Philip's childhood away in Brazil, working as a telegraph superintendent. In 1897, having enjoyed some time in Brazil, Philip and his two siblings were brought back to England by their mother. Philip was sent to be a boarder at Hadleigh House School in Littlehampton, Sussex, before going on to Bedford Grammar School for his secondary education. From there he went to the University of London. Having qualified as a civil engineer, he would return to Brazil before living and working for most of his adult life in Argentina, having clearly developed a taste for life in South America.

Philip Arnold Foy.

An all-rounder who batted right-handed and bowled at fast-medium pace, he played as a young man for Bedfordshire in Minor Counties cricket but by 1912 he was, as the *Bedfordshire Times* states, 'doing well in the Argentine'. The reporter was in fact referring to his cricketing exploits. *The Cricketer* furnishes us with more details, confirming that in the MCC tour of Argentina in 1912, led by Lord Hawke, Foy took 39 wickets for Argentina at 14 apiece and that he also dismissed the great Archie MacLaren for a pair in one match.

Philip returned to Europe and served with distinction in the Royal Engineers during the First World War. After enlisting as a second lieutenant in November 1914, he rose to the rank of captain in the 42nd Division of the Signals Corps of the Royal Engineers by the time of his demobilisation in February 1919. He was mentioned three times in despatches and awarded the military cross in 1917 for conspicuous gallantry and devotion to duty while a second lieutenant (and acting captain). He had taken command of divisional duties 'at a time when they were in a very precarious state owing to exceptionally heavy hostile shelling', though it is hard to imagine shelling being anything other than hostile. For a fortnight he maintained communications, leading by example and supervising the work of his men while the bombardment continued.

In 1918 he had been elected to the Institute of Civil Engineers and he would reside for a while in England. Although his debut in 1919 was underwhelming, with the *Western Daily Press* reporting that he 'did not do anything special' but that 'his fielding was sound', he went on to make some valuable contributions for the county of his birth, with three five-wicket hauls that included an impressive 5 for 37 versus

Philip Foy – 'the county wished he could have played more often'.

Warwickshire and a career-best of 6 for 68. In 1920 he took 31 wickets and over the course of his brief and fragmentary career he bagged 47 victims for Somerset at 21.59. A highest score of 72 confirms that he was also a capable batsman. As David Foot observes in *Sunshine, Cider and Sixes*, 'the county wished he could have played more often'.

Thereafter, Philip Foy made Buenos Aires his home, working as a civil engineer, primarily in the construction and maintenance of railways on behalf of the Buenos Aires Southern Railway Company, certainly for some of the time and possibly throughout his working life. He continued to play cricket, captaining the Southern Suburbs team. He represented his adoptive country on a number of occasions until 1930 and was active thereafter on the organisational front. The *Buenos Aires Herald* notes in connection with Sir Theodore Brinckman's tour of 1938 that it was Philip Foy 'on whom has fallen the brunt of the work'. He appears never to have been married, travelling alone on any trips to England, including his visit in 1930, on the death of his mother.

Philip Foy died at the age of sixty-five on 12 February 1957 in Adrogué, Buenos Aires Province, Argentina.

1920

"A record … of seven wins as against ten defeats is nothing to boast about … [although] several times when beaten they only went down after a hard fight."

The Cricketer

Championship Position: 10 of 16

There was a welcome return to three-day fixtures. Once again the bowlers led the way in a number of low-scoring and rain-affected matches. Jack White was the principal wicket taker, assisted by Jim Bridges. Ernie Robson and Philip Foy each made useful contributions with the ball. *The Cricketer* notes that 'one heard laments of the number of catches dropped'. With more assistance from the fielders, the bowlers might perhaps have wrapped up more games.

It was unfortunate that Randall Johnson should have broken a bone in his wrist while batting for Gentlemen versus Players in June. He and Dar Lyon had been the leading batsmen in a poor bunch. According to *The Cricketer*, the Somerset batting 'seldom rose above a respectable mediocrity'. During a match against Sussex, Dudley Rippon went into meltdown, still suffering from the effects of his war experiences. Twin brother Sydney got his head down and made a century. Dudley never played first-class cricket again. Among the debutants, Dar Lyon, a batsman and sometime wicket-keeper, would make a lasting impression and Raymond Robertson-Glasgow was an important member of the bowling attack, although his greatest legacy would be his literary output.

This was to be the last season in which Len Braund appeared. He had played twenty-three times for England and in his prime was regarded by many as the world's finest all-rounder. He completed the double each year between 1901 and 1903, amassing nearly 4,500 runs and taking 426 wickets over the three seasons. In addition, he was an outstanding close fielder.

The appointment of Sam Woods as the club's new Secretary was an attempt to offer employment to the unemployable. He was given a salary and expenses of £240 per annum. With a bat or a ball in his hand, Sam Woods had been an inspiration: less so with a pen and paper at his disposal. His shambolic though well-intentioned efforts would result in a precipitous fall in membership.

With more than 15,000 first-class runs and over a 1,000 wickets, Sam Woods had been a fine all-rounder and occasional match-winner in his playing days. Awarded England caps both at cricket and rugby, he also played cricket for Australia and captained Somerset for thirteen seasons. On the pitch he was inspirational and possessed of an indomitable spirit. He was, however, unemployable. Unable to settle at any job for long, he led a chaotic life. The decision to offer him the role of Secretary was an act of gratitude-cum-charity that was doomed to failure.

235
John Stanton Fleming Morrison
29 May 1920 v. Cambridge University, Cambridge

[signature: John Morrison]

One of those rare individuals who excelled at everything he turned his hand to, John Morrison was born in West Jesmond, Newcastle-upon-Tyne, on 17 April 1892, the first of two sons of John Fleming Morrison who had begun his career as a solicitor's clerk and had married Florence Emma (née Stanton), a solicitor's daughter. Sadly, he died when John Jnr was only four years old. Florence would remarry in 1900. A supremely gifted sportsman, John was sent to Charterhouse before going on to Trinity College, Cambridge. He was captain of the school First XI and headed the averages in his final year with four centuries that led to an invitation to play for the Public Schools XI. He is described as 'a punishing batsman who excelled especially in driving'. At Cambridge he won blues at golf, football and cricket, scoring two brilliant double-centuries in 1914 and returning to captain the university team in 1919. He played football for Corinthians, Sunderland and England and would possibly have been invited to play cricket for England, had he opted to commit more time to the game. He was, however, one of those amateurs who needed to combine his leisure pursuits with a business career.

During the First World War he served initially with the Royal Naval Air Service and then with the Royal Flying Corps. He was mentioned in despatches and awarded a DFC with bar. He and fellow Old Carthusian Raymond Robertson-Glasgow were both persuaded to play for Somerset (on the basis that no other first-class county had a claim on their services) although John Morrison would only appear once for the county. Both in *46 Not Out* and in *Cricket Prints*, Robertson-Glasgow's admiration bordering on adulation for the older man is apparent. Summarising John's career, he notes of his time at school that 'John Morrison kept wicket. His athletic deeds at soccer, cricket, and golf were current tradition when I was a small boy at Charterhouse. He was the inventor of the water-proof golf skirt as worn by himself, and of a unique implement for sucking up balls without stooping. A great character, John Morrison, and for years one of the shrewdest foursome players in the game [of golf].'

John Morrison's game for Somerset yielded 65 runs in

J. S. F. Morrison – a precociously talented sportsman.

John Morrison became a successful golf course designer.

two innings. Although he would go on to make further appearances in matches deemed first-class, his only other county games would be for his native Northumberland. He was more interested in the game of golf, winning the Belgian Amateur Golf Championship in 1929. He later committed his knowledge to print, editing the book *Around Golf*, published in 1939.

He excelled both at cricket and football.

As for his career, he joined the world-renowned golf course architects, Harry Colt and Hugh Alison (the latter an occasional Somerset cricketer prior to the First World War), becoming a partner in the firm in 1928. He was married in 1938 to Gwendoline Mary Cradock-Hartopp, with whom he had a daughter, Elizabeth Mary, born in Totnes, Devon.

With fellow members of the Royal Flying Corps – pictured (left to right) are C. E. Brisley, B. Travers, W. H. Greer and J. S. F. Morrison: the popular playwright Ben Travers later settled in Somerset, becoming a Vice-President of Somerset CCC.

During the Second World War, he served as a Group Captain in the RAF and is reputedly one of the first pilots to have landed an aeroplane on an aircraft carrier.

John Morrison died in Farnham, Surrey, on 28 January 1961 at the age of sixty-eight, able to look back on an extraordinarily full and fulfilled life.

236
John Alfred Stewart Jackson
29 May 1920 v. Cambridge University, Cambridge

John Alfred Stewart Jackson

Often referred to as 'J. A. S.', John Jackson was a man of boundless energy and ideas. A legend in his lifetime in Anglo-Chilean circles, he has left a lasting legacy in the college he founded, now regarded as one of the leading schools in the world.

The son of Alfred Louis Stewart Jackson, a stockbroker based in Chile, John was born in Valparaiso on 27 Dec 1898, when this was the main centre for the English community in Chile. Over time, the centre of gravity for British ex-pats shifted to Santiago. This was cemented when the Chamber of Commerce moved its offices from Valparaiso to Santiago in 1932. John Jackson had anticipated that change and had moved to Santiago.

He had been sent over to England as a boy to be educated at Cheltenham College, his father's alma mater. A boarder there from 1912 until 1917, he played for two years in the cricket XI, captaining them in his final year and also playing for the rugby XV and winning the racquets pairs in 1917. He attended Sandhurst and was offered a commission with the Rifle Brigade as a second lieutenant in 1918, immediately leaving for France, where he was wounded in action. The following year he was promoted to the rank of lieutenant but he resigned his commission in 1920 ahead of going up to Jesus College, Cambridge, where he remained for only two terms. His schooling in a neighbouring county was perhaps all that was needed for Somerset's captain John Daniell to welcome him into the fold. John Jackson played fourteen times for his adoptive county in 1920, averaging 23.00 and hitting one century. He was also selected to play for Cambridge University but failed to gain a blue. Later he played seven times for Chile and was captain of the side on

J. A. S. Jackson at Cheltenham College in 1916.

John Jackson – cricketer and headmaster.

their tour of Argentina in 1924/5. His brother, A. L. S. Jackson Jnr, played both for Chile and for Argentina.

On returning to Chile in 1922, John settled into the world of business before embarking on a change of direction. In 1928 he founded Grange School in Santiago, initially with twelve boarders. His plan was to replicate his own public school upbringing, stating that 'we want to form young people who will be useful to the country and are trustworthy'. Elsewhere he confirms that his key founding principles were to instil 'fair play', a 'spirit of service' and to make each boy an 'all-rounder'.

John Jackson clearly believed in setting a fine example to his pupils. One extant photograph shows him completing a steeplechase in front of the assembled pupils: a case of 'do as I do' not 'do as I say'. His methods worked. The school remains a thriving enterprise, still adhering to the values he espoused.

In 1935 he returned to England to be married to Marion Jean Fanny Richard Kirkpatrick, the daughter of William Kirkpatrick, the MP for Preston who had business interests in South America. The couple had met in Chile. He was thirty-six and she twenty-four.

Awarded an OBE in 1947 for his services to education, he was also instrumental in setting up a fire service for the English community in Santiago, although he died shortly before his plan had come to fruition. In recognition of his efforts, the 14th Fire Company of Santiago became known as *The British and Commonwealth Fire Rescue Company J. A. S. Jackson*. He had left his imprint on the Chilean city with two tangible testaments to his vision and drive.

John Jackson died on 13 March 1958 in Santiago, Chile, at the age of fifty-nine.

237
Malcolm Douglas Lyon
29 May 1920 v. Cambridge University, Cambridge

Raymond Robertson-Glasgow was in no doubt that Dar, as he was known, should have represented England, though 'Crusoe' admits that Lyon's 'wisecracks played sharply round Marylebone'. His irreverent humour and qualities as a 'wind-up artist' are evident in his short, easily digested and occasionally provocative book *Cricket* in which, for example, he lists sports in order of difficulty to master, with cricket at the top of the pile and lawn tennis a lowly thirteenth, behind ludo and spillikins. As it happens, he was a superb tennis player. As well as his cricket manual, he also wrote a novel entitled *A Village Match & After*. With wags such as Dar Lyon and Crusoe in tow, the team was able to laugh in the face of adversity.

Dar Lyon, whose 'wisecracks played sharply round Marylebone'.

Born in Caterham Valley, Surrey, on 22 April 1898, he was the son of Jeremiah Lyon, a financial adventurer who made a fortune in the rubber industry but was later declared a bankrupt after two expensive divorce settlements, a stock market collapse, a failed business venture named Wireless Music Ltd and overly generous donations to the Irish League of Nations Society (set up as an attempt to avert the First World War). He finally overreached himself with the purchase of Sudbourne Hall in Suffolk, which proved too great a drain on resources. Jeremiah Lyon could have added to his woes the cost of educating Dar at Rugby School.

J. L. Guise of Middlesex, batting in 1929 at Lord's: Dar Lyon is the wicket-keeper, with E. F. Longrigg at slip and R. A. Ingle fielding on the leg side.

M. D. Lyon – 'among the best batsmen who never gained a cap for England'.

Dar served as a second lieutenant in the Royal Field Artillery during the First World War and was wounded in action. After going up to Trinity College, Cambridge, he won blues as a wicket-keeper batsman. He was also president of the Footlights group, revealing his irreverent side. Able to display his talents as an accomplished piano-player who could adopt a multiplicity of styles, he also composed humorous songs.

Dar and his brother, Bev, were both fine cricketers and it is said that their father, Jeremiah, was based in Bristol when John Daniell persuaded him to toss a coin and decide which son should play for Gloucestershire and which for Somerset. Perhaps Jeremiah was aware that his sons would benefit from playing for different counties. David Foot describes their rivalry as 'single-minded ... when the brothers were locked in combat'. Where Bev won renown as an innovative captain, Dar was always regarded as something of a rebel. His ability remained unquestioned. The *Bath Chronicle* of 1920 describes him as 'the most promising young batsman who has played for Somerset since P. R. Johnson and Lionel Palairet made their debuts'. The excitement was heightened by Dar's century on his Championship debut. This would prove to be one of fourteen first-class centuries (including two double-centuries), twelve of them for Somerset. In 123 matches for the county he would average 30.98 and he would often share wicket-keeping duties, though Robertson-Glasgow states that 'Lyon's wicket-keeping varied from the brilliant to the blandly inattentive'. He writes elsewhere that 'he was a powerful man, over six feet in height ... a supreme artist, revelling in his triumphs and laughing at his failures'.

He worked in the legal profession, becoming a barrister and making a name for himself when he defended John Robinson in an infamous 'trunk murder case' that dominated headlines for a while in 1927. Robinson had attempted to dispose of the dismembered body of his victim – Mini Bonati – by leaving it in a trunk at Charing

Cross Station. Dar's defence failed to convince the jury and Robinson was sentenced to death by hanging.

Dar's personal life was at times a tangled web. He caused great stirrings and mutterings among the Somerset committee when he conducted an affair with Helen Alice Earle, the wife of teammate Guy Earle, a popular and affable Old Harrovian. It should be added that, judging by the correspondence around the time of the divorce, Earle seemed rather more relaxed about the episode than some members of the Somerset committee. In 1928, Dar and Helen were married, although they would in time divorce.

In 1929, he stood as a Liberal MP for Bury St Edmunds but failed to be elected. Never a man to be pigeon-holed, he scripted a film entitled *Ashes* which was enjoyed by the public but caused consternation at Lord's. One review summarises the plot, noting that 'Test Match peculiarities are burlesqued in clever and amusing fashion'. Lyon himself appears as the Australian captain in a match of no predefined length that lasts for sixty years until the final two men, confined to bath chairs, collapse and die. Lyon was by now also sending broadsides to the press, referring to 'the old dears' on the MCC Committee.

He continued to practise in law and was appointed a magistrate in Gambia in 1932. He would then become a magistrate in Kenya between 1945 and 1948 and Chief Justice in the Seychelles from 1948 until 1957. This period of his career was a particularly unhappy one. Dar was outspoken in his criticism of those in authority – notably Governor Selwyn-Clarke about whom he made remarks in court. He let it be known that he wanted out. The powers that be would have liked to have seen him replaced, too, but there was a stalemate. As one Foreign Office letter states: 'nobody would have him and it would be unfair to move him to play his organ in some other street'.

His final stint was as a judge in Uganda. In the meantime he had divorced Helen and was married in 1941 to Doreen Healey, a colliery examiner's daughter from Cheltenham, nineteen years his junior. He was serving at the time as a major in the Second World War

He died at St Leonard's-on-Sea, Sussex, on 17 February 1964 at the age of sixty-five. Peter Roebuck wrote that 'Lyon could never see a balloon without wanting to pop it, and sometimes those balloons contained water, so that he was drenched', adding that 'his life was more diverting if less fulfilled because of it'. On his career as a cricketer, *Wisden* noted that Lyon was 'considered by many to be among the best batsmen who never gained a cap for England'.

Dar Lyon himself once wrote that 'cricket was my first love and will be my last love'.

238
Montague Leslie Hambling
29 May 1920 v. Cambridge University, Cambridge

[signature]

Monty Hambling's parents were Herbert Montague and Annie (née Quick), she from Pill in Somerset and he born in London, a senior manager for the Board of Trade, also on the Royal Navy Reserve as a paymaster.

Monty was born on 6 December 1893 in Mitcham, Surrey, but his parents would move back to his mother's birthplace of Pill within a year of his birth. On leaving school, Monty was employed by Lloyds Bank as a trainee clerk. His career was interrupted by the First World War, when he served as a lance corporal in the Royal Gloucestershire Hussars. He was demobilised in July 1919, having been awarded the 1914/15 Star.

Returning to civilian life in the employ of Lloyds Bank, he was married in 1922 at Westbury-on-Trym to Kathleen Newton, daughter of a railway official. Kathleen was an able pianist and would often perform alongside her husband, who is described in teammate Raymond Robertson-Glasgow's autobiography *46 Not Out* as 'an accomplished amateur tenor'. Monty was certainly no blushing violet and is far removed from the stereotype of a bank manager. The local press carried reports of his performances in amateur dramatics and a photograph of him appearing in the comic role of Gregory in the Bristol Amateur Operatic Society's 1927 production of *Tom Jones*, provides ample demonstration of his taste for the thespian. An accompanying report informs us that he 'put in some very amusing incidents'.

Monty Hambling appearing for Somerset in 1921. Pictured left to right are: J. Daniell, E. Robson, M. L. Hambling and J. C. White.

Both Monty and his younger brother, Herbert, were employed as bank managers, with Monty managing the Bedminster branch of Lloyds for many years and Herbert managing the branch of Barclays in Romsey, Hampshire.

Monty was a successful club cricketer who captained the Bristol United Banks club and was both a useful batsman and fast bowler. He also appeared for Lodway CC. His successes at club level in the Bristol area brought him to the attention of Somerset, for whom he played on eighteen occasions, averaging 13.46 with the bat and scoring two half-centuries. He also took 24 wickets at 20.54 apiece, including an impressive return of 6 for 31 against Worcestershire.

In 1927 he was runner-up in the annual 'Sports News' Cup for best all-round club cricketer in the Bristol area. This was also the year in which he made his final appearance for the county. He continued to work as a bank manager until his retirement.

Monty Hambling died on 22 August 1960 at the age of sixty-six in Stoke Bishop, Bristol. He and Kathleen had had no children.

Monty Hambling – by day a bank manager, at night 'an accomplished amateur tenor'.

239
John Mitton
29 May 1920 v. Cambridge University, Cambridge

JMitton.

Born on 7 November 1895 in Cornholme, Lancashire (confusingly in the registration district of nearby Todmorden, Yorkshire), Jack Mitton was the son of a house painter, William Mitton, and after leaving school he was employed as a weaver, though his prowess as a sportsman would help him to seek new horizons.

A successful club bowler who was Weston-super-Mare's leading wicket-taker while he resided in Somerset in 1920, he was more widely known as a professional footballer rather than as a cricketer. The *Bath Chronicle* of May 1920 reports that 'Jack Mitton, the Exeter City half-back, has been signed on as a Somerset cricket professional and has joined the ground staff at Taunton. He is described as a medium to fast bowler, a useful bat and a splendid field.' His brother James also played for Exeter City. Still awaiting qualification by residence to play in Championship games, Jack only appeared in the two Varsity fixtures in 1920 before events moved on and he had left the Somerset ground staff. In his two matches, he took only one wicket at a cost of 100 runs and he averaged 15.00 with the bat. He went on to play as a professional in 1921 in Durham league cricket for Wearmouth CC. In 1922, he applied successfully to be re-classified as an amateur and continued playing cricket for pleasure for many years.

He enjoyed a more prolonged professional career as a footballer. A strongly-built man standing 5 ft 11 inches tall, he played primarily as a half-back but was versatile enough to be deployed as a centre-forward when the need arose. The *Derby Daily Telegraph* gives an account of his style, referring to 'this light-haired giant' and adding that 'he is a versatile sort, even if his long legs do give him a gawky, cumbersome style'.

Jack Mitton in the colours of Wolverhampton Wanderers FC.

Jack had begun his football career as a trainee with Burnley, but the First World War intervened and he joined the Coldstream Guards in 1914. He was released by the Army in 1916 to contribute to the war effort using his skills as a weaver with Joseph Webb & Sons, based in Bury, whose football team he played for. His war record therefore reads as 'at home' for the duration of hostilities and until his discharge in 1918. While working in the North West he met and in 1917 was married to Edith Pearson, with whom he had a daughter and three sons, one of whom would lose his life when shot down over Belgium during the Second World War.

During the 1919 and 1920 seasons he was with Exeter City, the latter date being the inaugural year of the Third Division. Jack's performances caught the eye of some First Division sides, with Sunderland and Liverpool vying for his services. The *Western Times* reported that 'Exeter City do not want to part with Mitton but the directors take the view that if a player desires to better himself it is their duty not to stand in his way'.

Between 1920 and 1924 he became a regular in the Sunderland team, initially as a right-half but stepping in and playing at centre-forward a number of times and also reverting to centre-half. Writing many years later in the *Sunderland Daily Echo*, 'Argus' recalls an incident where Mitton was standing approximately 30 to 40 yards from the goal and when a cross came over, he 'pivoted and hit it on the turn. Mitton stood searching the stand to see where the ball had landed, and Pearson, the old Albion goalkeeper, stood staring at Mitton. The ball was in the back of the net. A great goal – and pure luck.'

Between 1924 and 1927 he played for Wolverhampton Wanderers (then in the Second Division) and was a virtual ever-present until his transfer to Southampton, for whom he played for one season, although he continued to reside in Wolverhampton.

After ending his footballing career he became landlord of a succession of pubs in Wolverhampton, among them The Butler's Arms, Bushbury Lane, of which his wife, Edith, is listed as manageress in the 1939 census. For a while, their income was supplemented by Jack's employment as a bowling green groundsman. In the days before lucrative footballing contracts, the couple were working hard to support their family.

They remained in Wolverhampton until Edith's death, at which point Jack went to live with his daughter, Joan, in Norfolk. He died in Burnham Market, Norfolk, on 5 August 1983 at the age of eighty-seven.

Jack Mitton of Sunderland FC: later he became a pub landlord.

240
George Stephen Butler
2 June 1920 v. Oxford University, Oxford

George Butler was born in West Kennett, Wiltshire, on 16 December 1900. His father, William Stephen Butler, owned the Butler Brewery, which had been established in the first half of the Nineteenth Century by George's great-grandfather. It would be sold in 1921.

Educated at Marlborough College, he appeared for the First XI for five seasons from 1915 until 1919, in which year he was also selected to play at Lord's for a Public Schools XI for whom he top scored in their first innings. He also won the national squash

G. S. Butler at Marlborough College.

doubles for Marlborough, his opponents in the final being the Winchester pair of future England cricket captain Douglas Jardine and Middlesex cricketer R. H. Hill. He then went up to Keble College, Oxford, but failed to gain a blue.

George began as a batsman who was also a 'useful medium-paced bowler', as the *Bath Chronicle* described him during his time with New Lansdown CC (whom he captained while a schoolmaster in the city). He played only one match for Somerset and, looking at his subsequent career, Somerset would be justified in ruing a missed opportunity as he developed into a punishing batsman at club and Minor Counties level, noted for his 'timing and powerful off-side play'. Perhaps Somerset made advances which were rejected in favour of the county of his birth. It may also have been the case that his career rendered it impracticable for him to make himself available for Somerset. He often played for Wiltshire between 1920 and 1939, captaining them on occasions, and also appeared in a number of combined Minor Counties XI matches against touring sides in fixtures deemed first-class. In 1929, *The Cricketer* describes him as 'one of the best all-round cricketers in Minor Counties'. Playing for the Minor Counties against Wales in 1930, he scored 121, his only first-class century. *Wisden* reports that he 'played most enterprising cricket'. His one match for Somerset, by contrast, had been against Oxford University in 1920 and he had made only 7 and 2 in a low-scoring match that was over inside two days.

G. S. Butler played Minor Counties cricket while head-master-proprietor of Winchester Lodge School.

He was married in Purley in 1925 to Paula Wolfenden, after a two-year engagement. Her late father had owned a manufacturing business. George was still teaching in Bath at the time, but soon started up a preparatory school – Winchester Lodge in Torquay, Devon – of which he was the proprietor-headmaster. In advertisements he extolled the healthy schooling afforded pupils, noting its charmed position and the school's 'excellent feeding and health record'.

Despite his commitments, George captained the Torquay cricket club for a number of years, also playing for Devon on occasions and continuing to score big centuries throughout the

WINCHESTER LODGE SCHOOL
TORQUAY.
Head Master: G. S. BUTLER.

BOYS' PREPARATORY SCHOOL FOR THE ROYAL NAVY & PUBLIC SCHOOLS.

Wonderful Position, 450ft. above sea level, and facing due South.

EXCELLENT FEEDING AND HEALTH RECORD.

EXHIBITIONS, TOTAL VALUE £90, GAINED AT PUBLIC SCHOOLS DURING THE YEAR.

INSPECTED AND RECOGNIZED BY THE BOARD OF EDUCATION.

BY KIND PERMISSON OF THE WARDEN AND FELLOWS OF KEBLE COLLEGE, OXFORD

G. S. Butler in the Keble College XI.

1930s at club and Minor Counties level. He also remained a brilliant squash player, winning the Devon Squash Championship year in and year out during the 1930s. His skills extended to hockey, at which he played for Devon.

Having decided to relinquish his role as proprietor of the Winchester Lodge prep school, he enjoyed a second career as a farmer after he purchased Kingston Farm in Kingswear, Devon. He would pass on the farm to his son, Jeremy.

George Butler died at Kingswear on 21 September 1969 at the age of sixty-eight.

241
Francis Edward Spurway
2 June 1920 v. Oxford University, Oxford

Francis Spurway sits on the knee of his father, Rev. E. P. Spurway, a Somerset cricketer from the Victorian Age.

Francis Spurway was born in Winchester on 8 August 1894. His father, former Somerset cricketer Edward Popham Spurway, would become Rector of Heathfield, near Taunton, after having learned the ropes within the Church of England, initially as a curate at Newbury. Francis and his brother, Michael, who would also play for Somerset, were brought up at Heathfield when Edward inherited the living.

Educated at King's School, Bruton, Francis went on to St John's College, Oxford. From the outset, he was destined for a life in the ministry, though he served in the Somerset Light Infantry during the First World War, rising to the rank of acting captain in 1917. He would later become a chaplain in the Royal Army Chaplain's Department. His first ecclesiastical appointment was as a curate at St Andrew's, Taunton, where he was ordained a deacon in 1922 and a priest in 1923. He remained there until 1926, becoming very involved in youth work. For a short while he worked for the Toc H youth organisation as a padre, residing in and overseeing a hostel in Birmingham, before returning in 1927 to Somerset, specifically to Bishop's Hull, near Taunton, in order to replace Arthur Hook (another of Somerset's cricketing clergymen) as the vicar of St John's.

He played as a wicket-keeper and according to the *Western Daily Press* was responsible for some 'brilliant exhibitions'. The newspaper calls him the 'finest keeper since

F. E. Spurway in the St John's College XI.

Francis Spurway – a wicket-keeper described as 'a worthy successor to his brilliant forerunners'.

the days of A. E. Newton' asserting that 'his certainty on the leg side and his quickness of action' made him 'a worthy successor to his brilliant forerunners'. Less worthy of superlatives with a bat in hand, he made his highest score of 35 on his debut, and never matched that performance. In twenty-three appearances he averaged 9.37. He was also a keen rugby and hockey player.

He was married in 1935 to Avis Odeyne Hodgson, a clergyman's daughter. The couple would have two daughters. Avis was a remarkable woman and it is easy to understand why Francis was captivated by her. She would become a worthy recipient of an MBE award in recognition of her unstinting support for the St Dunstan's charity, set up to support soldiers who had lost their sight or suffered vision impairment as a result of the First World War. Avis would remain a loyal supporter and activist for the cause for five decades. She had set aside an early ambition to become an actress on the basis of parental disapproval. Her work as a nurse during the war led to her involvement with St Dunstan's. This began with her coxing crews of blind rowers, an interest that stemmed from being a member of a family of rowing blues. She later set up the charity's first sports club in Birmingham, a model that was copied in Manchester. Enlisting the help of the Birchfield Harriers, she encouraged many blind young men to overcome their fears and take up sport. She would go on to cajole the charity into persuading others to take part in international competitions for the disabled and would have been delighted by the later success of the Paralympics. Her infectious enthusiasm is apparent in some of the tales she related about her young charges, fresh from the war. They are recorded in the St Dunstan's newsletter:

> *Oh, it was great fun. The regatta dinner was marvellous ... but in those days we were expected to get them home on ordinary public transport ... I can remember going around Oxford Circus with them all, Drummer Downs sitting up in the front of the bus with a large bottle of beer and one of the semi-sighted men jumping off the bus. I don't know what happened to him. I couldn't leave the others to go after him! Awful! Then getting them to the right billets ... How the landladies put up with it, I don't know... but I loved them, so I would do anything for them.*

From 1936 until 1947 Francis was offering pastoral care of his own as the vicar of Tichfield, Hampshire, and then, for more than twenty years, of Holmwood in Surrey. Many will have felt that they owed the couple a great deal. Francis died at the age of eighty-six at Mount House in the village of Halse, near Taunton, on 30 December 1980. Avis died at their home a little over seven years later on New Year's Day in 1988.

242
Leonard Warwick Greenwood
2 June 1920 v. Oxford University, Oxford

Leonard N. Greenwood

Leonard's parents were Emily Clara (née Warwick) and Frederick William Thompson Greenwood, the latter for many years the vicar of St Mary's, Market Drayton. Leonard was born in Toxteth Park, Liverpool, on 25 March 1899 and educated first at Old Hall School in Wellington, Shropshire, and then at Winchester College, where in 1917 he completed 'a brilliant innings of 141' against Harrow.

Immediately on leaving school, he enlisted with the Royal Flying Corps in August 1917. After training as a pilot, he was commissioned as a second lieutenant and attached to 90 Squadron in October 1918. Formed in Shawbury, Shropshire, the squadron never in fact saw action. Within two months of receiving his commission, Leonard had been admitted to military hospital although details are elusive. He received his discharge at the end of January 1919.

Thereafter, he went up to New College, Oxford, where he was a member of the Oxford University XI who played Gentlemen in the opening first-class fixture after the First World War. He failed, however, to gain a blue, although he was invited to represent Somerset by their captain, John Daniell. Leonard had been a teammate at Winchester College of fellow debutant, Somerset-born William Baldock, who no doubt facilitated the introduction. His acquaintance with Somerset cricket would be a passing one. In his only appearance for them, Leonard made 16 and 0.

After graduating over a shortened period, he became a teacher in March 1921 at Abberley Hall, a preparatory school nestling in ninety acres of the Worcestershire countryside. He would remain there for the rest of his working life, a much-loved teacher known to pupils as 'LWG' or 'Grinder'. From 1921 until 1939 he was an assistant master and then from 1939 until 1961 he was one of three men who shared the role of headmaster. Finally, between 1961 and 1964 he opted to become an assistant master once more. On three occasions he played for Worcestershire, though with no great distinction, as his first-class average of 7.28 attests.

He was married in Upton, Worcestershire, in 1934 to Violet Elizabeth Rowlatt, known as Betty. They would have two children – Martin and Gillian – and spent many

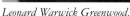

Leonard Warwick Greenwood.

L. W. Greenwood – for forty-three years a teacher at Abberley Hall in Worcestershire.

years based in the school, taking on a pastoral role as stand-in parents for the boarders. Gillian would become the Hon. Gillian Clare Seager when she was married to Hon. Douglas Leighton Seager, with whom she emigrated to Vancouver.

Perhaps Leonard's mind had been on his own forthcoming nuptials when in 1933, as a local press report informs us, he had the misfortune to speed across a crossroads on his way from Worcestershire to Lansdown before being hotly pursued by the police car that had had to give way to him. This was a minor indiscretion and an example of ill-luck in what appears to have been an otherwise blessed and blameless life. In a tribute, fellow joint-headmaster Gilbert Ashton writes of Leonard's 'thoroughness and clarity of expression, and his ability to understand and dispel a boy's difficulties and give him confidence'. He was an inspirational teacher and – perhaps unusually – his sermons in the school chapel were looked forward to for their insight and wit. A caring man, he was, however, possessed of a 'passion for punctuality' with reprisals for those who transgressed. He was a committed Christian and very actively involved in charitable work through freemasonry. For thirty-seven years he edited the school magazine, organised school plays and assiduously updated biographical records of the school's alumni. His other interests included singing, which began when he was a chorister at Winchester College and continued throughout his life until he performed as a bass singer with the Worcester Choral Society. He was an avid collector of private press books, including rare editions from William Morris's Kelmscott Press. Such was his expertise that he was asked to oversee the library at Worcester Cathedral.

Leonard and Betty retired to Astley, near Stourport, Worcestershire, and he died there on 20 July 1982 at the age of eighty-three. His life of unstinting service is commemorated on a plaque in the Abberley Hall school chapel.

243
William Frederick Baldock
2 June 1920 v. Oxford University, Oxford

William Baldock was born in Wellington, Somerset, on 1 August 1900. The son of Lt. Col. William Stanford Baldock and his wife, Mary (née Elworthy), of Foxdown, Wellington, he had a good cricketing pedigree. His father had played for Hampshire during that county's first brush with first-class status in the 1880s and his paternal grandfather (also William) had played for Gentlemen of Kent between 1842 and 1849. Educated at Winchester College (as was his father and his two younger brothers), William Jnr then went to Oriel College, Oxford, where he obtained a diploma in Forestry in 1921 before being awarded a degree in 1922. On graduating, he was offered a role in the Colonial Office Forestry Service, working in Tanganyika (Tanzania), and this would remain his place of work until 1939.

William would make ten first-class appearances for Somerset. Having first played as a nineteen-year-old, he would represent the county again in 1936 after an absence of 15 years, when he was granted an extended period of leave in order to be married in Taunton to Joan Clinton (née Daniell), the daughter of former Somerset captain (and future President) John Daniell. His wedding apart, the highlight of his

William Baldock – first played for Somerset as a nineteen-year-old.

W. F. Baldock – a life in the Colonial Office Forestry Service was ended brutally while a prisoner of war.

sojourn was his 63 not out when, on a cold day in 1936, Harold Gimblett, opening the innings for the first time, set about the All-Indian attack with a swashbuckling century that paved the way for an onslaught where Somerset scored 496 in five hours. Over the course of his ten games for the county William Baldock would average 17.00 with the bat.

For a while he and Joan divided their time between Tanganyika and Taunton until he was offered a role in Malaya as the Conservator of Forests. This would in fact prove an unfortunate turn of events when Japan set its sights on conquering the Malay States. While Joan returned to Taunton, already pregnant, William joined the 2nd (Selangor) Battalion of the Federated Malay States Volunteer Defence Force. Their son, named John Webbstone Baldock, was born on 21 April 1940, but William would never see his only child. He was taken prisoner by the invading Japanese Army while acting as an intelligence officer and reported as 'missing in action'. In a shameful war crime, he was, we are informed, 'shot by the Japanese Army after he had been captured'. His death is given as having occurred at Jabor Valley, Terengganu, Malaysia, on 30 December 1941. He was forty-one years old. His place of burial is unknown.

His grieving wife at least had the consolation of watching their son grow up and make his way in the world after – inevitably perhaps – being schooled at Winchester College as his father and grandfather before him had been.

244
Frederic Alexander Waldock
5 June 1920 v. Warwickshire, Bath

Frederic Waldock was born in Colombo, Ceylon, on 16 March 1898. His grandfather – an architect, Baptist minister and for a period secretary of the Baptist Translation Society – had left England for Ceylon (Sri Lanka) in 1862 to help in the building of the Cinnamon Gardens Baptist Church in Colombo. He remained there as a minister, bringing up his family. Among them was Frederic William Meredith Waldock (father of Frederic Alexander) a tea broker who was married in 1897 to Lizzie Kyd (née Souter).

Frederic Alexander was the first of five children. As a young boy he was sent to board first at Forest School, Walthamstow, and then to Uppingham School, where he proved an outstanding all-round sportsman, as did his three brothers who also attended the school. On leaving Uppingham, he served with the Royal Field Artillery, quickly rising to the rank of captain. Frederic went up to Hertford College, Oxford. Whilst there he made his initial first-class appearance in 1919 alongside fellow Somerset cricketer Leonard Greenwood against Gentlemen. He went on to win blues both at rugby and cricket.

F. A. Waldock in the Uppingham School hockey XI.

At the time of his Somerset debut he was residing at Shepton Mallet, possibly with a relative, adding authenticity to Somerset's claims on his services. He is variously described in local press reports as 'a fine left-handed all-rounder' and 'a steady left-hander'. In nineteen first-class games for Oxford University, he averaged 24.20 with the bat and took 24 wickets, including a best bowling analysis of 7 for 46. In seventeen matches for Somerset, he would average 22.51, with three half-centuries to his name. He was never called upon to bowl for them.

He in fact played for Somerset in two spells. In 1920, he appeared for them during the summer vacation but he left the country without completing his degree in order to pursue work as a tea broker in Kenya. It was his intention at the time to settle there permanently. However, by 1924 he was back in England and playing for Somerset, though the association was limited to four games in the month of May. If he had intended to appear in future years, his plans would have changed on the death of his father in October 1924. This resulted in Frederic Jnr's having to look after the family interests in Sri Lanka, becoming a partner in Keell & Waldock, based at Australia Buildings in Columbo. The company were brokers of produce, exchange, freight and shares. Despite his business commitments, he maintained his links with England, returning briefly in 1927 for his marriage in Farnborough, Hampshire, to Muriel Francis Walker, the daughter of a lieutenant colonel in the Royal Army Medical Corps.

Frederic played cricket for Ceylon, including in two first-class fixtures, one against

Frederic Alexander Waldock.

F. A. Waldock appearing for Somerset (left) and seen (far left, right) with younger brother C. H. M. Waldock who played for Oxford Authentics.

the visiting MCC side in an exhibition match in 1936. Using his prerogative as captain, he declared at 149 for 4 (while himself on 23 not out), knowing that monsoon rains were on the way and that the 5,000-strong crowd had all come to see Wally Hammond batting. In the event, Hammond made 46 of a total of 232 for 5.

During the Second World War he served as a lieutenant colonel in the 61st Infantry Division. After the cessation of hostilities, his son, Frederick [sic], attended Uppingham, impressing as his father had done and captaining the school rugby XV.

Frederic and Muriel continued to be based in Sri Lanka (visiting England on a regular basis) until 1955 when they retired to South Petherton in Somerset. His death occurred in Galmington, Taunton, on 4 July 1959. He was sixty-one years old. For the final four years of his life, Frederic had settled in the county that had embraced him as a young man.

245
Charles Fremantle Bishop
26 June 1920 v. Leicestershire, Leicester

Charles Fremantle Bishop, who played only two times for Somerset – once in 1920 and then in1921 – is listed incorrectly in some sources as Charles Frederick Bishop. He was born on 24 February 1899 at The Vicarage, Winterbourne Down, in Gloucestershire. His father was Frederick William Fremantle Bishop, vicar of Winterbourne Down and his mother was Laura (née Evans). Charles was a pupil at Kings College,

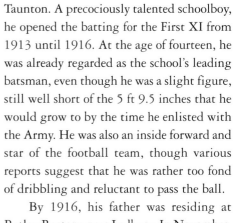

Taunton. A precociously talented schoolboy, he opened the batting for the First XI from 1913 until 1916. At the age of fourteen, he was already regarded as the school's leading batsman, even though he was a slight figure, still well short of the 5 ft 9.5 inches that he would grow to by the time he enlisted with the Army. He was also an inside forward and star of the football team, though various reports suggest that he was rather too fond of dribbling and reluctant to pass the ball.

By 1916, his father was residing at Putley Rectory, near Ledbury. In November, Charles enlisted but was deemed too young for active service and placed on the reserve list. The following year he became a cadet in the Royal Flying Corps but was finally posted to France in March 1918 where he joined the Middlesex Regiment until October 1918, falling victim to a gas attack. He returned home and was not declared fit for further service until February 1919, when he enlisted with the King's Royal Rifle Corps. His return to the fray was clearly ill-judged and too early, with further references to the effects of gas poisoning and his final discharge from duty in February 1920 when he was deemed no longer fit for active service.

C. F. Bishop at fourteen (top) and as captain of the King's College First XI (above).

After the war he made his two appearances for Somerset, who would have recalled the exploits of the boy wonder, the *Bath Chronicle* noting the introduction of the 'young amateur'. But with an average of only 3.00, his performances were hardly stellar, perhaps because of the lingering impact of his war injuries. Unbowed by the disappointment, the *Aluredian*, the magazine of King's College, refers to the fresh honours conferred on the Old Aluredians by 'the Rippon brothers [Dudley and Sydney] and Bishop'.

By 1923, a *Western Daily Press* report refers to him as 'a schoolmaster, and quite a good bat whose home is at Ledbury', adding that 'he will probably play on occasions' for Gloucestershire. He was playing cricket for Ledbury CC at that time, presumably living with his parents. In a subsequent issue, the same paper mentions that 'he had a trial with Somerset and had shaped well' but that he also 'has a qualification for Gloucestershire' In the end, Gloucestershire never came calling.

He became a schoolmaster, although he was never in one place for long. The *Aluredian* tracks his progress. By 1921, he was teaching in Wales and in that same year was appointed Sports Master at Winton House School, Winchester. By 1923, he was at the University School in Hastings but before the year was out he had taken up a teaching post in an S. P. G. School in Rhodesia. Here he would meet his future wife, Dorothy Mary Charge. Dorothy had worked as a governess for a family in Spalding, Lincolnshire, before leaving in November 1924 to take up a teaching post in Domestic Science in Rhodesia. There is a strong possibility that she taught at the same school as Charles. They returned to England together in 1926 in order to be married.

By June 1926, he was based at Cobham but lodging at the home of his future parents-in-law at West Bridgford, Nottingham. The wedding took place in August 1926 but their marriage was tragically shortlived. Charles departed for Egypt on the *Ormonde* (Orient Line) on 19 January 1929 for yet another teaching appointment – probably at the British Boys School, which was set up that year in Alexandria. He gives The Welcome Inn, St Martin's Court, as his address, hinting at the possibility that all was not well in his marriage and he was seeking a clean break, though this is speculation. His wife, Dorothy, remained in England. Having disembarked at Port Said, Charles Bishop died at the age of twenty-nine on 5 February 1929 at the Victoria Hospital in Cairo – a week after arriving in the country. Details of the cause of death remain elusive.

We are left to wonder whether or not he ever recovered fully from his gas attack. Perhaps he might otherwise have fulfilled his early promise and developed into a fine county cricketer.

246
Raymond Charles Robertson-Glasgow
21 July 1920 v. Essex, Leyton

Raymond Robertson-Glasgow was generally referred to within the cricketing fraternity as 'Crusoe'. He is said to have earned the moniker when he bowled C. P. McGahey in

R. C. Robertson-Glasgow
– dubbed 'Crusoe' by
C. P. McGahey of Essex.

1920 with a full toss. On returning to the pavilion the Essex batsman observed in an expletive-laden aside that he had been bowled by 'an old ——— I thought was dead two thousand years ago called Robinson Crusoe'. McGahey's sense of the timeline of history and the demarcation between fact and fiction might both have been decidedly suspect, but the name stuck. Others, such as his county captain, John Daniell, referred to him as 'Glasgie'.

Crusoe was born on 15 July 1901 in Murrayfield, Edinburgh, the son of Robert Purdon Robertson-Glasgow and his wife, Muriel Barbara (née Wilson). Crusoe and his brother, Bobs, were brought up in some comfort, although they appear to have spent most of their time in the company not of their parents but of their chauffeur, Harry Plumb, while their father fished, shot and managed the estate. Harry was a man of firm opinions who resolutely refused to risk taking the family car above 19.5 mph and on hearing that his two charges were to be despatched to Hindhead Prep School informed them that if they were going to school they would need to 'know cricket'. Harry was of the view that bowling was all that mattered in the game and set the boys practising with a tennis ball in the stable yard. Thus began Crusoe's cricketing odyssey.

He later won a scholarship to Charterhouse where he excelled both intellectually and as a cricketer, winning an exhibition to Corpus Christi, Oxford, to read Classics. Always able to balance the academic and sporting aspects of his life, he became a successful member of the Oxford XI, attracting Somerset's eye. As a Scot, he belonged to no county. Furthermore, Rev. Archie Wickham, Somerset's eccentric wicket-keeper from the Golden Age, was his great uncle, and Crusoe's cousins, the Foxcrofts, lived at Hinton Charterhouse. As far as John Daniell was concerned, here was a Somerset man through and through.

Crusoe appeared an easy-going fellow, extraordinarily bright but able to relate to anyone. He was also hugely disorganised, never learned to drive a car and was notoriously forgetful, once mislaying his kit and having to complete a game in his black, leather-soled shoes, which rather hampered his run-up and delivery. He would play for Oxford University for four years between 1919 and 1923 and for sixteen seasons for Somerset from 1920 until 1935. To his 146 wickets for Oxford University were

Crusoe – bowling.

Crusoe – relaxing in a deckchair between Jack White and Sam Woods.

added 238 for Somerset at 26.35 apiece, including seventeen 5-wicket hauls. Very much a tail-ender, he would recall that he was paired by his captain with Jim Bridges, and told: 'You two clowns are Number 10 and 11 and you can sort out between you what order you want to bat in.' He managed an average of 14.02 over the course of his Somerset career, surprising himself and his teammates with three half-centuries. In *Cricket, Lovely Cricket*, Frank Lee describes Crusoe the innovator and the eccentric. He is said – though the claim has surely been made for others – to have developed the notion of dampening one side of the ball to accentuate swing. On the other side of the coin, in a match against Glamorgan, there was much consternation when Somerset became aware that they had shrunk to ten men, only for Crusoe to appear shortly afterwards from behind the sightscreen, clutching an ice-cream and announcing: 'This should put me right.' He is also said on one occasion to have bowled a doughnut to Bev Lyon of Gloucestershire immediately after one tea interval.

For much of his career, Crusoe was only available during school vacations. After graduating, he had returned to teach at his prep school – Hindhead – and would remain there until being offered a job as a journalist in 1933, initially as a golf correspondent at the *Morning Post*. He had previously submitted poems and articles that had impressed the editor. Very soon he was covering other sports, including cricket, and working in turn for the *Daily Telegraph*, *The Observer* and finally the *Sunday Times*. He wrote with great wit and warmth, which some saw disapprovingly as flippancy. They were wrong. His writing has stood the test of time and remains as entertaining and readable as ever. Crusoe wrote to inform and not to impress and wore his erudition lightly. His work as a journalist was supplemented with income from the books he had authored – invariably engaging – with titles as various as *How to Become a Test Cricketer* and *I Was Himmler's Aunt*.

Behind the wit and the gregariousness there lurked the spectre of manic depression that dogged him throughout his adult life. Friends were also concerned that during the 1920s and early part of the 1930s he was displaying the signs of alcoholism. Depression and strong drink: the one perhaps fed the other. He made the first attempt on his own life in the early 1930s and it would leave him with a scar on his neck. He was later at St Aiden's Hospital in Northampton when he was nursed by Elizabeth Hutton, whom he was married to in 1943. Both by then in their forties, there was never a question of any children for the two soulmates who had found love and companionship late.

Crusoe was still writing with great verve and wit, still bringing joy to others. A. P. (Sandy) Singleton said of him that: 'He carried a small red memo book which he referred to as 'the washing book' and in which he occasionally made notes. Wherever he was, one could hear his bellow of laughter, and the whole scene brightened up at once, and cricket became fun.' But behind the joy were the tears of the clown. On 4 March 1965, snowdrifts had marooned him in his home in Buckhold, Berkshire, and Elizabeth went out to clear a pathway. By the time she returned, her husband's life was ebbing away after another suicide attempt. The ambulance was called but could not make it in time in the atrocious conditions. Depression had claimed the last laugh. He was sixty-three at the time.

R. C. Robertson-Glasgow in the Somerset XI who played Hampshire at Dean Park, Bournemouth, in August 1920. He helped his side to a comfortable win with match figures of 7 for 64.
LEFT TO RIGHT: S. G. U. Considine, J. Bridges, J. C. W. MacBryan, J. A. S. Jackson,
M. D. Lyon, F. A. Waldock, J. C. White, J. Daniell, S. G. McAulay (Scorer),
R. C. Robertson-Glasgow, L. C. Braund, E. Robson.

1921

"I will do my best to leave the old county with a good side of eleven amateurs."

John Daniell (Somerset Captain)

Championship Position: 10 of 17

Glamorgan were accorded first-class status, increasing the number of counties to seventeen. At the annual meeting in February, John Daniell was re-elected captain and reaffirmed his belief that Somerset should be committed to amateurism.

Once again, Jack White was the pick of the bowlers, supported by Ernie Robson. At Worcester, White took ten wickets in an innings, the first Somerset man to have done so since E. J. Tyler in 1895. Tyler had been his coach at Taunton School. White had learned well.

The fielding was moribund. The *Northern Whig* notes 'an epidemic of missed chances'. Exempted from criticism is Somerset's veteran wicket-keeper, Harry Chidgey, who had first played for the county in 1900. One of six men invited to keep wicket during the 1921 season, his twenty dismissals included ten stumpings, which trumped the combined efforts of the other five keepers. Jack MacBryan and Randall Johnson led the county's batting averages, with three of Somerset's seven centuries compiled by Johnson. Among a multiplicity of debutants, many of them plundered from Oxbridge, Mervyn Hill was a useful addition behind the stumps and Tom Lowry would become a towering figure – literally and metaphorically – in New Zealand cricket.

1921 marked the death of Herbert Tremenheere Hewett, who ranks as one of the finest of Somerset's captains. A forceful left-handed opening batsman and uncompromising leader, he, more than any other player, had been responsible for Somerset's admission to the County Championship back in 1891.

247
George Edward Hunt
14 May 1921 v. Gloucestershire, Taunton

George Hunt, whose brother, Hubert would also play for Somerset, was born on 30 September 1896 in the village of Pill. His father worked for many years for the Bristol Docks. George and Hubert were beneficiaries of Lodway CC's forward-thinking policy of coaching and encouraging promising local talent, affording youngsters an early opportunity to develop their skills in competitive fixtures. It would yield up a number of Somerset cricketers. George was arguably the most successful of them. In his *History of the Lodway Cricket Club*, Mike Lovell notes that:

> *George was a brilliant club player .... On the occasional Saturday when he was free to play for Lodway, the news would spread round the village and an unusually big gate would gather at Ham Green. The spectators expected fireworks and they were rarely disappointed. George was equally proficient with both bat and ball and was a brilliant fielder.*

During the First World War he served as a private in the Somerset Light Infantry, fighting in France from September 1915 and later transferring to the Royal Ambulance

Service Corps. After returning to civilian life and performing wonders for Lodway with regular wickets as well as innings that included 'towering sixes over the old row of fine chestnut trees' he stepped up to the first-class game.

County Championship cricket proved more challenging. First appearing for Somerset in 1921, George Hunt is perhaps the archetype of a journeyman county pro. Regarded as an excellent close fielder, he played as an all-rounder over eleven seasons without ever quite hitting the heights. He made nearly 5,000 runs (including one century) at an average of 15.42 and took 386 wickets at 32.87 apiece, bowling right-arm medium pace. He

George Edward Hunt.

G. E. Hunt – a journey-man pro but an outstanding fielder.

also took 199 catches. During the winter he kept fit by playing football as a centre forward or inside right for Taunton Town.

The *Taunton Courier* of July 1937 notes his absence from the match against Gloucestershire after a run of appearances in eighty consecutive Championship matches. A reporter writes that 'although not in the forefront of our players, Hunt has rendered Somerset good service', adding that during his unbroken run 'his aggregate figures for this period are not impressive, the batting average ranging about 14, and the bowling analysis being in the region of 30. This, however, does not take into account his fielding, or of the fact that most of his best performances have been produced when most needed.' In 1925, he bore the brunt of the bowling when Jack White was unavailable for much of the season.

If dependability was a strength, then adaptability and a creative approach to problem-solving should also be added to the list of his virtues. In 1930, towards the end of the Somerset innings, Bill Voce of Nottinghamshire was aiming a barrage of deliveries at the ribcage of George, who was batting at number ten. We are informed that 'an agitated Hunt switched to a left-handed guard, trying to prevent Voce from hitting him. He scored 17, and helped Somerset add 33 for the last two wickets.'

His contract was terminated by Somerset at the end of 1931 but he was awarded a Testimonial Fund, including a collection at a match of his choosing – Somerset versus Lancashire at Weston-super-Mare – where £12 was raised. George was taken on as a pro by Kilmarnock CC until he resigned in 1934 and was replaced by his younger brother, Hubert, who had completed a club double the preceding season with 1,179 runs and 104 wickets for Lodway CC.

George was married in 1922 to Maud Amelia (née Waldron) and they would have one son together. He was still describing himself as a professional cricketer at the outset of the Second World War, although he was supplementing his income with work as a general labourer. During the war he also acted as a special constable and air raid warden in Portishead. Peter Roebuck informs us in *From Sammy to Jimmy* that George became a carpet salesman after his career as a professional cricketer had ended.

He died in Bristol on 22 January 1959 at the age of sixty-two.

248
Kenneth Guy Blaikie
18 May 1921 v. Oxford University, Oxford

KG Blaikie

Guy Blaikie, also sometimes referred to as 'Bill', was a hugely impressive person – a sportsman, scientist and businessman – although he had no immediately apparent links with the county who claimed his services. Here was another case of commendable opportunism on the part of John Daniell.

Guy was born in Johannesburg on 8 May 1897 and was not yet three years old when his father was killed at the Siege of Ladysmith in 1900. He was raised and educated in South Africa, and when war broke out he joined the 4th Mounted Rifles, an expeditionary force of 67,000 South Africans charged with laying claim to German South West Africa. In 1917, having come to England with his mother, Margaret, he joined the Royal Field Artillery and was wounded in action in 1918 and demobilised in 1919. He was a Rhodes Scholar, his entry to St John's College, Oxford, having been delayed because of the First World War.

At Oxford, he quickly established himself as a leading light in his college's cricket, hockey and lawn tennis teams. A hard-hitting left-handed batsman and medium-paced left-arm bowler, he was in and out of the University XI until his career blossomed in 1924 when he topped the Oxford University averages. *Wisden* reports that against MCC at Lord's, he 'astonished his critics by the vigour of his left-handed batting' when he scored 120. He followed this with a barnstorming century against Gloucestershire and then a score of 48 in the Varsity match, when he 'hit with amazing brilliancy'.

He was only ever an occasional player for Somerset, appearing for them in nine matches. His batting average was 22.35, including two half-centuries for his adoptive county. He also took 15 wickets at an average of 28.80. The 1923 season would be his last for Somerset and after further appearances for Oxford University in 1924 he forsook first-class cricket in order to pursue his career.

He had been invited to work as a chemist for Shawinigan Chemicals Ltd in Quebec (at the time the Canadian Electro Products Co.) and he accepted the post. He would remain with the company throughout his working life, making the city of Shawinigan his home. Rising through the ranks, he

Guy Blaikie – an impressive sportsman, scientist and businessman.

Kenneth Guy Blaikie.

would become their head of research and a widely respected figure within the chemical manufacturing industry. He remained an active sportsman. In his new environment he quickly mastered golf, fly-fishing, skiing and curling, becoming the President of the Shawinigan Curling Club.

He was married in 1932 to Mary Petrie Black and they would have two children, Peter and Jane. Guy and Mary also continued to care for his widowed mother, who lived with the family. Peter, who attended St John's College, as his father had done, became a prominent lawyer and politician in Quebec.

Guy Blaikie served in the Second World War as a major with the 81st Field Battery, which in 1946 became one of the sub-units of the 62nd Field Artillery Regiment of Shawinigan. He was added to the retired list with the rank of major in 1967, shortly before his death in Lennoxville, Quebec, on 8 June 1968 at the age of seventy-one. He lies buried there in the Malvern Cemetery.

249
John Ewan Frazer
18 May 1921 v. Oxford University, Oxford

The tragic, early death of Jack Frazer would occasion much grief. He is described in one report as 'one of the most impressive and lovable of Oxford's young men'. His father, a man credited with inaugurating the Australian Open Golf Championship, was a doctor who had studied at Balliol.

Jack was born in Woollahra, Sydney, on 2 April 1901 and was educated in England, firstly at a prep school in Herne Hill and then at Winchester College. He proved a brilliant pupil and won an exhibition to Balliol. Over 6 feet tall, we are variously told that 'he was a fellow of fine physique' and that he was 'the very flower of manhood'. Selection for Somerset resulted from John Daniell's marvellous nose for talent whom no other county had yet claimed. As it happened, in this particular instance, Sussex came forward immediately afterwards and called on Jack's services. A left-handed batsman, he was originally an all-rounder but never bowled in first-class cricket. His contemporary and great friend at Winchester, future England captain Douglas Jardine, wrote that Jack's ability to bowl 'mysteriously

John Ewan Frazer.

Jack Frazer – 'the very flower of manhood'.

deserted him – possibly a result of gymnastics'. We are left to ponder the precise meaning of Jardine's observation. Perhaps he was referring to a wrist injury. It is clear, however, that Jack was a keen gymnast as one later tribute praises him for the time and effort he expended in Physical Education training for young men from the deprived East End of London.

He was at Oxford between 1920 and 1924 and won blues for cricket and football (playing as a left wing). Squeezed into his busy schedule was a cricketing tour of Canada in 1923 with a combined group of Oxford and Cambridge undergraduates. His one game for Somerset – where he scored 4 and 14 – was something of an aberration, given that all his Championship games were for Sussex, for whom he played on twenty-three occasions up until 1924. It is also said that his disappointing first-class performances resulted from deteriorating eyesight.

After graduating from Balliol with a First, he acted for a while as a Chemistry demonstrator at the university before taking up a position as a bank official in East Grinstead. While based there, Jack played cricket for the East

Grinstead club. In January 1927 he went to Wolfgang, near Davos, on a skiing holiday with his mother and father. He was trying out the course with some companions, commencing at the Parsenn hut and following the route of the course for the British cross-country ski championship scheduled to take place the following day. A press report informs us that 'near Wasserscherde, about 50 minutes run from the hut, where the ascent begins, he was taking a short, steep slope when he fell forward, apparently striking a hidden rock'. He had cut his chin and both his skis were broken, but there were no signs of internal injury. He was nevertheless taken to Davos Hospital, where his condition suddenly deteriorated and he died that same afternoon. The date was 2 January 1927 and Jack was only twenty-five years old. A report of his death informs us that 'he was a first-class skier' and that the British championships were postponed by a day.

His obituary in *The Times* states that 'Frazer was undoubtedly one of the most brilliant all-round men of his generation and all who knew him felt he would have gone far'. Indeed, the various records of his life and death all extol his many virtues. The Cantelupe Golf Club (at Royal Ashdown, East Sussex), of which he had been a member, inaugurated the 'Jack Frazer Memorial Cup' in the year of his death. Perhaps the grieving parents derived a modicum of comfort from the fact that Jack's younger brother, Charles, following the fine example set by his sibling, went up to Oxford in 1927 and played for the Varsity XI.

J. E. Frazer – 'one of the most impressive and lovable of Oxford's young men'.

250
Louis Edgar Wharton
18 May 1921 v. Oxford University, Oxford

Louis Wharton was born in Port of Spain on 18 January 1896. He was a member of a wealthy merchant family whose forbears were early settlers in Trinidad after its seizure by the British in 1797. His father, Louis Anthony Wharton, was educated at St Mary's

College in Port of Spain, where he won an Island Scholarship to study at London University. Called to the bar at Gray's Inn in 1884 and later to King's Council, Louis Snr is said to have been a 'fervent Catholic'. In July 1909 he brought his two sons – Louis Jnr and Ralph – to England, where they were educated in Berkshire at the Douai School, run by Benedictine monks. In September 1915, Louis Jnr enlisted as a gunner with the Honorary Company of Artillery and served in Egypt, Sinai and Palestine before accepting a commission as a second lieutenant with the Royal Field Artillery in June 1917. He relinquished his commission on completion of service in October 1920, although he was added to the reserve list.

By this time he was studying at Oriel College, Oxford, and he would represent the university at cricket, without gaining his blue, often playing alongside fellow Somerset recruit, Raymond Robertson-Glasgow. Louis did however win blues in successive years for football and was given a trial for England in 1920 when he appeared for the Amateurs of The South versus The North.

Having been persuaded to represent Somerset, he threw in his lot with the county and would play for them eleven times during 1921 and 1922. Averaging 21.00 with the bat, he made some useful contributions, including three half-centuries. One reporter suggests that Louis had a tendency to take too many risks and to play the ball in the air. On one occasion, in 1922, P. F. C. Williams of Gloucestershire shaped to catch him on the boundary but was hampered by a number of spectators who had spilled over and were lying on the ground within the boundary. Louis survived but moments later, undaunted, he yielded up another catch. This time it was held.

He only ever took one wicket at a cost of 175 runs. That wicket had come on his debut. A diminutive figure, he was very quick in the outfield. *The Cricketer* states that 'even when he did not make runs, [he] was worth a place in the side for his out-fielding' and the *Taunton Courier* describes him in 1921 as a 'lucky discovery', although in truth, John Daniell's assiduous networking took all luck out of the equation. The latter reporter also calls Louis 'a brilliant field'. By 1922 the same man had revised his opinion, stating that 'L. E. Wharton, who showed brilliant form in the field last season, was poor. His fielding was feeble and he missed some easy chances.' Louis was clearly suffering an off day.

Louis Edgar Wharton.

By 1923 he had ceased playing for Somerset, though he retained his links with the West Country, delivering speeches in support of his friend Stanley Tubbs, the prospective Conservative candidate for Stroud. Tubbs lost the seat to Freddie Guest, the Liberal candidate and sometime Secretary of State for Air, a post concerned with the country's defences rather than ensuring the continuing supply of oxygen.

Louis was married to Hilda Koch Davies in 1924. Hilda's father, Albert, was a city financier – half-German and half-English. Given the prevailing mood of hostility to all things Germanic, he went to great lengths to hide his origins. Similarly, Hilda never used the Koch middle name, not even on her marriage certificate. Louis and Hilda divided their time between Port of Spain and London whilst he built his career as a barrister. They completed their permanent move to Trinidad on the 30 September 1930, accompanied by their son Richard, born in London in 1928.

A press report of October 1931 confirms that he was acting as Port of Spain's magistrate when adjudicating over the matter of nine French felons who had escaped the brutal and notorious 'Devil's Island' prison, rowing more than 600 miles. On arrival at Port of Spain they are described as 'nine human scarecrows, exhausted, starving and blistered by the tropical sun'. The report fails to inform us how Louis resolved the conflicting pulls of compassion for the nine men and the need to retain cordial relations with the French Consulate.

Louis and Hilda made a brief return to England in 1948 where, like his father before him, he was appointed King's Council. He died in Port of Spain on 31 December 1957. He was sixty-one. Hilda returned to England a year later and lived there for a further thirty-nine years.

251
Cuthbert Fairbanks-Smith
18 May 1921 v. Oxford University, Oxford

Cuthbert Fairbanks Smith (who later hyphenated his name) was born on 18 March 1885 in Lee, London, at that time in the county of Kent. He was the son of the vicar of Lee, Rev. Lewis Smith, and his wife Edith (née Fairbanks), a rector's daughter. Cuthbert was educated at a boarding school run by the Rev. Lewis Evans in Butlers Green, Parkfield, Hayward's Heath, and later at Bradfield College in Berkshire. He and his elder brother, Oswald, eschewed family tradition and opted for careers in the Army.

At the age of eighteen, Cuthbert joined the Royal Berkshire Regiment as a second lieutenant, transferring a year later to the Middlesex Regiment. Promoted to lieutenant in 1906, he was married in 1909 to Gladys Clara Frances (née Ward) and the couple left immediately for India where Cuthbert had been seconded. It was later reported that while based in Calcutta he conducted an affair with Jean Corrie (née Burnyeat) the wife of Major William Corrie, Cuthbert's fellow officer, who was the son of a general in the Indian Army. It was revealed at a divorce hearing that when Jean returned to England in July 1912 to see her two children and her father, she was accompanied by Cuthbert. Major Corrie was granted a decree nisi in April 1913 and given custody of his two young daughters. The affair between Jean and Cuthbert did not last and Jean

Cuthbert Fairbanks-Smith – 'always starting up new ventures that invariably failed'.

would return to live with her ex-husband in later life. For his part, it is claimed that Cuthbert refused to grant his wife Gladys the divorce she had requested. It must be assumed that Cuthbert relented once he had later decided the time was right for him to become remarried.

Cuthbert's dalliance proved a less-than-astute career move: he was posted for a while to the Princess Patricia's Canadian Light Infantry in Canada. During the First World War, after having been promoted to the rank of major, he was invalided in France in January 1915 with knee injuries. After having been incapacitated for six weeks by 'dislocation of the semi-lunar cartilage', he resigned his commission in September 1915, before subsequently joining his younger brother Lionel in the Durham Light Infantry for the remainder of the war.

He played in Somerset's two Varsity games in 1921, when he was already thirty-six years old. He was at least able to claim a tenuous link with Somerset on the basis that an uncle, originally from Denver, was a housemaster at Clifton College. As *Wisden* recounts, Somerset were 'in such a plight' that they were obliged to draft in four newcomers, including Cuthbert, who would eke out a first-class average of 3.00 in his two first-class matches.

He travelled to New York and Canada on frequent occasions during the late 1920s and early 1930s, giving his home address as the Garrick Club. He worked briefly for the Radio Research Department, resigning in 1931, and it must have been either through this employment, his theatrical friends at the Garrick Club or his contacts in New York that he became involved with the film industry. By the mid-1930s, he was styling himself as Major Fairbanks-Smith, Motion Picture Studio Executive, on his many trips to New York. He was advising the Hollywood film industry over British manners, customs and accents. In 1934, he crossed the Atlantic on at least eight occasions, also finding time to be married to Genevieve Hammerly in Manhattan. His second marriage, like his first, was a brief one. By 1939, he was working as the hotel manager at the Hog's Back Hotel, a large country hotel between Farnham and Guildford, a few miles from the family home at Pennybont, Guildford.

Cuthbert was living at the hotel with Barbara Eva Gough, a free-spirited artist from St Ives in Cornwall who referred to him as 'Cuffy' and who adopted the name of Barbara Fairbanks-Smith. She was 26 years his junior and although they presented themselves as man and wife, they were never married. Cuthbert and Barbara moved out to Shamley Green during the Second World War and then retired to Middleton-on-Sea, Sussex. He died there on 25 May 1948 at the age of sixty-three. One member of the family describes him as 'something of a black sheep, always starting up new ventures that invariably failed'. The judgement is perhaps a little harsh but the trajectory of his life had certainly been unpredictable.

Barbara returned to St Ives where – known once more as Barbara Gough – she ended her days in the Headlands Nursing Home.

252
Thomas Coleman Lowry
21 May 1921 v. Cambridge University, Cambridge

T. C. Lowry

Over six feet tall, well built and a charismatic presence, Tom Lowry was, according to Somerset teammate Raymond Robertson-Glasgow, 'a leader in a thousand' and although he took with some success to batting, bowling and wicket-keeping, it was for his qualities as a captain that he won most renown in cricketing circles. He was, as Robertson-Glasgow wrote, 'a man first and a cricketer second, but it was a close finish'.

Born at Okawa (near Fernhill) in Hawke's Bay, New Zealand, on 17 February 1898, he was the son of Thomas Henry Lowry, a wealthy sheep farmer and racehorse breeder and a Cambridge graduate. His mother, 'Marsie' (née Ward), was the daughter of a man said to be one of the richest in New Zealand, although the Lowry clan were hardly

Thomas Coleman Lowry.

short of money of their own, the Okawa sheep station having been established in 1846 by Tom's grandfather (also a Thomas and a Cantabrian).

Educated first at the Heretaunga College in Hastings and then at Christ's College, Canterbury, Tom was captain of both the school rugby XV and the cricket XI. This

Tom Lowry – 'a leader in a thousand'.

rather set the tone for the rest of his life.

On leaving school he trained at the New Zealand Flying School in Auckland and was commissioned as a second lieutenant in the Royal Flying Corps in February 1919, three months after the end of the First World War. His time in the military was shortlived and he went up to Jesus College, Cambridge, in 1921. Peter Roebuck describes Tom Lowry as 'a loud New Zealander who was a member of the 'Hellfire' club at Cambridge – to qualify for which a man had to blow three smoke rings and spit through them'. Already gaining a reputation as an aggressive stroke-maker, Tom was invited to join Archie MacLaren's tour of New Zealand in 1922-23. Although he was in the running for a blue as a wicket-keeper batsman, he was not in fact selected to play in the Varsity match until 1923 after he had 'strengthened his defence without spoiling his forcing strokes'. He went on to captain the Cambridge University XI the following year. Demonstrating their eye for emerging talent and their powers of persuasion, Somerset talked him into representing them between 1921 and 1924. In 46 matches he would average 24.26 with the bat and effect 40 catches and 16 stumpings.

Showing admirable versatility, he would also take 1 wicket at a cost of 21 runs. It is said that in those matches where he was captain of various teams, including New Zealand, he would sometimes decide to bowl when bored with keeping and he would certainly enjoy some success with the ball.

After his experiences as a captain for Cambridge, he would go on to establish his reputation as a leader whether leading a tour of the USA by MCC, or taking the helm at Wellington, whom he led for six successful seasons. He later led the New Zealand side who toured England, surprising those who had written off the tourists' chances. He is described as an active captain, leading the fight from the front, never prepared to let a game drift and happy to try out unorthodox methods to wrest back momentum. As a person, he could fill a room with his commanding presence and was forthright in his opinions but always down to earth.

In 1933 he was married to Margaret Gertrude Russell, known as Margot, whose parents owned a neighbouring farm. Tom and Margot would go on to farm land of their own at Maowhango near Taihape and in 1942 they would inherit yet more property and land in Queensland. There was then a homecoming in 1944 when, after the death of his father, Tom returned to Okawa to manage the family sheep station and stud. Between 1944 and his death in 1976, he established a reputation as a fine breeder of racehorses and also served on the council of the New Zealand Thoroughbred Breeders' Association, for fourteen years as President. From 1950 until 1953 he was also President of the New Zealand Cricket Council. In addition, he held a number of company directorships.

Tom Lowry died on 20 July 1976 at the age of seventy-eight at the Memorial Hospital in Hastings, New Zealand, the running of the family holdings having passed to his son, also Tom, who was one of four children. The cricketer and journalist Digby Jephson reported that one could feel the 'strong magnetic influence of one man over ten' when Lowry captained a side. This appears to have been true in all walks of his full and active life.

253
George Woodcock
21 May 1921 v. Cambridge University, Cambridge

George Woodcock was born in Warrington on 21 April 1894. His father, William, was a gas stove fitter and his mother, Margaret Martha (née Hill) the daughter of a railway engine driver. George would prove a bright young man, able to rise above his working-class roots. He won a place at the Boteler Grammar School in Warrington, where he was head boy in his final year and was awarded a Crabtree Exhibition to study History and Maths at St Catharine's College, Cambridge. The scholarship was granted to students who were academically gifted and were deemed likely to add to the social life of the college. With a reputation already established in Warrington as a successful schoolboy with both bat and ball, George played cricket, hockey and football for the college. Regularly among the runs and wickets, a highpoint was a swashbuckling 172 against Downing College in 1914.

He obtained his BA in 1915. Although his army records begin in January 1916, it is almost certain from the details handed down by George himself via his son that he signed up for the war effort as part of a Pals regiment in July 1915 and served briefly in France before being identified as officer material when he revealed that he had graduated from Cambridge. He was appointed a second lieutenant with the Lancashire Fusiliers in 1916 before serving as a lieutenant with the King's Own Royal Lancaster Regiment, including a spell in Salonika where he suffered with malaria.

After the war he acted briefly as an assistant schoolmaster at his old school, Boteler Grammar. He had left for Ely Theological College – enjoying club cricket and also football for Ely City FC – when Somerset invited him to play for them against Cambridge. Also in the side was his friend from his St Catharine's days, Conrad Baker. In his only game for Somerset, George made scores of 5 and 63 and, bowling thirty-eight overs of right-arm medium pace, took 4 wickets for 119. Somerset surely pleaded, to no avail, for him to join their ranks on a more permanent basis.

George Woodcock – a brilliant scholar and superb all-round sportsman.

Ordained in 1921, his first appointment was as an assistant curate at Halsall, Lancashire. He remained at Halsall until 1925, when he became the Organising Secretary of the Liverpool branch of the Waifs and Strays Society, later renamed the Children's Society, which ran homes for destitute children and arranged for many of them to be fostered. His pastoral work included coaching boys at sports and he worked closely with Liverpool FC, being offered the use of their facilities at Anfield.

Over this period he figured regularly in club cricket in the Lancashire Leagues, primarily for Ormskirk and then Northern. He also represented the Clergy of Lancashire in their annual fixture with the Clergy of Yorkshire. The *Lancashire Evening Post* of July 1926 gives an account of his blistering 136 in 70 minutes at Bradford:

> *Woodcock's brilliant exhibition caused quite a sensation among the spectators. He knocked two balls out of the ground into the roadway, while another hit travelled over the pavilion. At the close of the game … one habitué of Park-avenue {sic}, referring to Woodcock, asked: "What are Lancashire County thinking about, not getting hold of him?" adding, "I wish we had him in Yorkshire."*

The truth of the matter was that George had no appetite for three-day fixtures, believing there were other priorities in his life and loathing the snobbery inherent in the game. Although he was a wholehearted player who took great delight in dismissing

Reverend George Woodcock.

George Woodcock – had no appetite for first-class cricket, preferring to deploy his talents for the greater good.

batsmen or clubbing the ball to all corners of the ground, he had no wish to indulge in the first-class game.

As an aside, it is claimed that the reference in his good friend Rev. Awdry's *Thomas the Tank Engine* to a six landing in a train and being carried from Elsbridge to Ffarquhar was inspired by George Woodcock, whose maternal grandfather and uncles were engine drivers who would pull up their trains to watch him in action. He had accomplished a similar feat when a ball struck in Lancashire was reputedly carried to Yorkshire. Such a claim is, of course, far from unique in cricketing folklore.

In January 1932 George became the vicar of Hale in Lancashire, remaining there until 1939, when he was appointed an army chaplain with the rank of major for the duration of the war. In 1939 he was married to Winifred Edith Cox, whose father was a shipping clerk and later a sink manufacturer. Winifred was fifteen years younger than George and together they had two sons.

In 1947, he became the vicar of St Athanasius in Kirkdale, Liverpool, having orchestrated the rebuilding of the church after it was bombed. He remained there until 1951 when he took up a similar role in St Thomas, Lydiate, a village in the Liverpool Diocese. In 1961 he became rector of Stour Provost, near Gillingham in Dorset. This would be his final appointment, with George retiring to Bruton in Somerset in 1965. He died at St Martin's Hospital in Bath on 22 February 1968 at the age of seventy-three.

This remarkable man had decided early in his life that creating a better world was a more productive use of his time than a tiresome round of County Championship matches.

254
Edward Conrad Baker
21 May 1921 v. Cambridge University, Cambridge

E. C. Baker

Known as Conrad, he sometimes signed himself as 'C. E. Baker'. Somerset would have known that Conrad Baker's appearance against his alma mater was strictly a one-off. Sussex had already claimed him as one of their own. He was born in Carmarthen, Wales, on 7 January 1892, though he was brought up in Brighton, where his father had taken the family, as a result of his role as an inspector of schools. Conrad was educated at Brighton College. He was offered an Exhibition to study History at St Catharine's College, Cambridge and in fact gained a BA in Law and History. Arriving at Cambridge in 1912, he was soon drafted into the Varsity team, enjoying a remarkable early flowering in his career with 22 first-class wickets at an average of 10.54. A competent batsman primarily noted for his bowling, the St Catharine's Society magazine refers to him as 'a very fast bowler'. Between 1912 and 1914 he would appear both for Cambridge University and Sussex. After graduating in 1914, he served during the First World War initially with the Royal Fusiliers, 3rd Battalion of the City of London Regiment. He saw service in Gallipoli before being discharged on medical grounds in May 1917 with the rank of captain. A year later, towards the end of the war, he enrolled as an officer cadet in the Royal Flying Corps. He left the RFC in 1919, shortly after his marriage on 4 January 1919 at St

Conrad Baker – Cambridge University, Sussex and Somerset cricketer and later a renowned economist.

Mary's, Teddington, to Marie Clare (née Scott), the daughter of a company director.

He made just one appearance for Somerset, along with his friend George Woodcock. It is perhaps to be expected that in the topsy-turvy world of Somersetshire cricket this successful bowler should fail with the ball, taking 0 for 87, but come away with scores of 0 and 63 not out, the latter as part of a 9th-wicket stand of 128 with Woodcock.

After his brief appearance for Somerset, Conrad went into partnership with a former

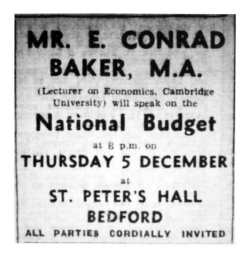

MR. E. CONRAD BAKER, M.A.

(Lecturer on Economics, Cambridge University) will speak on the

National Budget

at 8 p.m. on

THURSDAY 5 DECEMBER

at

ST. PETER'S HALL
BEDFORD

ALL PARTIES CORDIALLY INVITED

RFC colleague, Gilbert Harriman, and together they formed Baker, Harriman & Co, a firm of stockbrokers operating in Singapore. During this time he played in a first-class fixture for the Straits Settlements XI. The partnership with Harriman was dissolved in 1927. Gilbert moved to Hong Kong and later became President of the Sydney Stock Exchange, while Conrad returned to England. He was subsequently appointed a senior History master at Kingston-upon-Thames Grammar School. Then, in 1932, at the age of forty, he was offered the position of Headmaster at Crewkerne Grammar School, welcomed into the bosom of the county who had briefly claimed him as a young man. His stay in Crewkerne was shortlived. In May 1937 he resigned and returned to Cambridge University as a Director of Studies, involving himself with the Army Education Corps and commanding the Infantry Unit at Cambridge University from 1935 up to the outbreak of the Second World War. Thereafter he was appointed a Professor of Economics with the Cambridge Extra Mural Board, originally set up in 1873 to take education beyond the confines of the university. He travelled to various parts of the East of England, delivering courses of lectures and also, as 'E. Conrad Baker, M. A.', writing books and pamphlets on economic matters, attempting to explain issues in a way that could be digested by the layman. He can therefore be added to the swollen ranks of Somerset cricketers who have enjoyed literary success.

Having ventured opinions on the Bretton Woods Agreement and the relatively high level of taxation under the Attlee government of 1945, he became actively involved in politics, becoming the prospective Conservative candidate for Great Yarmouth and Gorleston in 1947. By the time of the 1950 election, the constituency had been renamed as Yarmouth. He came second, losing by 1,162 votes to the Labour candidate. At about this time Conrad's marriage to Marie Clare ended. He would subsequently be married to Mabel Whitworth in Maidenhead in 1964.

Conrad Baker died at Islet Park, Maidenhead in Berkshire on 8 April 1969 at the age of seventy-seven.

255
Walter Sydney Whiting
28 May 1921 v. Middlesex, Bath

Walter Whiting was born on 23 October 1888 in Bath, one of ten children of George Whiting, an ironmonger, cutler and saw manufacturer, who had purchased the business in 1873. A description of the 'handsome and commodious' shop on Walcot Street, Bath, in *Progress Commerce* gives a picture of the wiles deployed by George to ensnare his customers:

> *On entering, the first feature of interest is the bold and pertinent query, "Why are Whiting's knives like the Briish Army" to which the obvious reply, "Because they cannot be beaten," is appended.*

The article goes on to list some of the 'interesting novelties' in display cabinets, intended to convey a reassuring sense of expertise. They included an ingeniously designed and superbly crafted pocket-knife with 128 blades, which had been on display since the shop was founded in 1828, a pair of scissors eighteen inches long and beside them 'half a dozen pairs of Lilliputian scissors, three quarters of an inch long'. To the rear of the premises stood the manufacturing and repair workshops where it was claimed that some 400 to 500 items were sharpened weekly.

Walter was educated at King Edward's School, Bath. Whereas some of George Whiting's offspring followed their father into the ironmongery business, Walter opted for a career as a clerk in a solicitors' office. He was a talented all-round sportsman. A versatile footballer, he played in a variety of forward positions for Bath City FC and as a cricketer he bowled leg-breaks and was for many years one of the mainstays of a strong Bath CC side.

He was invited to play for Somerset on eight occasions between 1921 and 1923 and proved by no means out of his depth with a batting average of 14.77 and 27 wickets at 23.92 including 4 for 28 in the first Middlesex innings on his debut. Returning to club cricket he would remain vice-

Walter Whiting – a long-serving member of Bath CC and regarded as a fine coach and mentor.

captain of the club for a total of twenty years, stepping in regularly to captain the Bath team. Over the course of his career he scored ten centuries for the club and took more than 1,000 wickets. A local press reports states that 'in one season for the First XI he had the unique experience of performing the hat trick on four occasions'.

He was regarded as an outstanding coach and mentor to the young members of the Bath club. In 1928, Somerset introduced an Under-25s tournament where each district was captained by an older player. Walter was chosen to captain Bath Area and led his charges to victory in the inaugural competition. In later life he became a keen golfer and a member of the Kingsdown Golf Club.

He had been married on 9 September 1916 in the Methodist chapel in West Derby, Liverpool, to Annie Caldicott Littler, a milliner. He was still working at the time as a solicitor's clerk. The couple would have no children. A loyal member of one cricket club and rooted in one city, he also remained with the same practice throughout his working life. He was promoted to the position of Managing Clerk at Titley, Long and Co. (later Titley, Long and Volle) as early as the 1930s and would remain in that position until the early 1950s.

After a period of illness, with local press reports of his suffering from pneumonia, he died at the age of sixty-three on 15 January 1952 in Combe Park, Bath.

256
William Arthur Burgess
28 May 1921 v. Middlesex, Bath

He was known to friends and family as Archie. Peter Roebuck refers to Archie Burgess as 'a hitter from Minehead', doing something of a disservice to an all-rounder who, having appeared for Somerset on seven occasions across the 1921 and 1922 seasons, went on to achieve the double of 1,000 runs and 100 wickets for Minehead. The *Wells Journal* of 1923 reported that 'this is believed to be the first time a Somerset cricketer has achieved this feat in local cricket', adding that 'owing to the glut of talent at the disposal of Somerset this season, Burgess did not find a place in the county XI'. In his games for the county he had averaged 17.58 with the bat, including one half-century and took 6 wickets at 41.00 apiece.

Archie was born in Minehead on 31 January 1888. His mother, Mary Jane (née Floyd) was a farmer's daughter from Bossington and his father, John, a building contractor who would later name his company John Burgess and Sons. John's offspring, Sidney and

Archie, both entered the fold on leaving school. The brothers would become joint owners of the thriving business in 1934 on the death of their father. The family firm was very successful, taking on apprentices and being responsible for the building of many houses in the area, together with projects such as an extension to the Minehead Public Swimming Baths.

In 1915, he was married to Dorothy May Cox, the daughter of Herbert Cox, who owned and edited the *West Somerset Free Press*. Prior to their marriage, Dorothy and Archie had lived near to each other on Tregonwell Road and no doubt mixed in the same social circles.

Archie Burgess was active in local politics, becoming Chairman for a period, in the mid-1930s, of the Minehead Urban District Council. There are clear indications of a deep-rooted concern for his fellow men. As an example, a local press report informs us that he was the driving force behind a new scheme to help financially distressed areas of his home town, as part of the celebrations of the coronation of King Edward the Eighth. In the event, by abdicating, the monarch inadvertently saved the burghers of Minehead some possibly unwanted expenditure.

By this time, Archie had begun to turn his hand to lawn bowls and, demonstrating his natural flair as a sportsman, he proved a success, winning the Somerset singles title in 1949. That same year he was appointed President of the Minehead Rotary Club.

He died in Minehead on 20 June 1970, aged eighty-two, by then a wealthy man. He had no children but was survived by his wife, Dorothy.

Archie Burgess of Minehead CC – seen (top) as a young man and (bottom, right) seated with fellow Somerset cricketer, Algy Bligh.

257
Harry George Pruett
11 June 1921 v. Derbyshire, Bath

Harry George Pruett [signature]

Harry Pruett's birth certificate is a work of fiction that had him registered as Harry Doel, the son of 'Fanny Elizabeth (née Dawes)' and 'Henry George Doel'. The truth is that his mother Fanny Doel was unmarried and had never been a Dawes. Furthermore, Henry George Doel did not exist. The deception had been orchestrated by her lover, Thomas Pruett. It was all a subplot in an audacious plan by Thomas to dispense with his wife and begin a new life.

Harry Pruett seen (top, left) with E. G. Northway v Yorkshire at Huddersfield, 1926: he found more fame as a golfer than as a cricketer.

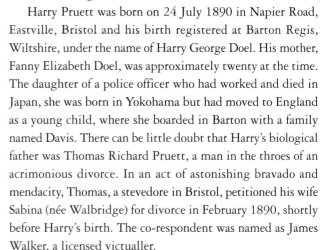

Harry Pruett was born on 24 July 1890 in Napier Road, Eastville, Bristol and his birth registered at Barton Regis, Wiltshire, under the name of Harry George Doel. His mother, Fanny Elizabeth Doel, was approximately twenty at the time. The daughter of a police officer who had worked and died in Japan, she was born in Yokohama but had moved to England as a young child, where she boarded in Barton with a family named Davis. There can be little doubt that Harry's biological father was Thomas Richard Pruett, a man in the throes of an acrimonious divorce. In an act of astonishing bravado and mendacity, Thomas, a stevedore in Bristol, petitioned his wife Sabina (née Walbridge) for divorce in February 1890, shortly before Harry's birth. The co-respondent was named as James Walker, a licensed victualler.

Thomas and Sabina had been married in 1870 and had had five children between 1873 and 1882. The four-day hearing in the High Court commenced in November 1890. In support of his claim, Thomas stated that neighbours had informed him 'that they have seen different men entering the house at night and have seen them come out again the following morning'. Sabina and Walker denied the accusations and she counter-petitioned, alleging that on numerous occasions Thomas had beaten her, that he had deserted her and the children, leaving her destitute, and that in June 1889 he came to the house, abused her and struck her in the face and body with his fist. In consequence of this assault, Thomas had entered a written agreement to pay his wife fifteen shillings a week in maintenance in order to escape imprisonment. The final piece of the jigsaw was that since April 1889 and to the date of the hearing, Thomas had lived and habitually committed adultery with Fanny Doel. Sabina also counter-petitioned for custody of the children.

It should be noted that Thomas was indeed by now living with Fanny and their son Harry and yet – astonishingly – adultery by Sabina was found to be proven by the jury but Thomas was found not to have transgressed. Thomas was awarded costs against Walker and gained custody of the children.

It is unclear how much Harry knew about the

ESTABLISHED 1882.

T. Pruett & Sons,

Offices:

59 QUEEN SQUARE,
BRISTOL

Tel. Address: Pronto, Bristol
Day Telephone: 23779 Bristol
Night „ 67152 Bristol

Stevedores, Contractors,
Steam Hoist Owners

Harry Pruett inherited his father's thriving stevedore business in Bristol

subterfuge as he grew to adulthood bearing the surname of Pruett. During the war, he joined up with the Royal Engineers as a motor cycle despatch rider and was wounded at Ypres in May 1915. Later that year he was married to Evelyn Mabel (née Roberts) with whom he would have a son and two daughters. In marked contrast to his parents, Harry appears to have enjoyed a long and happy marriage.

His father's stevedore business in the Bristol docks continued to thrive and Harry would in time become the principal of T. Pruett and Sons of Queen's Square, Bristol. In the meantime, as Thomas prepared him for his future role, Harry found time to indulge in sporting activity. He featured regularly in club cricket as a left-arm bowler, particularly for Bristol Wayfarers and for a Bristol Schoolmasters side who embraced players from other professions. He was offered a trial with Gloucestershire in May 1921 and performed well with a seven-wicket haul for a Gloucestershire XI versus Cirencester & District. It is therefore a surprise that he should have made his first-class debut the following month for Somerset. He would only play for them on one further occasion – in 1926. He took no first-class wickets, at a cost of 49 runs and averaged 1.75 with the bat, suggesting that Gloucestershire had made the correct decision in rejecting him. Harry's greatest sporting prowess was as a golfer. He was a member of the Shirehampton Golf Club in Bristol and enjoyed success at club and county level, at one point holding the course record. He had also become a director of Bristol City FC in the early 1920s, although he and five fellow directors were suspended in 1923 after questions were asked about the possible rigging of the results of certain fixtures. The suspension was lifted by the Football League in 1926. Later, Harry became a racehorse owner, with one press report stating that his horse, Sonza, had in 1938 won the Rajah Cup at Cheltenham, presented by Rajah Badahur of Rajmagar.

Harry Pruett died at the Chesterfield Nursing Home in Clifton on 22 January 1948 at the age of fifty-seven. His ashes were scattered in the Bristol Channel, not far from the Bristol Docks where his family had made their living.

258
Edward Peter Collings
13 July 1921 v. Worcestershire, Taunton

Edward Collings was the son of Colonel Godfrey Disney Collings and his wife, Johanna Katherine. He was born on 30 January 1892 in Lichfield in Staffordshire and educated between 1905 and 1908 at The King's School, Canterbury. He played for the school's First XI for two years, the school magazine of 1908 reporting that 'he bowled a good deal slower than last year and with greater steadiness, but without much sting'. He is also described as a 'very fair field'. As for his batting, we are informed that he 'can hit, but has no defence'. On leaving The King's School, he attended the Army School in Maidenhead. Whereas his brother, Alexander Godfrey, went on to become a schoolmaster at Worksop College, Edward left school at eighteen to join the Army. He was trained at the Royal Military College at Sandhurst and in March 1912 he joined the 30th Foot (East Lancashire) Regiment as a second lieutenant. There was some dispute over the events that followed. Edward would later claim, as part of his application for paid sick-leave and in order to secure the pension he hoped for, that he had been given leave in order to assist in the running of a tea plantation in Assam. This version of events would be challenged by the Army, who would claim that he had resigned his commission only to rejoin at the onset of the First World War. In the absence of any proof to the contrary, his view prevailed, although subsequent events would suggest that this had blotted his copybook.

For the duration of the war and beyond, he served with the 6th Royal Fusiliers (City of London) Regiment and would suffer a wound in his left shoulder at Gallipoli in April 1915. Thenceforth his involvement was limited by ill health and he would in fact only see further active service for a fortnight in 1916 and for five months in 1917. He would remain in the military until 1925, when he resigned his commission, by then a captain. This was the point at which the arguments surfaced over the nature of his previous separation from the Army and the debate ensued over the size of his pension pot.

He had been married on 23 May 1914 at All Saints Cathedral, Allahabad, to Dorothy Jessie (née Penwarden), the daughter of an engineer who worked with the Indian government. He and Dorothy would have a son, Adrian Edward Penwarden Collings, and they would subsequently fight over custody at the time of their divorce, which resulted from her affair with a Mr R. H. Read.

By the 1920s, Edward's father had retired to Bath and the returning son began to play club cricket for Bath and Lansdown, where he was regarded as a useful right-arm fast-medium bowler. He played four times for Somerset – twice in 1921 and two more times in 1925 – but with only limited success. His two wickets came at the cost of 78.00 runs apiece and he averaged 6.00 with the bat.

In 1927, by now living in Marlborough and a company secretary, he was married to Nora Spencer Mitchell, the daughter of a retired colonel. They would have no children together. A press report reveals that his 'health broke down' in 1928 with the result that he was obliged to give up cricket for a year. His seems not to have been the most robust of constitutions.

E. P. Collings of Bath CC and Lansdown CC – he blotted his copybook with the Army.

His application to join the Army Reserve at the start of the Second World War was rejected with the words 'not accepted' writ bold and heavily underscored, offering telling evidence of the Army's continued disenchantment with him.

He died at Combe Down outside Bath on 14 September 1968 at the age of seventy-six.

259
Thomas Egerton Seymour Francis
3 August 1921 v. Glamorgan, Weston-super-Mare

In *Rugger: The History, Theory and Practice of Rugby Football*, former England international Sir Wavell Wakefield writes that:

I noticed during my term in office at Cambridge that harm is done by excessive Press write-ups of schoolboy {rugby} football. T. E. S. Francis, for example, came up from Tonbridge with a great reputation as a stand-off half, but in his first few matches for the 'Varsity he played against halves of International class … and soon realised how much he had to learn. In his case no harm was done for he was big enough to learn his lesson.

Indeed, he was a good learner. Good enough to gain four England caps.

Known as 'Tim', he was born on 21 November 1902 in Uitenhage, near Port Elizabeth. His father was Percy James Francis, a London-born accountant who had been posted to South Africa and was married to Annie Edith (née Smith). Tim was educated at Tonbridge School before going up to Pembroke College, Cambridge. An all-round sportsman, he won rugby blues in 1922 and the two succeeding years and gained his cricketing blue in 1925. In his history of Somerset cricket, Peter Roebuck states that, with his usual eye for the main chance, John Daniell asked Tim if he had anywhere to stay during the summer vacation and invited him to reside with the Daniells for the

duration. It is certainly a fact that on a return trip to England in April 1922 he gave his destination as Somerset.

Tim Francis would play for the county on sixteen occasions between 1921 and 1925. A right-handed batsman who occasionally turned his arm, he averaged a modest 9.08 and took no wickets at a cost of 19 runs. Looking for positives, his obituary in the Somerset Year Book would later state that he was 'neat, and always immaculately turned out'. Perhaps he spent too short a while at the crease to become in any way dishevelled. He enjoyed more success at rugby, playing for Blackheath and the Barbarians as well as Cambridge University and England. In a series of cigarette cards entitled *Famous Rugby Players*, Ogden's notes that he 'never really fulfilled his promise as a stand-off half' and consequently moved to centre, which was the position in which he gained his four England caps.

After graduating, he returned to Southern Africa, where he would continue to be involved in cricket and rugby circles in various capacities. He made one final first-class appearance as captain of an Eastern Province team who were defeated by MCC on their 1927/8 tour of South Africa. He was married on 17 September 1930 to Margaret Glenton at St George's

T. E. S. 'Tim' Francis – gained four England rugby caps.

Church, Parktown, Johannesburg. She was the daughter of Frederick Glenton, a successful merchant, based in Cape Town. Margaret had studied at the Royal College of Music and had taught for a while in London.

He would be awarded the OBE in 1965 'for services to sport, particularly cricket and rugby football'. Outside the world of sport he was a company director, based primarily in Southern Rhodesia (now Zimbabwe).

Tim Francis died at the age of sixty-six on 24 February 1969 in Kumalo, Bulawayo, Zimbabwe. His death was attributed to heart failure, coronary thrombosis and asthma: a cocktail of ailments strong enough to floor even the ablest of sportsmen.

260
Charles Arthur Winter
3 August 1921 v. Glamorgan, Weston-super-Mare

He was generally referred to as Arthur. His father, Charles Edgar Winter, born in Wellington, Somerset, had been a protégée of Harry Fox, the man who had helped to establish county teams at rugby and cricket. Encouraged by Fox, Charles Edgar had appeared as a teenager for Somerset at both sports. A fast bowler, he had made useful contributions but had never quite hit the heights. Charles was married to Edith Ellen (née Hedditch) and by the time of Arthur's birth on 24 December 1903 in Stroud Green, North London, he was working as an agent for Fox Brothers woollen goods in the capital. In time he would build up his own clothing concern.

The business proved profitable enough for Arthur to be educated privately. Initially he was sent – along with two brothers and a sister – to Hart House School, a tiny institution run by his uncle, Walter Potter, who was married to Blanche (née Winter), the sister of Charles Edgar. Given that the siblings accounted for four of the five pupils, the place must have seemed a home from home. He then went on to Repton School, where he was captain of the school cricket XI for two years and, following in the paternal footsteps, appeared for Somerset as a teenager. Like his father before

Charles Arthur Winter at Repton.

*C. A. Winter as captain
of the Repton First XI.*

him, he was a right-arm pace bowler who was no mug with the bat. In *Repton Cricket (1901-1951),* F. R. D'O Monro observes that 'Winter bowled fast and well but tired rather soon'. A local press report, announcing his forthcoming debut for the county, makes a similar observation, suggesting that 'he may make a good fast bowler as well as a useful bat, if only he would go at things with a little more vim'. In the event he would play twenty-six first-class matches for Somerset, taking 15 wickets at 38.13 each and averaging 10.92 with the bat.

He was married in 1930 to Raemonde Martin, whose father, Oscar Harry Martin, also worked in the London cloth manufacturing business, having originally run a factory in Huddersfield making worsted cloth. At the time of his marriage, Arthur listed his job as Company Secretary and prior to this he had described himself as a Continental Sales Manager, suggesting that he was very possibly continuing in the family business.

Charles Arthur Winter was a member of the Somerset XI who played Hampshire at Dean Park, Bournemouth, in 1922: despite a masterful innings of 156 by Jack MacBryan, Somerset conspired to pluck defeat from the jaws of victory.
LEFT TO RIGHT: A. Young, E. Robson, T. E. S. Francis, S. G. U. Considine, C. A. Winter, A. G. Marshall, T. C. Lowry, J. Bridges, J. C. White, R. C. Robertson-Glasgow, J. C. W. MacBryan.

The 1939 census records him and Raemonde living in Wallingford without children but with a housekeeper, his occupation given intriguingly as 'fruit and poultry'. Inserted in another hand are the words 'incapacitated: retired'. He would have been thirty-five at the time – too early, in the normal course of events to have retired. It is worth noting that 1939 was the year in which Arthur's father, by then seventy-three, was married for a second time, on this occasion to a woman forty years his junior. Perhaps this was the spur for Charles Edgar to sell the business. We are left to wonder whether or not relations between father and son were strained at the time.

Arthur Winter was gazetted into the Royal Electrical and Mechanical Engineers in May 1944 as a second lieutenant, suggesting that whatever the reasons for his incapacitation in 1939, the setback had not been of a permanent nature.

He and Raemonde moved to Farnham Common, Buckinghamshire, where her father had resided. Arthur died there on 4 March 1982 at the age of seventy-eight.

261
Mervyn Llewellyn Hill
20 August 1921 v. Sussex, Weston-super-Mare

Mervyn was the elder of the two sons of Vernon Tickell Hill, a hard-hitting batsman who had figured prominently in Somerset's early years of County Championship cricket and would become President of the club in 1930. Born on 23 June 1902 in Llandaff, Cardiff, Mervyn was educated at Eton College and was in the First XI in 1920 and 1921, developing into a fine wicket-keeper. He went up to Pembroke College, Cambridge, where he played for the University XI but failed to win a blue. He would play for Somerset and Glamorgan. In his first seven first-class innings, he mustered only three runs in total. But things looked up and, taking his cue from his father, he made three swashbuckling half-centuries in his career. His average over forty-two games was 11.17 and he effected 66 dismissals, including 25 stumpings.

When playing for Gentlemen versus Players in 1925 at The Oval, it is said that he surprised Gubby Allen by standing up to the wicket (which, unbeknown to the bowler, he always did) as Allen sent down his pacey deliveries. He will have pleased his teammate yet more when he came in at

Mervyn Hill – 'a man of easy temperament'.

Mervyn Llewellyn Hill.

number eleven and held his ground while Allen went on to chalk up his maiden first-class century. In 1926, Mervyn played his small and generally overlooked part in cricketing history when with Surrey only moments away from a ten-wicket victory and Jack Hobbs just three short of his record-breaking century that would take him past W G Grace's aggregate, he appeared deliberately to miss a stumping opportunity with Hobbs well out of his crease. It is certainly in keeping with his personality to have done so: cricket for him

Mervyn and Patricia Hill on their wedding day in 1936.

was something to be enjoyed, not marred by competitive edge. Mervyn took part in a trail-blazing MCC tour of Indian, Ceylon, Pakistan, Bangladesh and Burma in 1926/7. Obliged to delay his departure owing to ill health, he joined his teammates when the tour was already underway. The following season, his first-class career began to peter out as professional wicket-keeper Wally Luckes became a regular fixture in the Somerset team.

In 1933 Mervyn became the land agent for Sir John Amory, residing at Home Farm, Knightshayes, in Devon. He turned out for the Devon cricket team on a number of occasions, sometimes as captain. He was married in 1936 to Patricia Barton, in Slad, Gloucestershire. They would have three sons: Vernon, Victor and Gerald, the last of these born in 1946.

In 1945, Mervyn purchased a farm of his own – Collipriest Farm, near Tiverton. He acted as Secretary of the Devon Landowners Association and was a member of the council of the Bath and West Show. Sadly, he had less than three years to develop his farming business before he died unexpectedly whilst in a solicitor's office in Little Cottage Street in Westminster. His death in Westminster on 27 February 1948 at the age of only forty-five was sudden, resulting from the congenital heart condition he had endured since birth, though it had never curbed his zest for life.

Peter Roebuck describes him as 'a man of easy temperament, as strong as a Suffolk punch' and teammate Raymond Robertson-Glasgow says of him that he was 'an artist at working, sleeping and eating: epicurean by taste, he could be a mighty hitter'. His niece, Guinea, describes Mervyn as 'a great character, enormous fun and a great enthusiast.' His younger brother, Evelyn, a contrasting figure in every way – tall, slim, reserved and happiest in the background – also played for Somerset.

1922

"Robson made the winning hit, a six over the pavilion
off Hearne, on the stroke of time and to the
accompaniment of wild enthusiasm."

Taunton Courier

Championship Position: 10 of 17

At their end-of-season dinner, Somerset celebrated securing a mid-table position
despite fielding a largely amateur side and playing the game in a fine spirit. And
yet most of the toasts were for the old pro, Ernie Robson, after his winning six at the
eleventh hour against Middlesex at Weston-super-Mare. He had been immediately
handed a cheque for £50 by an 'anonymous donor' who turned out to be Jeremiah
Lyon, father of Somerset cricketer, M. D. Lyon. Jeremiah earned and lost money in
prodigious amounts and with dizzying speed and was later declared a bankrupt.
Perhaps he was too generous for his own good. Robson was later awarded a marble
clock and presented with the match ball, mounted on a silver stand. While Somerset
were reliving the glory of one heady winning shot, Yorkshire were celebrating winning
the County Championship. The North was a foreign place: they did things differently
there.

It was true that Somerset were a better side than their position suggested and that,
as one report had it, 'several times the side was robbed of a win by bad weather or just
an irritating insufficiency of time'. In six of their seven draws they had accumulated a
first innings lead.

Jack White and Jack MacBryan led the way with bat and ball respectively. *The
Cricketer* reports that 'J. C. W. MacBryan was the outstanding batsman ... who besides
getting runs with great consistency got them in beautiful style'. He scored two of the
county's three centuries and was well supported by Ulick Considine who showed 'rare
grit and not a little skill' in making just short of 1,000 runs. There was a welcome
return from Ceylon (Sri Lanka) by Bill Greswell. Although past his devastating best
as a swing bowler, he still took 71 wickets to add to Jack White's 146 victims. Ernie
Robson and Jim Bridges offered valuable support.

Among the debutants, Guy Earle would, in the best Somerset tradition, win renown for the astonishing power of his hitting, if not for his skills as a builder of innings.

December 1922 marked the passing of the President, Henry Murray-Anderdon, a hugely influential figure. Murray-Anderdon's tireless work as an administrator and patron had been instrumental in the club's continued survival. Without his unflagging support, Somerset could well have opted to forgo their first-class status in the lean years prior to the First World War.

Ernie Robson – an unassuming Yorkshireman, he had served Somerset well since 1895.

262
Guy Fife Earle
31 May 1922 v. Oxford University, Oxford

Guy Earle was born on 24 August 1891 in Newcastle-on-Tyne. Owing to the fact that his paternal grandfather, a businessman based in Liverpool, had left a staggering fortune, he would never be obliged to work, although he did spend time in the military. His father, Cecil Arthur Earle was a lieutenant in the Royal Artillery who died in Bengal at the age of only twenty-seven, leaving his widow Lizzie Isabella (née Scott) to bring up four-year-old Guy and his younger brother, Eric. Guy was sent to Harrow, where he gained a reputation as a fast bowler and fearsome hitter, playing for the First XI from 1907 until 1910, when he captained the side. It is said that such was his prodigious power that whenever he was at the crease, the fielders on the three adjoining pitches kept a wary eye on proceedings, expecting one of his thunderous missiles to come winging their way.

On leaving Harrow he became a gentleman cadet at Sandhurst, whom he played for alongside fellow Somerset cricketer Jack MacBryan. He was offered a commission with the Rifle Brigade and served in the First World War. Wounded at Neuve Chapelle in March 1915, he recovered and eventually resigned his commission with the rank of captain in 1919.

MR G.F. EARLE
THE HERCULEAN, HURRICANE HITTER

Having played for Surrey on four occasions (two times before and twice after the war), he took up residence for a while at his mother's home in Minehead and threw in his lot with Somerset. He would prove a hitter in the finest Somerset tradition, giving Herbert Fowler and Arthur Wellard a good run for their money for the title of mightiest of the Somersetshire smiters. He was an imposing figure, 6 ft 3 in tall and 'broad as a barn', as Peter Roebuck put it. Frank Lee states in *Cricket, Lovely Cricket* that Earle 'used bats weighing five or six ounces heavier than most, and always insisted on hitting the bowling out of sight or dying in the attempt'. It is said that as he came in to bat, the rowing boats were manned in readiness to fish the ball out of the River Tone. Whilst this may be an apocryphal tale, it is certainly the case that he emptied the bar each time he strode to the crease. To loiter around finishing your pint was to risk missing the show. He would plant his leg forward and shape to heave every delivery out of the ground, one noteworthy six landing the other side of the River Tone. The *Taunton Courier* furnishes us with a useful summary of his technique:

He does not play himself in. From the first ball to the last he is always attacking the bowling, and although on some occasions he skies the ball unintentionally, he generally places his shots well and with plenty of power behind them.

He in fact averaged 18.96 in 152 matches for Somerset, betraying the truth that the flurries of excitement were often all too brief. To his one century were added twenty 50s. He also chipped in with 86 wickets at 28.45 apiece. He captained Somerset on three occasions, including a match against Gloucestershire when he compiled what Peter Roebuck describes as one of his 'brief and brutish' innings, reaching his half-century in fifteen minutes.

As a man of independent means, he was able to join tours of New Zealand, the Indian sub-continent and Egypt. While in Egypt in 1932 he was involved in a motor accident that, although it did not cause major injury, cut short his sporting career. He never took part in any serious cricket again.

Guy Earle – his innings were generally 'brief and brutish'.

His personal life was as tangled and complex as his batting was straightforward and predictable. In 1918 he was married to Isabel Bridget Boughton-Knight, with whom he had a daughter, Audrey Bridget. He was divorced in 1922, having initially failed to adhere to a court order demanding that he restore his wife's conjugal rights. His marriage to Helen Alice Elliot took place in 1924 but was dissolved in 1927 after teammate Dar Lyon had purloined her. The divorce proceedings confirm that the marriage was over more or less before it had begun, with the union only ever consummated while they enjoyed their honeymoon on the Isle of Mull. Lyon is clearly the co-respondent referred to anonymously as 'some man' in the citing of Helen's adultery. Earle was seemingly relaxed over his new status as a cuckold and not a man to bear grudges.

Guy was married for a third and final time in 1935 to Bridget Joan Sherston. They would have three children. He enjoyed the countryside and was never happier than with a fishing rod in his hand, ensnaring salmon in Scotland. During the Second World War, he cast his rod aside when he was called into service as a squadron leader in the Auxiliary Air Force in an administrative capacity.

He died at the age of seventy-five on 30 December 1966 in Maperton, near Wincanton. Perhaps his epitaphs should be left to two of his teammates. Raymond Robertson-Glasgow writes that Guy Earle 'had that rare and enviable spirit which sees no good in opponents ... soon to become useful, if reluctant, accessories to acts of prodigious violence'. By way of comparison, Frank Lee describes him as 'kind and considerate' and 'well loved by all'. A gentle giant, his thoughts turned to aggression only when he held a cricket bat in his hand.

263
Terence George Owen Cole
31 May 1922 v. Oxford University, Oxford

Terence Cole was born on 14 November 1877 at Llanrhaiadr in Denbighshire, Wales, and would become something of a cricketing nomad, making first-class appearances for Cambridge University, MCC, Lancashire, Lord Brackley's XI (on a tour of the West Indies), Derbyshire and Somerset, as well as appearing for his native Denbighshire. Given this, it is perhaps surprising that he mustered only twenty first-class games.

His father – Francis Burton Cole – was a captain in the 7th Royal Fusiliers and when Terence's mother died before her son's fourth birthday, Francis quickly remarried. Terence was soon sent off to Harrow School, and through it all he retained a sunny disposition. A contemporaneous report describes him as being 'possessed of a fine sense of humour' and in many of the images of him, he displays a smiling countenance. He certainly had reason to be cheerful when in1897 in the annual fixture against Eton at Lord's, he amassed a record-breaking 142 runs versus Harrow's great rivals. He was presented with a miniature golden bat inscribed with his exploits and he would retain it as a treasured possession for the rest of his life. The record stood until 1913, when it was surpassed by Geoffrey Wilson, who went on to play for Yorkshire. Terence also represented Harrow at fives.

On leaving school, he went up to Trinity Hall, Cambridge, where he played for the Varsity side in 1898 but failed to win his blue. A right-handed batsman and slow left-arm bowler, he never hit the heights in a fragmented first-class career spread over twenty-four years. In twenty matches he averaged 15.59 with the bat and took no wickets, conceding 17 runs.

After graduating he trained briefly as an engineer before aborting the idea and becoming a land agent based for a while in the Liverpool area and engaging in club cricket, while making one unsuccessful appearance for Lancashire in 1904. He then lived for a period before the First World War in Duckmanton, near Chesterfield, continuing his work as a land agent and turning out on six occasions for Derbyshire.

T. G. O. Cole – he won plaudits at Harrow but never hit the heights as a first-class cricketer.

During the war he joined the Denbighshire Yeomanry and served in Turkey under Field Marshall Allenby. After the cessation of hostilities he moved – by now a captain –to the Taunton area: firstly to Sherford House in the town and then to Stoke Court in Stoke St Mary. He became very active with the Somerset Stragglers team, as a participant and administrator. His only game for Somerset, when he was forty-four years of age, yielded 19 runs in his two innings.

By this stage of his life, his major passion was hunting with the Taunton Vale Foxhounds and later with the West Somerset Foxhounds. Almost inevitably, he engaged in the other associated activities of shooting and fishing. Terence was a very keen supporter of the Boy Scout movement and a friend of Baden-Powell, whom he accompanied on a trip to Jamaica in 1904, laying the ground for the establishment of a branch of the movement there, six years later. He was married in 1916 to Audrey Isabelle Katherine Mutter. She was forty-two at the time and he thirty-nine, so that there was never any likelihood of children. Perhaps his involvement with the scouts provided him with a substitute family. He was similarly a huge supporter of the hospital at Taunton and a frequent visitor. He also remained for much of his life involved with the parish church at Thurlbear, serving for a period as a churchwarden.

During the Second World War he was appointed a platoon commander in the home guard. A very popular, easy-going man, he did not live to see the end of the war, dying at Stoke St Mary on 15 December 1944 at the age of sixty-seven.

264
Alpin Erroll Thomson
31 May 1922 v. Oxford University, Oxford

A. E. Thomson – 'if he drank less he would probably be a better officer'.

Alpin Erroll Thomson was born in Perth, Western Australia on 14 May 1893. He was the son of Alpin Fowler Thomson and his wife, Ada Henrietta. Alpin Snr was Under Secretary for Railways in Western Australia, and would later retire to Wellington in Somerset, providing the son's link with the county. Alpin Jnr enjoyed or endured a peripatetic life. After enrolling at the age of thirteen at the Osborne Naval College on the Isle of Wight he later trained at the Britannia Naval College at Dartmouth.

His first appointment was as a midshipman on HMS *Superior* and then in 1914 he was appointed a sub-lieutenant on HMS *Circe*. He would serve as a sub-lieutenant until 1916 when he was promoted to the rank of lieutenant, serving on the HMS *Gloucester* before being deployed on the minesweeper HMS *Kempton*. He won the Distinguished Service Cross (DSC) in 1917 for showing great fortitude and presence of mind when HMS *Kempton* hit a mine. He subsequently commanded HMS *Melton* and HMS *Tring*.

On 17 August 1918 he was married to Sophia (née Bedell-Sivright), with whom he would have a daughter, who became an actress. The Bedell-Sivrights were prominent in the Scottish social scene with Sophia's brother, David (known as 'Darkie'), a captain of the British rugby team (later the British Lions) and described as the toughest forward to have played rugby for Scotland.

After the war Alpin qualified as a military Physical Training instructor. Short and powerfully built, he was a useful sportsman who played rugby for Scotland at a time when he was representing the Combined Services. He and fellow officer Cecil MacKenzie (who appears to have excelled at every sport known to man) played together over the 1921 season with Thomson selected as a three-quarter for the matches against France, Wales and England. Although he scored one try, his handling of the ball was pilloried by the correspondent in *The Times*, who at least conceded that Alpin had a good turn of pace. Unable to resist a pun, the reporter informs us that the two naval officers were 'all at sea'.

Somerset's leading light, John Daniell, had an unshakeable belief that being a good rugby player was ample reason for a man's inclusion in the Somerset cricket team. His faith was rarely rewarded. Alpin Thomson appeared only twice for the county – against Oxford University in 1922 and against Hampshire at the United Services Ground in Portsmouth in 1923. Described as a fast-medium right-arm bowler, he only bowled in the first of these games, taking 3 wickets at 36.00 runs apiece. As a batsman, he never troubled the scorers. He also played for the Royal Navy at this time.

His annual performance reviews suggest that there were issues with his conduct. Entries include 'leadership and influence good, not always too tactful' and separately we are informed that he was 'impatient of discipline and excitable and unbalanced', that his 'influence on younger officers tends to be bad' and finally that 'if he drank less he would probably be a better officer'. He was neither the first nor the last rugby player to have attracted such criticism. Maybe such concerns lay behind his secondment to the RAF at Leuchars, near Dundee, and his subsequent transfer to the role of office instructor with the Royal Naval Volunteer Reserves from 1932 until his retirement in 1936.

While based at Leuchars he played for Fifeshire at cricket (appearing during the 1932 season) and at the Grange club at Edinburgh (in 1933). He also began to appear regularly in golf tournaments, representing the St Andrews New Club.

Following his divorce from Sophia in 1938, he was married for a second time in 1945. His partner was Mary Elizabeth, widow of Alexander Lindsay, with whom she had resided at Craigsanquhar House, Fife. Alexander had been the director of a confectionary and preserve manufacturing business, also representing Scotland at cricket. It is clear that Alpin and Mary were already co-habiting prior to Alexander's death. As an aside, Alexander Lindsay had in 1909 become the first man to score 1,000 runs in a season of county cricket in Scotland.

Alpin Thomson retired to Hawridge in Buckinghamshire where he died on 6 March 1960 at the age of sixty-six. His wife, Mary, lived for another twenty-two years.

265
Algernon Stuart Bligh
7 June 1922 v. Derbyshire, Taunton

Algernon S. Bligh

Algy Bligh was born on 6 October 1888 in Marylebone, London, and brought up first in Dulverton and then in Minehead. He was able to claim descent from the Earls of Darnley. His father, Lodovick, was a JP of independent means, the third generation of Blighs to have played cricket for Kent. Indeed, his great uncle, Ivo Bligh – who became the 8th Earl of Darnley – found fame as the England captain who won The Ashes in 1882-3. In the more distant past, another ancestor was Captain Bligh, who was famously cast adrift by the mutineers of the *Bounty* but successfully navigated his acolytes for over 4,000 nautical miles to safety.

The Blighs were cricket-obsessed. A letter from Edward Hawtrey, the headmaster of Algy's prep school, St Michael's, spells out in detail cricket's place on the curriculum, offering reassurances to Lodovick. Algy's father was clearly not interested in the school's academic record. He had in fact named his first son Harroweton in celebration of the fact that the child was born on 9 July 1887, the day after the fixture between the two institutions at Lord's. Harroweton would die in infancy and would never have to bear the cross of his name.

Sent to Eton College, Algy hit the headlines when a fire broke out at the school and two boys, trapped by the iron bars at the windows, were consumed by the flames, whereas he found the strength to remove the bars at his window, escaping in his night-clothes. On leaving school he went on to study at the Royal College of Agriculture at Cirencester, though he would only ever use his knowledge of horticulture in the management of his beloved fruit garden at Amberley House in Minehead. Indeed, he was a man of means whose only inclination was the pursuit of hobbies rather than any career. Among these hobbies, cricket was preeminent.

Algy Bligh was a modest man, uncomfortable with the idea of leading others, although his obsession with data made him an inveterate organiser. He signed up to the war effort with the 3rd Public Schools Brigade (later the 20th Battalion of the Royal Fusiliers) and saw action on the Western Front as a private. Despite the pleadings of his family he was reluctant to take up a commission as an officer. When all else had failed, Lt Col R. M. Dodington sent him a letter resorting to emotional blackmail, claiming that Algy was causing great distress to his mother and demanding that he should accept a commission as a second lieutenant with the Devonshire Regiment.

The writer also expresses the hope that Algy is recovering from his 'cases of spotted fever'. He received his commission in December 1918 and resigned from the Army in 1921.

He played for Somerset on four-teen occasions over a five-year period, averaging 17.50 with the bat and taking no wickets for 14 runs. He is described in one press report as 'a batsman who was very difficult to dislodge and a hard hitter'. He enjoyed a purple patch in early June 1925 with scores of 73 not out and 71 but his run of form was shortlived. At club level he played for many years with a great deal of success for Minehead CC and Somerset Stragglers, primarily as a wicket-keeper batsman.

Algernon Stuart Bligh.

He was an introverted but confident man who went quietly, even eccentrically, about his business and loved nothing more than communing with nature or engaging in sport. He was, however, inclined to firmly-held views and would speak out against what he perceived as any injustice or cheating. He was also said by Raymond Robertson-Glasgow to have made his feelings abun-dantly clear to an umpire when he believed he had been unfairly given out LBW. His unpreparedness or inability to engage in a nuanced debate was evident at the time of his divorce in 1936. Frustrated that his wife, the mother of his first two children, would not agree to a separation, he allegedly made her life miserable. Algy had been married in 1922 to Dora Joan (née Lovelace). After his divorce in 1937, he was married the following year to Emily Mabel Dorothy (née Larway), with whom he would have two daughters, born when he was well into his fifties.

With no employment, he found plenty of time to indulge his passions, which included not only cricket but also fox hunting. He was incensed that his pleasure was being diminished in 1934 when he claimed that foxes were 'being wilfully poisoned to spoil sport in the district.' He asserted that 'it appears to have been done from sheer maliciousness and selfishness and I think we are entitled to a little fairer treatment'.

A. S. Bligh – a willing soldier but a reluctant leader.

This might perhaps have been a pithy if unwitting summary of a fox's perspective on Algy and his fellow members of the hunt. He rode with the Minehead Harriers and was for a while joint master along with his sister. The two of them had stepped in to save the hunt when it was in a financially parlous state, although he soon stood down as a result of unease among other members of the hunt over his divorce from Dora, who was a popular figure.

Algy was a familiar presence in the countryside, regularly walking around the rides, pruning back the hedgerows to the benefit not just of the hunt but users of footpaths. Indeed he was rarely ever seen without a tool of some sort in his hand, tidying the countryside or his garden. When not walking, he might be seen cycling, in particular to church at least twice on a Sunday. On those occasions when he drove – for example to football matches, with Bristol City, Exeter City and Swindon Town all falling within his orbit – Algy kept a detailed record of miles travelled, totting it up each week, for no known reason beyond curiosity. He also kept a log of every number plate spotted at a time when cars were something of a novelty. Perhaps a trifle more conventional was his enthusiasm for philately.

Another more unexpected obsession was wasps, or more precisely their extermination. It apparently won him the sobriquet 'Minehead's champion wasp killer'. In one particularly productive season he destroyed 144 wasps' nests, thus exterminating about half a million wasps. It seems that he was on a one-man mission to rid West Somerset of anything he regarded as vermin – foxes and wasps being foremost in his sights.

On a more positive note, he was an enthusiastic promoter of and participant in sports of many kinds in Minehead, coached the Ladies' Hockey XI and was a leading light in mixed tennis. He acted as an unpaid groundsman to the cricket, tennis and hockey clubs and playfully inserted 'Groundsman' as his occupation on some official documents. He also offered his services as a referee. He did so until the very last. On the day before his death he had taken charge of a football match in the morning and a hockey match in the after-noon before complaining of feeling unwell. He died in his sleep at his beloved Amberley House in Minehead on 27 December 1952 at the age of sixty-four. The obituaries were full of praise for a 'warm-hearted' and 'kind and courte-ous' and 'humble' man. His daughter, Heather, should perhaps have the last word. She recounts how, despite all his interests, he always had time for his family. She has happy memories of falling asleep as Algy, banned by his wife from listening to the Ashes Tests taking place in Australia, would secretly steal into her bedroom and turn on the radio in the middle of the night to listen to the commentary, lying on the bed beside her while she drifted back to sleep. This glorious eccentric had no greater obsession than cricket and no greater love than family.

Algy Bligh – 'Minehead's champion wasp killer'.

266
James Jones
28 August 1922 v. Warwickshire, Taunton

James Jones, known as Jim, was born on 15 February 1895 in Blackwell, Derbyshire, the son of William Jones, a miner, and his wife, Sarah. Their sons, particularly James and his older brother, Harry, showed great promise as young sportsmen, with Harry playing football for Nottingham Forest and England and Jim enjoying a successful career as a professional cricketer. Their father had been a useful club cricketer who became a groundsman after he retired from the pits.

In 1909, at the age of only fourteen, Jim was severely injured, when his right arm was crushed in a mining accident at Blackwell colliery. Having returned to work after an eleven-week stay in hospital, he became an engine driver, transporting coal from the mine to nearby stations. By the outbreak of the First World War, his mother had died and the family had moved to Worksop. As a result of his injury, Jim was not enlisted until December 1915 and thereafter he served with the Labour Centre, Northern Command, until 1918.

At 5 ft 7 inches tall and possessed of a slight frame, Jim was able to overcome the restricted movement in his right arm and develop into a forceful left-handed batsman and a well-regarded wicket-keeper. His performances for Manton Colliery were sufficiently impressive for the Chard club side in Somerset to engage him as a pro. He caught Somerset's eye with some hard-hitting knocks and tidy displays behind the stumps. Over the 1922 and 1923 seasons he played seventeen times for the county,

Jim Jones of Somerset and Glamorgan.

although in many of those matches, the amateur M. D. Lyon was given precedence as the side's wicket-keeper. Singing his praises, the *Taunton Courier* reports that 'the Chard man scored freely all round the wicket, had an admirable defence and drove with power'. He only averaged 14.36, with a highest score of 70 for Somerset, but he would double this batting average during the latter part of his first-class career, suggesting that his output for Somerset does not reflect his ability. He also effected 16 dismissals for the county (which would rise to 40 in all first-class matches).

Whilst playing for Chard, he met his future wife, Edna Adeline Marjorie (née Worner), whose father was by then a retired police inspector. After leaving for Bermuda in the autumn of 1923 to take up a coaching appointment, before subsequently being employed by Gowerton CC in South Wales, Jim returned to be married to Madge, as he always referred to her, in November 1924. Thereafter, he took up a number of professional appointments, playing for Gowerton until 1927, for Neath in 1928 and 1929 and finally for Briton Ferry. Having qualified by residence to play for Glamorgan, he represented the county eight times over the 1928 and 1929 seasons. He was also selected to play twice for Wales in 1929, thus joining his brother Harry among the ranks of international sportsmen. In the 1930s, he took up a coaching position at Denstone College. A son, Arwyn, had been born in Swansea in 1925 and a daughter, Frances, was born in 1933, in Ashbourne, where Jim was based while employed by the college. His final coaching position saw the family moved to Hammersmith.

Jim Jones (top, left) with Cyril Smart (top, right) of Warwickshire and Glamorgan and (bottom) with his son, Arwyn.

In 1944 he became the licensee of The Old Duke on King Street, Bristol. Jim's daughter, Frances, describes her father as 'a generous man' whom she saw too little of as a child, having been evacuated during the war to stay with friends of the family in Briton Ferry and then watching as her father worked hard as a publican for seven days a week. Frances adds that 'his customers included the dockers from the river nearby, the prosperous solicitors from Queen Square and the actors from the Bristol Old Vic in King Street. These last included Julian Slade and Dorothy Reynolds, who wrote *Salad Days* in The Old Duke. The musical was premiered in Bristol in 1954, before touring nationally and then overseas.' Jim Jones did not live to witness this. He had still been managing the business when he died of heart failure on 19 December 1953 at the age of fifty-eight. He was survived by his wife and two children.

References in some sources to 'J.M. Jones' are erroneous.

1923

"When I was appointed two years ago there were many doubters as to my business capabilities and I feel those doubts have proved well founded."
Sam Woods (Secretary and Former Captain)

Championship Position: 9 of 17

Revered former Somerset wicket-keeper A. E. Newton was appointed President following the death of Henry Murray-Anderdon. One of his first duties was to chair the annual meeting of members at Taunton in March 1923. It proved an acrimonious affair. There had been a mutinous response to the request for members and patrons to dig deep into their pockets when they believed that the deficit of £447 resulted from the profligacy and incompetence of the committee. Sam Woods surprised the meeting by falling on his sword, admitting that the role of Secretary was beyond him. Sam's replacement was Alan Francis Davey, who, since arriving from Canada, had proved his credentials as Secretary of the Somerset Agricultural Association. He would remain in the post until 1931.

Ernest R. Norton – a Taunton dentist with a practice in Bath Place offering 'artificial teeth and painless extractions at moderate prices' - launched an appeal to raise funds for a new scoreboard. A local press report notes that the existing scoreboards were 'in a dilapidated condition and ... difficult to read'. The appeal would prove a success and his extraction of funds from the hard-pressed supporters was hopefully as painless as his tooth-pulling.

On the field of play there appeared to be more harmony. Somerset were regarded as a good fielding side, displaying 'considerable skill and quickness' where their captain, John Daniell, 'set them an example which they followed with enthusiasm'. Jack White again led the bowling attack, coming in with nearly 150 wickets, with his metronomic precision. In the absence of Bill Greswell, back in Ceylon, Jim Bridges took on the main supporting role, with suggestions that he was over-bowled, working his way through minor injuries until the undergraduates – notably Robertson-Glasgow

– appeared on the scene. Jack MacBryan was once more the leading batsman, with over 1,500 runs, including four centuries. Dar Lyon was the only other man to top 1,000 runs.

One local newspaper notes that 'in R. A. Ingle, Somerset have found a most promising cricketer'. The debutant would go on to captain the team in later years. In keeping with the club's ethos, no new professionals were taken on.

Jack White – he would take 2,355 wickets at 18.58 apiece over the course of his extraordinary first-class career, which ran from 1909 until 1937.

267
Percival Charles Ewens
14 July 1923 v. Derbyshire, Chesterfield

C. P. Ewens.

He was referred to as 'Sonny', very occasionally in formal situations as Charles, but never as Percival or Percy, and he often signed his name as 'C. P. Ewens'. Sonny was in fact a hugely influential figure in the Taunton area. A successful businessman, he was also an active sportsman and later a generous benefactor.

Born in Yeovil on 23 November 1882, he was the son of Edward Samuel (known as Sam) and Sarah Annie (known as Annie) Ewens, the third of their eight children who survived into adulthood. Sam was a skilled leather glove cutter who, along with other members of his family, worked in and later ran a glove manufacturing company. The business rode some storms, including a less-than-amicable parting of the ways with a business partner, Alexander Henry Cobb, in 1901. Cobb, who was later exposed as something of a chancer, successfully claimed a substantial pay-off which resulted in

Sonny Ewens – enjoying his cricket in Taunton and his shooting at Bisley.

Sam's having to sell the family home, but he recovered through a combination of hard work and business acumen.

The company continued to operate throughout the First World War. While three brothers saw active service – with one of them, Lionel, killed in action at Passchendaele in 1917 – Sonny helped with the family business, setting up and managing the Taunton branch of operations in 1915. A military arbitration report confirms that his exceptional skills as a selector and buyer of leather were critical to the enterprise. He would no doubt have proved a useful soldier, having won the Lord Lieutenant's Cup for shooting at Bisley in 1911 and 1913, but the military's loss was industry's gain. By day, Sonny served with the Territorial branch of the Somerset Light Infantry (with whom he would retain his links for nearly fourteen years) and in the early mornings and evenings he played his part in business, based first in Thomas Street and then larger premises in Bridge Street, Taunton. As well as overseeing the purchasing of leather and the cutting process, Sonny would drive around to outworkers based in villages between Taunton and Yeovil. Although glove making was never hugely lucrative, the business flourished and continued to do so during the subsequent decades.

P. C. Ewens – he owned a glove manufacturing business and was a generous benefactor.

On 27 December 1915 he was married to Edith Mary (née Pitcher), the daughter of Charles Pitcher, who for many years owned The Mermaid Hotel in Yeovil. Sonny and Edith would have three sons (two of whom would join their father's firm). Edith's brother, Charles Jnr, was actively involved and would remain a partner in the business. The generally held view is that the Pitchers brought wealth and business acumen to the enterprise while the Ewens family brought glove making skills.

Peter Roebuck asserts in his history of Somerset CCC that Sonny was a bankrupt who relied on charity from other amateurs such as 'Box' Case. The source of this anecdote is unknown, but the observation is entirely wide of the mark. Sonny Ewens lived a comfortable life and witness to this is the fact that he and his wife, Edith, purchased Priory Park in 1927 for the then eye-watering sum of £3,000, owning both the land and the pavilion that was used by Taunton Town FC for many years before the football club moved and Sonny and Edith sold the playing field and facilities to Taunton RFC.

As well as being a generous benefactor to Taunton Town, for whom he also served on the committee and was made an Honorary Life Member in 1930, Sonny had been a useful outside right in his younger days, playing for Yeovil Casuals FC (now Yeovil Town) and ending the 1903-4 season as their leading scorer.

In his very first competitive game of cricket, playing as a Yeovil schoolboy for Preston, he was hit above the eye by the ball and required five stitches, though his appetite for the game was not dulled by the experience. A right-handed batsman, he would go on to play for Taunton, Somerset Stragglers and – on seven occasions between 1923 and 1926 – for Somerset. He came away with a first-class average of 16.28. A more lasting contribution to Somerset's cause was the Baker Cup, inaugurated in 1935 in memory of Herbert Baker, the groundsman of Taunton School and a popular club cricketer who had died aged thirty. The trophy is competed for by club sides in the

Taunton area, culminating in a final at the County Ground. Sonny had set up and helped to fund the competition and he remained Chairman from 1935 until his death in 1961.

In later years, he took up skittles. A skilled practitioner, he was appointed President of the Taunton and District Skittles League. In November 1960, his left leg was amputated after a period of serious illness, but he refused to be bowed by the setback. As an obituary would state, 'the sense of humour and kindly consideration for others that made him so well liked were characteristic of him till the end.'

His final hours were spent at the County Ground. On 21 July 1961, he was presenting the cup and medals at the final of the Evening Cricket League (featuring Somerset Police and Staplegrove) when he slumped into his wheelchair. Moments earlier, he had been joking about his final appearance for Taunton Old Crocks where he had run a five when the ball had been lost in long grass at a ground less well manicured than Somerset's. Breathless for a considerable while, he had eventually recovered from that particular trauma.

On this occasion, though, an ambulance was called but he was declared dead on arrival at the Musgrove Park Hospital, Taunton. He was seventy-eight years old at the time. Only days later, a minute's silence was held at the final of the Baker Cup where the President, former Somerset cricketer Dr Leslie Marshall, gave a short address:

He died here a few days ago after watching a match and presenting medals to the winners – probably the way he would have chosen to die. Sonny Ewens was the originator of this competition in the 1930s and due to his drive and enthusiasm, the competition became the success it has. We owe him a great deal for his work and keenness.

A fitting tribute to a great supporter of cricket in Somerset and a generous benefactor to sport in general in the area.

268
Reginald Addington Ingle
22 August 1923 v. Essex, Taunton

Reg or Reggie Ingle was born in Penzance, Cornwall, on 5 November 1903. His father, Frank Seaton Ingle was already a solicitor with a practice in Bath. Frank's wife, Maria Harriette Augusta (née Taylor), a vicar's daughter, had decamped to a lodging house in Penzance, purportedly for rest and recuperation. Reggie had been born there a mere six and a half months after the wedding. This was common practice in such cases among the well-heeled and mother and son returned to the family home in Bath after Maria's prolonged absence. No one – including Rev. Taylor – was any the wiser.

He was educated at Oundle School in Northamptonshire and was coached there by former Somerset professional Bill Montgomery whose presence in the Somerset side had, in the first decade of the twentieth century, caused a major falling out with Surrey, from whom he had been poached. Reggie then went up to Jesus College, Cambridge, but not before he had already been drafted into the Somerset side as a promising nineteen-year-old who was due to play for Incogniti at Sidmouth but was summoned to the County Ground at Taunton. He did not disappoint, scoring a half-century on his debut. At Cambridge, he played for the University XI but failed to gain a blue.

He followed in his father's footsteps and became a solicitor, welcomed as a partner in the practice of F. S. & R. A. Ingle, based in a building that fronted both Gay Street and Old King Street in Bath.

Always immaculately turned out, apart perhaps from his faded county cap, Reggie is described as 'an adventurous stroke player, not great at building an innings'. He averaged 19.03 with the bat over 309 matches for the county, although the fact that he suffered badly from hay fever may have adversely affected his aggregate. Included among his

R. A. Ingle (top) as captain of the Oundle School XI, coached by former Somerset cricketer Bill Montgomery (above).

performances were ten centuries (two of which came in one match, against Middlesex in 1928) and 34 half-centuries.

Reggie Ingle's main service to Somerset was as a captain. The team responded to his skills as a man manager. Bill Andrews regarded him as a 'considerate' leader, his approach in stark contrast to the cold indifference of his predecessor, Jack White. He combined thoughtfulness with an unerring rectitude, offering encouragement to the more diffident among the professionals but coming down hard on any miscreants – pro and amateur alike. R. J. O. Meyer, for example was pilloried for having deliberately handed a duff betting tip to some of the more gullible members of the team and the great Arthur Wellard was banned for two games for an undisclosed indiscretion in Blackpool during Ingle's first year as captain. Reggie was no respecter of persons. Although gentlemanly, he was also inclined to swear without inhibition when the

Reg Ingle – Somerset captain and a debonair solicitor, much in demand at social functions.

mood took him.

He was prone to disconcerting fluctuations in intensity, sometimes urging his troops from the front, sometimes seemingly indifferent – in the words of Raymond Robertson-Glasgow, 'opening telegrams at cover point and distantly inquiring of his bowlers whether they would be agreeable to temporary relief'. His methods generally worked, given that between 1932 and 1937 inclusive, he twice led Somerset to the top half of the Championship table.

He was regarded as an eligible bachelor and in great demand at social functions from hunt balls to beauty pageants. In 1932 he was engaged to the actress Jean Colin, who was enjoying success in London's West End at the time. Their engagement generated great excitement in the local media and was conducted under the glare of press scrutiny. It was later broken off amicably and in 1936 he was married to Pansy Narayanee Peters, known as Pip. They would have three children.

There are varying reports as to the reasons for Reggie Ingle's replacement as captain at the end of the 1937 season. The official version put it down to the increasing demands of his legal practice. However, there was talk of behind the scenes manoeuvring. Frank Lee writes in his memoirs that the appointment of Bunty Longrigg as the new leader lifted the club from its lethargy. Reggie Ingle certainly appears to have lost his appetite for the game and as early as October 1934 had been quoted as saying that three-day cricket was 'dull and many people wonder why amateurs play'. He was also disillusioned with the set-up at the County Ground and felt undervalued, not least for his tireless fundraising efforts, not matched in other parts of the county.

He played a handful of games in 1938 and in 1939. Perhaps he was determined to make a point when, as his swansong, he stepped in and captained the team against Hampshire at Bournemouth in 1939, leading Somerset to an innings victory. There followed an intractable breakdown in relations, with Reggie vowing to have nothing further to do with the club. He was too discrete or too well versed in the dangers of litigation ever to go public with his grievances.

After retiring from his work as a solicitor, Reggie lived for many years in Timsbury keeping to his vow never to set foot inside any of the county's cricket grounds. This self-imposed exile lasted until 1977 when, following the award of honorary life membership, he attended the Weston Festival and enjoyed the occasion, reminiscing with old colleagues such as Bill Andrews. He ended his days in a nursing home in Oakhill where he died (not in Bath as many sources suggest) at the age of eighty-nine on 19 December 1992.

R. A. Ingle batting against Middlesex at Lord's in 1930: the wicket-keeper is W. F. F. Price.

1924

"The amateur talent stands out head and shoulders
above other counties, but we must look ahead ...
The question of finding good professionals must be
given careful consideration."

A. F. Davey (Somerset CCC Secretary)

Championship Position: 8 of 17

A E. Newton had relinquished the reins as President and it would be an annual
appointment for a number of years. Secretary A. F. Davey was winning plaudits
for having turned things around financially. Membership numbers were rising dramat-
ically and the money was coming in. Even another simmering row about whether the
Weston Festival should be run locally or centrally was quickly quashed. Everyone
agreed that Alan Davey should be trusted to take control. He also had the farsighted-
ness to suggest that the cult of amateurism was in danger of holding Somerset back.

The team performed well – very well on occasions, such as the match against
Hampshire on a peach of a wicket at Bath, where they amassed 675 for 9 declared.
Once again, Jack MacBryan was the leading run-maker, his efforts resulting in an
England call-up. Sadly, the match was severely rain-affected and Jack faced not a single
delivery: it was to be his only Test Match appearance. He was once again well
supported by Dar Lyon, 'whose drive', in the words of writer Ron Roberts, 'was as
rollicking and as penetrating as his sense of humour'. Predictably, Jack White claimed
his annual haul of nearly 150 wickets. Jim Bridges fell just short of 100, his worthy
performances including a hat trick away against Derbyshire.

Among the debutants was Wally Luckes of the Bridgwater club. His contributions
were infrequent in the early days, owing to the diagnosis of a heart condition, but he
became one of the country's leading first-class wicket-keepers over many years.

This was the last season in which the much-loved veteran Ernie Robson would
appear, by now looking decidedly ill. Cancer would claim him before he was able to
embark on a planned career as a first-class umpire. He would have made a great one,
too: fair-minded and always entirely unruffled.

Jack MacBryan – an elegant and technically sound batsman who had made his debut in 1911, he hit sixteen first-class centuries for Somerset. Awarded one England cap in a rain-affected match, he never had the opportunity to bat for his country. He was more actively involved when winning a gold medal as a member of the Great Britain hockey team at the 1920 Olympics.

269
Walter Thomas Luckes
31 May 1924 v. Sussex, Hove

W.T. Luckes

His surname is pronounced 'Luck-ease'. Wally was born on 1 January 1901 in Lambeth, London, where his father was a fireman, although both parents – Walter Snr and Elizabeth – hailed from Bridgwater.

Short and neat, Wally was an undemonstrative but superb wicket-keeper whom his colleagues rated highly. Raymond Robertson-Glasgow wrote:

> *He is consistent, cardinally sound in method and temperament ... Quite often he is brilliant, but this brilliance is so unspoiled by the vice of flamboyancy that it generally escapes the notice of all but the bowler, the slips, the non-striker and the bowler's umpire.*

Wally Luckes – 'cardinally sound in method and temperament'.

Having caught Somerset's eye with some useful performances at club level for Bridgwater, he made his first-class debut in 1924. Wally did not become a regular until the 1927 season but a debilitating heart condition was diagnosed while he was attending the coaching school run by Major Aubrey Faulkner. This curtailed his appearances between 1929 and 1931, when he kept his eye in with Bridgwater, whilst also working as an electrician for the South Western Electricity Board. Some mythology has arisen over his having been paid by Somerset while he recuperated, but the evidence suggests otherwise. Professional contracts at the time were draconian and stipulated that in the event of illness, pros would not be paid. (Ever conscious of the need to cut costs, the committee even refused to pay for lodgings when Somerset visited Gloucestershire, regarding it as akin to a home fixture.) The truth is that Wally was required to prove his fitness at Bridgwater while Frank Lee was deemed to be doing a competent job as a wicket-keeper batsman. He eventually returned to become a mainstay of the Somerset team for two decades. He was married in 1931 to Winifred Annie Norman, a postman's daughter from Bridgwater. Their only child - a daughter, Janet – was born two years later.

By the 1934 season he was gaining widespread renown for his ability as a keeper. As the *Sunday Post* noted, 'in four successive matches, Luckes had not a single bye in an aggregate of 1577. Also when Kent made 577 at Taunton there was but one bye in it.' In 1946, he was the most successful wicket-keeper in the country with 76 dismissals to his name. He also made useful contributions with the bat, with an average of 16.22 over 365 matches. As Robertson-Glasgow notes in a tribute to his former team-mate, 'illness forced him down the batting order', where he was regarded as 'an unwelcome opponent' by bowlers who believed, mistakenly, that they were about to wrap up the Somerset innings.

Well into his forties by the post-war period, he was ready to retire from first-class cricket and finally did so when Somerset found an able replacement in Harold Stephenson, another quietly effective wicket-keeper. Wally played his last game for Somerset in 1949. The following year he was granted a Testimonial season by the county, as a reward for his years of service. The many events staged around the county were well attended, a measure of the esteem in which he was held.

Still living in Bridgwater, he would once again play cricket for the town in which his parents had both been born and in which he had lived for many years. He returned full-time to his work as an electrician and then continued to live in Bridgwater after his retirement. He died in the town on 27 October 1982 at the age of eighty-one.

W. T. Luckes – 'brilliance ... unspoiled by the vice of flamboyancy'.

270
Frederick Henry Baitup
21 June 1924 v. Derbyshire, Burton-on-Trent

Fred Baitup was born in Tunbridge Wells, Kent, on 9 January 1896, one of twelve children of Albert Baitup, an agricultural labourer and jobbing gardener, and his wife, Lucy. Fred and his siblings were brought up in a crowded house at 51 Nelson Street and he was still living with his parents when he was taken on as butcher's apprentice by a Mr Hoad.

But Fred had been blessed with sufficient talent as a cricketer to attract interest and by 1913 had been offered a job by Kent, working as a member of the groundstaff. After a season with the county side, he volunteered at the commencement of the First World

Fred Baitup – 'a young man full of vim and vitality'.

F. H. Baitup – a hostile fast-medium bowler and hard-hitting batsman.

War, joining the Royal West Kents and fighting in the ill-fated Dardanelles campaign against the Ottoman Empire and then in Egypt and Palestine, where he was wounded in Gaza in April 1917 while serving as a lance corporal. He then returned to fight in Salonika before being demobilised.

He was re-employed as a member of the Kent ground-staff for three seasons. A newspaper report informs us that he broke his wrist while riding his motorcycle but must have staged a speedy recovery, given that he was offered the opportunity to join Chard, in Somerset, as their professional in 1922. A useful all-rounder, Fred was a hostile fast-medium right-arm bowler and a right-handed batsman capable of smiting the ball. He was also a good footballer, playing as a left winger for Tunbridge Wells before being signed in 1921 by Charlton Athletic, then in the Third Division South. He soon returned to play for Tunbridge Wells when he came home for the winter months, also making occasional appearances for the Newton's & Taunton team.

While at Chard he impressed Somerset and was offered a contract as a county professional in 1924. One report describes him as 'the county professional and scorer'. In the event, perhaps he did more scoring than playing, given that he would make just one appearance for Somerset, scoring 11 runs in his only innings and taking 0 for 8.

He was married in Taunton in 1924 to Margaret Barlow, with whom he would have a daughter. They left the town ahead of the following season, with Fred having joined Chorley CC in the Ribblesdale League, the club's Chairman describing the new recruit as 'a young man, full of vim and vitality', adding that he hoped that 'his influence and ability' would 'help to cement the team'. That engagement lasted for one full season before he was offered terms by the Leyland Motors team in Lancashire. By 1932, he was playing for Adlington in the Bolton League and then in 1933 he had been taken on by British Goodrich with one local paper attributing the team's success to 'the good bowling of F. Baitup and W. Bowden'.

Once his playing days were behind him, Fred was employed in clerical work. The 1939 census lists him as a stock control clerk in a rubber works. He would also spend a number of years deploying his wiry strength and fitness and the leadership qualities gleaned as a lance corporal, becoming Captain of the Burwash Voluntary Fire Brigade in the Sussex village.

He died at Whipps Cross Hospital in Leytonstone, Essex on 3 February 1991 at the age of ninety-five. To have overcome his tough start in life and to have demonstrated such longevity, Fred Baitup must have been made of sterner stuff than many a man.

271
Cecil Leach
27 August 1924 v. South Africa, Taunton

Cecil Leach

Some sources suggest that the man who played for Somerset was Edward Leach Cecil Leach, born in 1896 in the Featherstall area of Oldham, but this is incorrect. He was in fact born on 29 November 1894 in Littleborough, near Rochdale, the son of William Leach, a cotton weaver, and his wife, Sarah Jane (née Tattersall), and was named plain Cecil with no embellishments. As a teenager, he worked in the cotton mills, alongside other members of his family. The 1911 census lists him as a warehouse boy, aged sixteen. His name soon began to appear in cricket matches played by Littleborough and this must have represented a merciful release from the work in the cotton mill.

In January 1916 he joined the Royal Navy. By that time he had become a cotton sizer, a mind-numbingly tedious job that involved applying a glue-like substance to prepared cotton, making it easier to work the raw material. He would have welcomed the change of career. Trained at Devonport, he subsequently served on a variety of ships including HMS *Isis*, HMS *Achilles* and HMS *Hector*.

After his demobilisation at the end of the war, Cecil played in Lancashire League cricket as an all-rounder, appearing on a regular basis in the Lancashire Second XI before forcing his way into the Lancashire side with a strong batting performance against Northumberland in June 1923. After making 79 on his first-class debut, his perform-ances fell away and by 1924, a season in which he only played for the county of his birth on one occasion, he threw in his lot with Somerset, being taken on by the Long Ashton club and offered employment at the Ashton Gate Brewery. He was given an airing against the South Africans and played in other non-Championship matches while he qualified by residency. A reporter, writing in the *Lancashire Evening News* notes that 'Cecil Leach, the young Lancastrian, who, after a spell on the ground staff here, went to Somerset, will complete his qualification next month and I am told that he promises to be an acquisition for the county'. Given that he was approaching thirty, the reference to his being 'young' is odd, though perhaps the reporter was confused by Cecil's look of

Cecil Leach at Old Trafford.

fresh-faced innocence and the fact that he was only 5 ft 5 inches tall, as testified by his Royal Navy enrolment papers.

The reporter had spoken too soon because in November 1926 Cecil slipped and fell while working at the Ashton Gate Brewery and fractured his arm. Regrettably, the bone was incorrectly set, hampering his performances as a cricketer thereafter. During the 1927 season, unable to play, he offered his services as an umpire in club cricket. He would not make his Championship debut until May 1928 and after four further games, Somerset decided they had seen enough. Cecil's batting average over a total of eight first-class matches was 6.84 and he took one wicket for 87 runs. Perhaps both parties were left to rue what might have been but for Cecil's injury. He remained rooted in North Somerset, playing cricket for Long Ashton and in 1929 marrying Edith Vining, who lived in the village and whose father worked for the Great Western Railway. They had a daughter, Shirley, and son, Renice (the latter a tribute to Cecil's older brother, also named Renice, who had been killed in a shell explosion on 14 April 1918, while serving with the Lancashire Fusiliers).

Cecil Leach – never the same cricketer after he broke his arm.

Cecil went on to become a groundsman and cricket coach at Prior Park College, where he lived with his family in a cottage in the college grounds, before working for many years for the Bristol Aeroplane Company. During the war, too old to serve in the forces, he was a special police constable in Bath. There are press reports of his having been a witness at a trial for assault. Cecil and Edith had been visiting their letting agent, having offered a room to evacuees, when they saw a man attack a member of staff, dragging her by the hair. Cecil, who intervened, described it as 'the dirtiest attack I have seen', informing the judge that it worsted anything he had witnessed in his days in the Navy.

He died in his home in Nailsea on 4 January 1973 at the age of seventy-eight. His daughter, Shirley, tells how she heard that Cecil was dying, overcome by bronchitis, but that he fought to stay alive so that she was there at his death. She says: 'My father and I adored each other and were inseparable while I was growing up, always enjoying our annual trips together to visit his sisters at their guest house in Southport. He was always smiling and joking.' Cecil's wife, Edith, lived to be 103 years old.

A talented cricketer whose career suffered a setback when he broke his arm, he was a popular figure who deserves to be restored to his rightful place in the cricketing archives.

1925

*"From a playing point of view this season has not
been very successful."*

Somerset CCC Committee Report

Championship Position: 15 of 17

Speaking in February at the annual dinner of the Bath Cricket Club, Secretary A. F.
Davey laid out his vision for the county. His aim was 'to see Somerset right up
with the leaders of the Championship. We also want to establish a Nursery, make good
improvements and help cricket generally throughout the county. That all means
money.'

The money came in. There was a profit of nearly £1,000, helped by good gates for
the Bank Holiday fixture against local rivals Gloucestershire, when the sun shone. The
crowds also came in mid-August in the hope that Jack Hobbs of Surrey would equal
W. G. Grace's career record of 126 centuries. He matched it in the first innings and
then surpassed it with a further century in the second innings. A. F. Davey used the
windfall wisely, investing £350 to replace the seating, described as 'in a deplorable
condition'. A further £200 was set aside as an opening deposit for a fund for a new
pavilion and grandstand. The performances might not have matched expectation but
Davey had exorcised the ghost of Sam Woods's chaotic tenure as Secretary.

As for the cricket, things started brightly when John Daniell, leading from the
front, hit scores of 174 not out and 108 against Essex at Taunton. Shortly thereafter
he suffered a knee injury that put him out of action. This setback was a blow to club
morale and heralded a disappointing season. Once again Jack MacBryan held the
batting together, with helpful contributions from Tom Young. Jack White, preeminent among the country's amateur bowlers, was, as ever, the major wicket-taker,
supported by Jim Bridges.

Among the debutants, Box Case would become an inelegant though perennial
presence, Bunty Longrigg would in time be appointed as club captain and London-
born Jack Lee, qualifying as a pro at Lansdown in Bath, would prove an excellent
investment.

272
Charles Sydney Barlow
9 May 1925 v. Kent, Gravesend

There can surely be few first-class cricketers who have had three species of bird named after them. In Charles Barlow's case, two of them are obscure sub-species but the third, known as Barlow's Lark (*Calendulauda barlowi*), is found in scrubland in South Africa and Namibia. It was named after the cricketer, rugby blue, businessman and philanthropist who had funded an expedition to find new species.

Known as 'Punch' (simply because his sister was named Judy), Charles Barlow was born on 18 May 1905, in Durban (and not 10 May 1905 as some sources state). His father, Major Ernest ('Billy') Barlow borrowed £1,000 in 1902 to form a company selling woollen goods and coats. After a while, the firm branched out into electrical supplies and from these humble beginnings a massive conglomerate would develop. Major Billy died in 1921, never having

C. S. Barlow at Clifton College.

recovered from his war wounds and for a while, Billy's friend and fellow director Frank Euting took over the reins while Punch learned about the business.

Punch had been sent to Rose Hall Prep School and then Clifton College where he was 'a steady, useful bat'. He then went on to Caius College, Cambridge, where, although he captained the Caius XI and was deemed 'a fine slip fielder', he was never selected for the University XI. He did however win a rugby blue in four successive years from 1923 until 1926, captaining the side in 1926. He also played on two occasions for the Barbarians. He would go on to captain the Natal rugby team. Also a fine golfer, he later founded and chaired the prestigious River Club at Sandton in South Africa. Finally, he excelled at polo, captaining a tour by South Africa of Argentina in 1952 until his horse died beneath him with the result that Punch's leg was broken.

He played two first-class games for Somerset, who had claimed him on the basis of his time at Clifton. Although he averaged only 6.00 with the bat and took just 2 wickets at 60 runs apiece, he did at least bag the wicket of the great Frank Woolley of Kent (who already had 215 runs to his name at the time).

On returning to South Africa, he worked in the family firm as a tractor salesman

Punch Barlow – captained the Cambridge University rugby XV.

in Natal and Orange Free State selling Caterpillar and Hyster machinery. His negotiation of the exclusive rights to the sale of Caterpillar crawlers proved his major coup. By 1929 Punch had become a director of the company and by 1937 its Managing Director.

During the Second World War he served as an intelligence officer in the 2nd South Africa Division and was given the rank of major, although titles embarrassed him: he was never one to make anything of status and was invariably described as 'a team man'. He would be appointed Chairman of the War Stores Disposal Board between 1945 and 1946 and would finally become Chairman of his company in 1948.

After the takeover of Rand Mines in 1971, he renamed the company Barlow Rand. At the time of his death, he was still active in the business and had overseen its growth from a relatively modest concern selling textiles and engineering supplies to the largest corporation in South Africa with more than 850 subsidiaries across 22 countries and a net value of 2 billion rand.

Throughout, Punch had insisted that his company should be run on ethical principles and that it should be at the forefront in offering management opportunities to the minority groups in the country. His stance against the injustices of apartheid was both brave and farsighted. He was also a noted philanthropist, setting up the C. S. Barlow Foundation in support of minority groups and technical schools. Beyond the worlds of sport and business, his hobbies were centred around wildlife and farming. He in fact purchased two farms, which he ran with a view to enhancing the environment. Vergelegen, purchased in 1941, was not retained after his divorce and in 1951 he purchased Bosch Hoek in the Pietermaritzburg district, planting innumerable trees and creating fishing lakes. He was also a senior figure in and benefactor to a number of wildlife charities and funded the ornithologist Austin Roberts's expedition to find and name new species of bird in South Africa. The discoveries included those birds named in Punch Barlow's honour.

Married to Margaret Eileen Cynthia Butcher in 1928, he would have two sons and two daughters. After his divorce he was married in 1950 to Kathleen Gallo (née Russell), known as Kate, with whom he would have no children.

Punch Barlow died of a heart attack on 1 June 1979 a few hours after having played a round of golf with Kate while on holiday in Sotogrande, Spain. He was seventy-three years old. Summing up his life, the *Dictionary of South African Biography* informs us that:

> *Barlow's success in business and industry was attributable to his energy and drive, the ability to think ahead and focus on major issues, and his gift of leadership. These qualities were combined with a fine sense of humour and a great sensitivity to people, situations, and environment. Humble and unassuming in speech and manner, detesting affectation and shunning publicity, he was a man of the highest personal integrity, with a strong sense of social responsibility.*

Punch Barlow – a hugely successful businessman and a philanthropic environmentalist.

P.W. Botha, then Prime Minister of South Africa, described him as 'an exceptionally pleasant man … he was indeed a great South African'. Perhaps Punch's quiet example and unflagging commitment to all that is good in the world had played its part in the dismantling of the apartheid regime.

273
Cecil Charles Coles Case
16 May 1925 v. Warwickshire, Edgbaston

C.C.C.Case.

He would often sign himself as 'C³ Case' or as 'C⁴' when pressed for time and faced with a queue of persistent autograph hunters. Cecil Case – referred to in cricketing circles as 'Box' Case – was born on 7 September 1895 in Frome. His father, George, variously a grazier and tanner, had spent much of his life building up the family fortune

before opting to be married in his mid-fifties (in 1892) to Louisa Coles, a girl thirty years his junior.

Cecil attended King's School, Bruton, where he came under the watchful eye of Somerset cricketers P. W. Vasey and C. J. Bowring, who instilled a sound batting technique. Too sound, some might say, for Box's wicket was one that had to be winkled out with great persistence. The problem was that runs rarely flowed from his bat as he dug in. Stanley Nelson, writing in *The People* in 1945, informs us that Box 'was the grimmest batsman I have ever seen. If determination deserved runs, Cecil Case deserved millions.'

In 1914, he was commissioned as a second lieutenant in the 3rd (Special Reservists) Dorset Regiment and arrived in France early in 1915. Wounded at Arras when a bullet entered the right side of his chest in May 1915, he was shipped home to England and was declared unfit for service at a number of Medical Board inspections, before being demobilised in 1919.

Box Case – 'the grimmest batsman I have ever seen'.

He first came into the Somerset side at the age of thirty, having made runs at club level. He made a slow start, cumbersome and unacquainted with flair or risk. He was, however, blessed with astonishing powers of concentration and dogged determination. *Wisden* later noted that 'if never a stylist, Case could often be relied upon to stay a collapse'. The very intensity of his cricket, allied to an absence of any grace of movement made him a subject of barracking from the Somerset crowds who liked to be entertained with pyrotechnics. But he was also unwittingly the source of much mirth.

Raymond Robertson-Glasgow says of Case that 'at first ... the pace of the game unhooked his deliberate machinery, and once, he was said to have been bowled while taking guard for the second time'. In the field he 'ran like a roll of thunder, but somehow he seldom had the legs of the ball'. But he persisted. In the end he made nine first-class centuries and came away with an average over 257 games of 22.09. On three occasions he topped 1,000 runs in a season. Opponents were bored into submission. A very occasional bowler, he took no wickets at a cost of 128 runs. His laborious attempts at field setting, always to no avail, were upset on at least one occasion when the batsman opted to change from a right-handed guard to left, kick-starting the whole process all over again.

Robertson-Glasgow recounts two tales that sum up Box's style of play. On one occasion, at Bath, he placed himself in position as a skyer from A. P. F. Chapman came his way. He 'slowly sank to a kneeling position; as the ball came nearer, so Case inclined himself ever more forwards, and, as one report put it "had the mortification of seeing the ball strike the turf a yard in front of him".' 'Crusoe' also recalls a shot that stuck forever in the memory of everyone at Old Trafford in 1930 when in arranging himself to defend against a top-spinner from Richard Tyldesley on a wet pitch, Box fell forward and, stranded in a prone position 'played the ball with his bat in front of his forehead'. Crusoe concludes that 'there was some sort of appeal; but it was a fair stroke'. Though not by any stretch an elegant one.

Teammate Frank Lee noted that 'after carefully playing a defensive stroke he would walk around and around in ever widening circles, bend down stiffly to play the next ball and then proceed to do it all again'. Lee's autobiography includes a number of tales of Box's being on the receiving end of pranks. He notes that Case 'could throw hard but with poor direction'. Knowing this, Jack Hobbs and Andrew Sandham of Surrey hatched a plan, shaping to take a quick single to Box, fielding at third man, before returning to their creases while he hurled the ball for four overthrows to mid-wicket.

C. C. C. Case – 'could often be relied upon to stay a collapse'.

Frank Lee then adds that 'with another ball played to Case, the batsmen were this time near to completing a second run when we heard Case, [still clinging to the ball and] calling out, "You don't kid me this time". What J. C. White said cannot I'm afraid be repeated here.' On another occasion, Frank Lee was the non-striker when Johnny Clay of Glamorgan bowled with a rubber ball. Such was the intensity of his concentration that Case earnestly called for a single, the only man in the ground apparently unaware that he had not played a regulation ball.

One of the many anecdotes attached to Box Case bears all the hallmarks of an apocryphal tale, but a contemporaneous match summary in the *Taunton Courier* confirms it to be true. Having ducked to avoid a vicious rib-tickler from Bill Voce in the home fixture against Notts in 1930, a befuddled Case dropped his bat as he stumbled against the wicket, picked up one of the stumps and headed towards the pavilion.

There was never a question of a career or marriage. He lived for his county cricket matches, thrived on his investments and survived with no need for female companionship, very probably regarding women as an alien species. A letter from C. W. W. Laverton MBE, who worked in a bank in Frome and was writing as a nonagenarian, informs us that:

He was a strange character – single; Occupation: "Gentleman", very unapproachable, undoubtedly wealthy and always insisted on having new banknotes. The pity was that he took no interest in local cricket and could so easily have been our coach, which was the one thing that we lacked.

Cecil Case died on 11 November 1969 in Keyford, Somerset, at the age of seventy-four.

274
Edward George Northway
23 May 1925 v. Derbyshire, Derby

Ned Northway – played cricket and rugby for Bath.

E. G. Northway as an officer in the RAF.

Known to friends and fellow cricketers as 'Ned', he was born on 30 October 1901 in Gampola in the district of Kandy, Ceylon, the son of Leon George Samuel James Northway and his wife Annie Cecilia. Edward was educated at the Convent School in Pulteney Road, Bath, and on leaving school was trained as an accountant, working for Mundy, Brewer & Johnson in the city of Bath.

An all-round sportsman, who played for the Bath rugby team and proved a useful right-handed batsman at club level with Bath CC, he played infrequently for Somerset. In eight appearances over the 1925 and 1926 seasons, he averaged 14.77 with a highest score of 55 not out. Then in September 1926 he joined the RAF as an accountant. He would play on a number of occasions for the RAF, including in three first-class fixtures.

In 1933 he was married in Karachi to Janet Gilmour (née Irving), who had also lived a peripatetic life, having been born in Hong Kong. They would have a son, Colin. Ned Northway enjoyed a successful career with the RAF. In 1934 he was made a flight lieutenant and then in 1941 he was appointed a wing commander. He was much decorated, receiving the OBE in the King's Honours List of 1941 for his services in the North Western Frontier of India. After the war he submitted naturalisation papers in order to become a British citizen. This was deemed necessary under the British Nationality Act of 1948, as he and both his parents had been born abroad. Prior to 1948, those born in Commonwealth countries had all enjoyed the status of British subjects. Hereafter, the concept of Commonwealth citizenship was eroded over time and replaced with separate national identities. In January 1949, by then having risen to the level of group captain, he was awarded the CBE.

He died on 4 August 1965 in Marylebone at the age of sixty-three. He was the cousin of R. P. Northway, who played for Somerset and Northamptonshire, until his career was ended by a tragic early death.

E. G. Northway seen flanked by J. Bridges and G. E. Hunt.

275
Esmé Thomas Lancelot Reed Haywood
13 June 1925 v. Sussex, Horsham

He disliked his given name of Esmé and from the moment he had any say in the matter was always referred to as Tom. He was born in Heene, Worthing, Sussex, on 23 August 1900. His father was Joseph Haywood, at the time a solicitor, married to Catherine Isabella (née Reed), ten years older than her husband and the daughter of a wealthy solicitor and land owner, Thomas Lancelot Reed (from whom Tom would inherit three of his four Christian names). In 1909 Tom's father, Joseph, was declared bankrupt and this would appear to have led to a cooling of relations with Catherine. He reverted to the title Captain although he had retired from the 3rd Welsh Regiment some nine years earlier. By the time of the 1911 census, Catherine was pointedly describing herself as a 'grass widow' and 'legally separated'. She would, though, retain cordial relations with her children.

After boarding at a prep school in Worthing, Tom went to Cheltenham College, again as a boarder. He was in the school rugby XV in 1918 and was an outstanding athlete. Oddly, he was not selected for the cricket XI although subsequent events would suggest that this is an aberration. He may have been injured or alternatively he may have been involved in athletics events.

Tom – perhaps benefitting from wealth on his mother's side – was able to indulge

E. T. L. R. Haywood at Cheltenham College.

in the luxury of completing two degrees. At the London School of Economics he graduated with a BSc and he came away from Christ's College, Cambridge, with a BA. Arriving at Christ's College in 1924, he would go on to represent Cambridge University at hockey, gaining blues in 1925, 1926 and 1927, captaining the side in the last year and winning frequent praise as an outstanding left back. He would also represent Dorset and the West of England. In 1926 he was being widely tipped as a double blue, expected to bat in the Cambridge XI, but an ankle injury sustained in the Varsity hockey match required surgery and put paid to that, although he returned to fitness in time to captain the hockey XI. By the following summer the moment had passed.

Tom played for Somerset on eight occasions between 1925 and 1927, averaging a modest 8.56 with the bat. The link with the county at this point is not immediately apparent but Somerset were nothing if not promiscuous in their preparedness to embrace all and sundry. He also made successful appearances for the Somerset Stragglers (for whom at least one century is recorded) and, later, playing where his career took him, with Dorset Rangers and North Devon.

His first teaching post was at Sedbergh, where the young Somerset and England cricketer Mandy Mitchell-Innes would be one of his pupils. In 1934, he was offered a teaching post at Canford School near Wimborne and remained there until 1938, when he was offered temporary position for two years at his alma mater, Cheltenham College. He was married that same year to Honoria Joy Bevan, with whom he would have two daughters. A son died in infancy. In 1940 he became Head of Modern Studies at Stowe School in Buckinghamshire but within a year had been offered the headmastership of Barnstaple Grammar School, where he would remain until his retirement, bringing up his family in a more settled and loving environment than he had known as a child.

Both daughters were married in Barnstaple – the latter in 1968 – and thereafter, Tom retired to Herefordshire where he died in the village of Fownhope on 8 January 1985 at the age of eighty-four. His daughter, Thea, says of him that:

> He was an exceptional father, loving, caring and loved a good laugh until tears ran down his face. He was a very intelligent academic and a stern disciplinarian at home, and as headmaster highly respected, always being fair to everyone. He had a thirst for knowledge and loved participating in or watching all forms of games played with a ball, particularly cricket.

Tom Haywood – for many years headmaster of Barnstaple Grammar School.

276
John William Lee
24 June 1925 v. Cambridge University, Cambridge

Born on 1 February 1902, Jack was one of three brothers – Harry and Frank were the others – who all began life as members of the Lord's groundstaff, with Harry enjoying a career with Middlesex and the two younger brothers offering their allegiance to Somerset. Their father, Henry, who was a fruiterer, played his part in encouraging Jack and Frank to try their luck with Somerset. Like many cricket followers, Henry regarded the county, with their reputation as entertainers and underdogs, as his 'second' team.

Having played just one game for Middlesex, Jack was taken on as a pro by the Lansdown club in Bath while he qualified for Somerset. His first outing for his new county, against Cambridge University, was not a success. Having made no runs and taken no wickets in his only game for Middlesex, he achieved something similar for Somerset with a pair, although he did take one expensive wicket. He developed, however, into a dependable opening batsman and a successful leg-break bowler. Over the course of 241 matches between 1925 and 1936 he averaged 21.10 with the bat,

Jack Lee – a dependable opening batsman and leg-break bowler.

scoring six centuries, including a highest score of 193 not out. At times, Somerset were reliant on Jack to hold an innings together with his steady approach, while wickets fell around him. He also claimed 493 wickets at 29.70 apiece.

He was married in Marylebone in 1930 to Agnes Gertrude (née Sennit). With family still based there, he had retained links with that part of London, though sadly Agnes's mother died a mere matter of days after the wedding. A myth has arisen – repeated, for example, in Peter Roebuck's history of Somerset cricket – that Jack played football for Arsenal but the Jack Lee signed by Arsenal in 1926 who then left for Chesterfield in 1928 is an entirely different man, a speedy winger who hailed from the North East.

Where Jack's brothers both turned successfully to umpiring after their playing days were over – older brother Harry proving his credentials when giving both of his brothers out LBW early in his career – Jack chose a different path. It came as a surprise to Somerset supporters when he was released by the county. He had been offered the role of coach and groundsman at Mill Hill School in London after the 1935 season and approached John Daniell, hoping to receive a counter-offer. Jack had good reason to believe that Somerset would extend his contract, given that he had topped 1,000 runs in each of the previous three seasons and had taken nearly 200 wickets over that same period. Daniell's disdain for professionals is well-documented but there are conflicting views as to whether Jack was dismissed or alternatively that John Daniell was concerned for the welfare of the pro and felt that a career as a coach offered greater financial security. Certainly the professionals in the team felt that Daniell was aware that Jack had voiced his concerns about the amateurism that

J. W. Lee – left Somerset to coach at Mill Hill School.

held sway at the county. Daniell would have considered this anarchic. On the other hand, Jack was invited to play the following August, suggesting no bitterness. Frank Lee is unequivocal in his autobiography, stating that having to leave for Mill Hill was 'a decision [Jack] regretted, as he was then at his full bent with both bat and ball'. Either way, from a Somerset perspective, it was not John Daniell's finest decision.

After a prolonged period in his new role and enjoying his cricket for London Counties, he joined the 208th Pioneer Corps as a private in the early part of the Second World War. On 20 June 1944, a fortnight after the D-Day landings, he was killed in action near Bazenville in Normandy. He was forty-two at the time. Jack lies buried in the Ryes War Cemetery in Bazenville. Many of his former teammates turned out for a testimonial match in Bath after the war in order to raise money for his widow, Agnes, and when the London Counties club was wound up in 1946, the remaining funds were handed to her.

277
Robert William Draper
24 June 1925 v. Cambridge University, Cambridge

Bob Draper was born on 20 January 1903. Although his grandmother cited Calcutta as his place of birth, it is more likely to have been in Mussoorie, India, where his parents resided and where he was baptised three months later. Walter, the son of a Dorset dairyman, worked for Fitch & Co., who ran a pharmacy and general merchants business in Northern India. He had married Magdelene (née Davis) in Calcutta in 1901 and they would remain in the region as he rose to become an export manager before leaving Fitch to start up his own business as a tailor, making suits to order. Bob was meanwhile sent to England where he was looked after by his grandmother, Lydia.

He was educated at King Edward's School. Bath. Here he played rugby for the school and captained the cricket First XI, proving a useful left-arm pace bowler who batted right-handed. On leaving school he opted for a career in law and was articled to Glyde, Kerslake and Co. in Bristol, passing his final Law Society exams in 1926.

He was married in 1930 to Kathleen Mary Rogers, known

Bob Draper – 'could really move the ball in the air'.

4.45pm DRAPER ALSO MAKES HIS FIRST "SLIP"

as Molly, with whom he would have two sons and a daughter. Bob then became a solicitor in the practice of Burgess, Sloane & Co. Prior to his marriage, he had appeared regularly for Bath CC but once he had moved to Clevedon and later to Portishead, he became a member of the successful Lodway team who could boast a number of occasional Somerset players in their ranks. A history of the Lodway club describes him as 'a fast left-armer who always opened the bowling and could really move the ball in the air. Bob took plenty of wickets but did not regard himself as a batsman although now and then he cut loose and smashed some short but sweet innings.' He captained the team for two years.

He played three times for Somerset: twice in 1925 and once in 1929. Acquitting himself well with the ball, he took 6 wickets at 36.83 apiece, his best performance being his 3 for 73 against Essex at Leyton, where he clearly troubled the batsmen with nearly half of his overs being maidens. His batting average was 4.00 over five innings.

During the Second World War he served as a squadron leader with the RAF Volunteer Reserve, working in administration. His efforts were recognised with the award of an MBE (Military Division) in 1945. Bob and Molly were by then living at the Manor House in Upper Milton, Wells, and after the war, with no appetite to return to the legal profession, he assisted his brother, Richard Jack, known as Jack, who had purchased a leather and sheepskin footwear company in Glastonbury in 1937. By 1948, with the brothers encountering problems as they struggled to obtain import licences to bring in the necessary equipment to convert their facilities to peace-time use, they looked to South Africa to expand their interests. It was apparent that, given the warmer climate there, they would need to explore other options and Jack was persuaded to buy a small paint-making factory. Bob left for Durban to run the company, followed three months later by his wife and children. After changing the name of the newly-purchased company from Elvic to Elvolac, the brothers began to build the business

R. W. Draper – a Bristol solicitor who became a successful entrepreneur in South Africa.

but it proved too small to support them both, so they agreed that Bob would buy Jack out and that the latter would focus on his existing business in England.

Adhering single-mindedly to the principle of managing for the long-term, reinvesting and eschewing short-termism, Bob ensured that the enterprise flourished and was sold in 1976 to Dulux. His son Bill continued to be employed in a senior capacity by Dulux, building up a new distribution concern. It is a measure of the success of the venture that it continues to thrive, run since 2002 by Bob's grandson.

Bob, meanwhile, had continued to work as a consultant, helping out in particular with his other son Rod's business. He also served on a number of boards and advisory bodies, including the South African Chamber of Industries.

He died in Durban at the age of eighty-four on 29 August 1987.

278
Frederick George Lee
4 July 1925 v. Yorkshire, Harrogate

Not related to the better-known Lee brothers, who hailed from London, Fred Lee was born in Chard on 24 May 1905. His parents, Ernest and Mary, were both lace workers in the town.

A useful club cricketer, Fred was employed as a professional player and groundsman for much of his adult life. The *Taunton Courier*, reporting on the Somerset trial match of 1929, informs us that he was a slow left-arm bowler. In ten matches for Somerset between 1925 and 1929, he took 11 wickets at 39.90 apiece and averaged 3.00 with the bat. He was for many years a member of the Taunton X1 and during the winters played football as a defender for Taunton Town FC.

Still working as a professional player-cum-groundsman, he was married in 1932 to Jessie Cruse, a Taunton girl and the daughter of a bricklayer. They had no children, with Jessie continuing to supplement their income by working as a 'patent turner', making shirt collars for the Van Heusen company. The Van Heusen family had patented the idea of semi-stiff collars attached to shirts to replace the old-fashioned stiff collars and had imported machinery from the United States, becoming a major employer in Taunton and

Fred Lee – a professional groundsman for many years at Taunton CC.

135

F.G. Lee.

Bishops Lydeard, later opening further sites in Bridgwater, Crewkerne and Watchet. The collars were used for Van Heusen shirts but also supplied to other shirt manufacturers and enjoyed global success. The Van Heusen Company was a major employer for many decades, finally closing down its West Country operations in 1990.

At the start of the Second World War, with Fred serving in the military, Jessie's parents moved into the couple's home at 1 Cranmer Road. On his return, Fred resumed his duties at Taunton CC and won acclaim as a fine coach to the younger club members. He championed the cause of these young players, arguing successfully that the membership costs for boys should be substantially lowered in order to encourage them to play. His powers as a left-arm spin bowler had not diminished. The 1949 season saw him still topping the Taunton bowling averages. He was also employed for a while as a cricketing coach by Wellington School.

He died in Taunton on 19 November 1977 at the age of seventy-two and a year after the death of his beloved Jessie.

279
Edmund Fallowfield Longrigg
12 August 1925 v. Hampshire, Bournemouth

Known as 'Bunty', he was the son of Major George Edmund Longrigg, a solicitor in Bath who later became President of Somerset CCC and was a leading light at the Lansdown club at Bath.

Born in Batheaston on 16 April 1906, Bunty was educated at Rugby, where he captained the First XI and won the national schoolboy rackets doubles. H. S. Altham wrote of Bunty in his review of Public Schools 'his record of 840 runs for an average of over 50 was remarkable', adding that 'above all he watches the ball, and is hard to bowl out'. Altham also praises his 'clever fielding near the wicket, and a capacity to bowl slows'. Bunty was introduced to first-class cricket as a nineteen-year-old when he was invited to bat at number three by his captain, John Daniell. He went up to Pembroke College, Cambridge, where he won blues in 1927 and 1928. Although his first-class appearances would be limited by his work as a solicitor in Bath, he would nevertheless play for Somerset on 219 occasions between 1925 and 1947, averaging 24.56 with the bat, with ten centuries to his name. By 1938, the *Taunton Courier* was claiming, perhaps with a hint of the partisan, that Bunty Longrigg was 'one of the most aggressive and attractive amateur batsmen in the country'. Between the years of 1938 and 1946 he was captain

Bunty Longrigg – established his reputation at Rugby School.

of Somerset, having replaced fellow Bath solicitor Reggie Ingle. There was talk of behind the scenes manoeuvring but some felt that Ingle had become rather too phlegmatic and that Longrigg would bring fresh ideas and enthusiasm to the cause. Frank Lee, writing in *Cricket, Lovely Cricket* was full of praise for his new captain, under whose leadership he claimed that 'the Somerset side was raised from its lethargy' and that the players 'became conscious of a new team spirit invading the side, and each one of us began to feel the necessity of .... giving everything we had to the game'. Lee adds that 'Longrigg had the interests of every player at heart'. Unlike many an amateur captain, Longrigg sought the opinions of his professionals and, once he had agreed a course of action, would adhere to it, with no recriminations. With a solicitor's sense of fair play, he also fought successfully for more extended contracts for the professionals, an innovation long resisted by the committee. The pros responded positively to such gestures.

Bunty had something of the look of Buzz Lightyear about him, although this seems not to have deterred his lady friends. A series of engagements was announced to great fanfare in the press, though they rarely threatened to go to infinity and

Tom Young (left) and Bunty Longrigg (right).

137

beyond. First up was Gwendoline Vaughan. But that was broken off. Then came Cecily Wollen, whose engagement to Bunty even made the front pages of the local press in 1932. But that was broken off. We are left to ponder the reasons. Mary Rooke Munden of Ilminster stayed the course and she and Bunty were wed in 1934, with teammate Dicky Burrough acting as best man, though that marriage ended in divorce. In 1948 he was married to Peggy Louise Trounson, her husband having been granted a decree nisi on the grounds of her affair with Bunty.

E. F. Longrigg – as captain he 'had the interests of every player at heart'.

He had begun his working life in his father's practice but would subsequently go into partnership with fellow Somerset cricketer Dicky Burrough, the offices of Longrigg & Burrough being situated on Gay Street, in Bath. During the Second World War he served in the RAF, having been appointed a flying officer in June 1941.

In later life, he became Chairman of Somerset CCC. He was forced to step down after talk of a player revolt when the amateur, Colin Atkinson, was appointed captain in place of Harold Stephenson. He was subsequently President from 1968 until 1970.

Bunty Longrigg died in the city of Bath on 23 July 1974 at the age of sixty-eight.

1926

"The financial statement shows the club to
be in a flourishing position."
Western Morning News

Change continued apace, orchestrated by the dynamic A. F. Davey. The county turned in another sizeable profit and membership was up still further, with subscriptions topping £3,000. Innumerable tons of earth had been brought in to create banking around much of the ground to ensure a better view for more spectators.

Somerset take the field against Sussex at Bath in 1926.
LEFT TO RIGHT: J. C. W. MacBryan, R. A. Ingle, C. C. C. Case, P. R. Johnson, A. Young, J. C.
White, G. F. Earle, J. Bridges, E. G. Northway, G. E. Hunt.

Seating was replaced and the capacity increased by 500. The President, Col H. M. Ridley had 'marked his year of office by a generous and acceptable gift of a new stand', subsequently known as 'The Ridley Stand', offering seating for 120 members and a temporary solution while money was raised for a new pavilion. The Somerset Stragglers had chipped in by donating a new sightscreen. The promised Nursery was introduced for the Easter holiday period, with free coaching sessions for schoolboys, guided by Tom Young and George Hunt.

It was a source of regret that the team's performance was mired in mediocrity. There were of course flurries of excitement. Witness to this is the match with Essex. Why was it that controversy came seeking Somerset again as it had done in the tied match against Sussex in 1919? This time the scores were level with two wickets remaining when Jim Bridges had Eastman caught by Guy Earle. With only one minute on the clock, the umpire removed the bails, rather than allowing the last Essex man to come in. He was technically correct. John Daniell sportingly offered to continue. His opposite number Perrin would have none of it. The umpire's decision was final. The match was declared a draw. MCC later overruled the umpire and deemed it a tie.

The match against Australia was a thoroughly enjoyable occasion played out in front of a record crowd for the County Ground. Dar Lyon hit a 'sublime' 136 but could neither chase down the required total nor avert defeat. For a couple of heady hours the crowd was buzzing, though. Less so at Knowle, where the experiment of playing at the Imperial Tobacco ground was spoilt by the inclement weather.

MacBryan and Lyon were again the pick of the batsmen and White and Bridges the most successful of the bowlers. None of the debutants made any lasting contribution to the cause.

280
Evelyn Vernon Llewellyn Hill
8 May 1926 v. Worcestershire, Worcester

E. V. L. Hill

Peter Roebuck informs us in *From Sammy to Jimmy* that Evelyn Hill 'was explosively fast for four overs, following which he was a spent force'. It might have been fairer to have pointed out that Evelyn, who had all the requirements of a pace bowler – height and a slim build, a fine action, aided by excellent coaching – was dogged by ill health. He suffered from a congenital weakness of the heart inherited from his mother, Gwynedd (or Guinea). It would often cause breathlessness and in his mother's, his brother's and his own case, would result in their early deaths. Evelyn had the ill luck also to be troubled by weak ankles that seriously impacted his enjoyment of sport.

The son of former Somerset cricketer Vernon Hill, Evelyn was born on 18 April 1907 in Cyntwell, Cardiff and, like his brother, fellow Somerset cricketer Mervyn, was sent to Eton. Here he gained a reputation as a very fast right-arm bowler. *Wisden* describes him in 1925 as Eton's 'greatest potential match-winner', adding that 'he does bowl fast and he does make the ball bounce, though as yet he lacks strength and stamina'. Strength and stamina enough, though, to be invited to play for the Lord's Schools side alongside Rugby School captain, Bunty Longrigg.

It had been assumed that Evelyn would go up to Oxford but this never happened. In a report in the *Yorkshire Post* of April 1927 we are told:

There is, I understand, a possibility that E. V. L. Hill, the Eton fast bowler of two seasons ago, may be up. Tall and with a high delivery, good judges formed excellent opinions of his promise. He missed Oxford for a year to regain his health, and if his sea trip has proved beneficial, he will unquestionably be an acquisition.

In the event, Evelyn chose not Oxford University but the Territorial branch (4th Battalion) of the Somerset Light Infantry, joining up as a second lieutenant in May 1927. Three years later, he was promoted to lieutenant. In the intervening period his health had recovered sufficiently for

E. V. L. Hill – 'tall and with a high delivery'.

him to play thirteen times for Somerset. In 1928 he hit a rich vein of form, taking 5 for 36 against Worcestershire, followed by 5 for 85 versus Surrey and then a 3-wicket haul in each innings against Middlesex. Perhaps he was overreaching himself because in the following game he broke down, forcing him to withdraw from the action. He never fully recovered and would only ever make one further appearance for the county. He had taken 33 first-class wickets at 32.03 apiece and averaged 16.75 with the bat. Evelyn and Somerset would be left to rue their misfortune after such a brief glimpse of the match-winning qualities first seen in his youth.

Evelyn Hill (standing in the foreground) with brother and fellow Somerset cricketer, Mervyn (seated on horse).

Having resigned his commission with the Somerset Light Infantry in 1933, he joined up again at the start of the Second World War, resigning his commission for a second time in 1952 with the rank of major and honorary lieutenant-colonel. His heart condition had meant that he was never allowed to engage in active service. He would retain the rank of lieutenant-colonel in civilian life.

Married in 1935 to Jessica Frances Sydney Smith, the daughter of the man who was for many years Town Clerk of Weston-super-Mare, he would have one son, Robert.

Evelyn died on 25 October 1953 at the age of only forty-six at Weston-super-Mare. Both of the cricketing brothers – one tall and rangy, the other rotund – had died young, with there being a certain inevitability about the sad events, given their medical histories.

281
Gerald Oscar Boundy
22 May 1926 v. Gloucestershire, Taunton

Gerald Boundy was born in Little Torrington, Devon on 17 July 1895. His father, John, was a carpenter who worked on the Swytham Manor estate but died when Gerald was not yet in his teens, leaving Emma (née Luxton) to bring up three sons and three daughters. Emma was obliged to move to Taunton where there were greater employment prospects for her offspring than at Little Torrington. The 1911 census confirms that she was still a full-time mother, housing five of her children, all of whom had found employment.

On leaving school, Gerald worked for an accountancy firm as a junior clerk, learning the trade, until his employment was interrupted by the First World War, where he served with the 4th Battalion of the Somerset Light Infantry, commissioned in 1917 as a second lieutenant and being demobilised in 1919. After returning to civilian life he qualified as an accountant, working at De Montfort Chambers in Hammet Street. It would prove a sound career choice with Gerald moving in time to the salubrious Mount Nebo district of Taunton. Inevitably, given his line of work, he was sometimes the harbinger of bad tidings. The example of Antony Bridger, an entrepreneur (though not one of a numerical persuasion) offers a window on the times. Mr Bridger had asked Gerald to audit his accounts, believing that he was making a profit, only to be told that he was

G. 0. Boundy – compiled a record number of runs for Taunton CC in 1929.

making a thumping loss and was seriously in debt. In an age before the widespread availability of television sets, he had opened cinemas in rented space in six small towns in an area from Bampton in Devon to Nether Stowey in Somerset. As a result of the light shone on his finances by Gerald Boundy, Antony Bridger was declared a bankrupt in 1929 and thus the inhabitants of those small towns were denied the delights of the cinematic experience.

Married in 1933 to Sophia Kate Hiscock – eighteen years his junior and the daughter of a bank clerk – Gerald and Kate, as she was known, would have a son and daughter. An inveterate committee man, he also offered his services as Treasurer to the St James's Assistant Curate's Fund, the previous incumbent having opted for the life of a monk. He was by then a well-known figure on the local sporting scene, for a while Treasurer of Taunton Town FC and a regular in the Taunton cricket team, whom he was captaining in 1933. He had also held the post of Secretary of Taunton CC since 1924 and was a member of the Somerset CCC committee. A right-handed batsman, he had compiled a record number of runs for Taunton in 1929 – well in excess of 1,000 in the season. He played in two first-class fixtures for Somerset, one in 1926 and another in 1930. His batting average of 7.33 is no doubt an accurate reflection of his ability: an excellent club batsman but short of first-class standard. Regrettably this description fits too many of the amateurs invited to represent the county.

Gerald continued to practice in Hammett Street until the early 1960s, by which time he and Kate were leading separate lives. He was residing at the Royal Pier Hotel in Weston-super-Mare at the time of his death. He breathed his last at the age of sixty-eight at the Royal Masonic Hospital in Hammersmith on 8 February 1964. Kate was remarried within two months but reverted to the name Boundy later in her life. She was survived by their two children.

282
Cecil Frederick Douglas Buttle
22 May 1926 v. Gloucestershire, Taunton

C.Buttle.

David Foot writes of Cec Buttle that he was 'the son of a sergeant major and had the shoulders and torso of a fast bowler'. Born in Norton Fitzwarren on 11 January 1906, Cec attended North Town School. Seemingly something of a young tearaway, he was made to appear in court as a twelve-year-old, had up, along with a gang of friends, for having committed wilful damage to the French Weir Free Bathing Station. 400 tiles had been broken, most of the coat hooks removed and a number of doors smashed. Cec and his gang were each fined four shillings. He had learned his lesson and by the age of fourteen was offered a job assisting Ernie Robson on the groundstaff at the County Ground, earning the princely sum of eight shillings a week. After Robson's departure, Cec was for many years assistant groundsman to the inimitable 'Fernie'. According to Peter Roebuck, Fernie was 'a Maltese cockney [born Fernando] with an air of distinction', who was fond of sitting in Scarlett's pub, issuing instructions to his staff, including Cec, while drinking bass with his chum, the tall and gangly Lord Portman. Locals still recall two sharp bends in the road between the villages of Orchard Portman and Staple Fitzpaine being referred to as 'Portman's Corners' on the basis that his lordship had been known to leave the road at those hazards, car and driver having to be rescued, the one needing repairs and the other in a state of advanced inebriation.

Cec Buttle would finally become Head Groundsman once Fernie had retired and he would remain in the role for thirty years. During his working life he witnessed

Cec Buttle – for many years Somerset's groundsman.

significant changes. He would reminisce about being sent to the local stables – Herd's of St James's Street – early each morning to secure the services of a hump-backed horse, the only one whose hooves fitted the specially made leather shoes that protected the turf as it helped to pull the heavy machinery. After the horse's sad demise, he would go to the labour exchange to summon men to pull the roller. Later still, he would be seen sitting astride the mower and heavy roller. He is as responsible as anyone for the County Ground becoming for so many years a batsman's paradise. In order to achieve the desired outcome he used marl (from a brick works in Wellington) that was crushed to a fine powder. He also advocated the use of worms to give a wicket 'air and pace'. Three weeks before a match he would draw the worms to the surface using mustard powder and remove them to another wicket. His advice was sought and his unconventional methods deployed at a number of grounds in the area, though the festival pitches proved more of a challenge. Once he arrived at the Bath ground two days before the festival to find 'knee-high grass'. Perhaps this was an exaggeration, but it is certainly true that despite his best efforts the festival pitches were often not fit for purpose. He would always stride onto the pitch at the fall of the ninth wicket to consult the fielding captain over which roller was required between innings. On one occasion at Bath, on a very poor wicket about which Cec could have done little, Cyril Washbrook, responded, inserting expletives, that Cec should get a chain harrow to level what looked little more than a ploughed field.

Cec was married in 1929 to Edith Love Lee, known as Edie, a longsuffering partner who lived with him for many years in a caravan in the car park at the ground. Edie 'laundered the towels for a penny each, drying them on a line in the Ridley Stand'. They had no children but their cats were a feature at the County Ground, visible on match days but keeping their distance during the greyhound meets held on a regular basis. He was a fast-medium bowler – very quick by club standards – and was regularly deployed in the nets at the County Ground. In his two matches for the county he averaged 2.66 with the bat and took no wickets, conceding 54 runs. He was also called on both by Somerset and their opponents at Taunton as a substitute fielder, though he reported that he regarded this as something of a chore. Used regularly as an umpire in non-first-class fixtures, including a number of Second XI matches, he was asked on one occasion to officiate in a first-class fixture against Yorkshire as emergency cover, though only at square leg.

He also served as a retained fireman for many decades, including a period with Somerset and England cricketer Harold Gimblett, during the Second World War. Harold apparently drove the silver Rolls Royce that had belonged to the late Somerset President, Henry Murray-Anderdon, to and from fires. Cec would recount that the sights they saw and the friends and colleagues killed broke Harold's spirit.

Having retired from the County Ground, he tended the wicket at Taunton Deane until his death at St Margaret's Hospice in Taunton on 15 December 1988 at the age of eighty-two. Not long before, he had joked with a reporter that 'old groundsmen never die, they just keep rolling along'.

283
William Ewart Berry
26 May 1926 v. Hampshire, Portsmouth

William Ewart Berry.

Listed incorrectly in the cricketing archives for many years, William Berry was in fact born in Bridgwater on 12 October 1897. An assiduous registrar has noted a time of birth of 4:40 am. William had chosen an inconvenient moment to arrive on the scene and the same might be said of his departure. His father, Samuel – awarded an MBE and the freedom of Bridgwater – ran a grocery business and was married to Ann Maria (née Vowles), a police officer's daughter. William was one of five children, including a twin brother, John Henry.

After being educated at West Buckland School, William would follow his father into the grocery business, becoming a director of Berry & Co, Wholesale Provisions Merchants of Dampiet Street, in Bridgwater.

During the First World War he served in the Royal Navy, joining the Volunteer Reserve early in 1916 as a signalman. Trained on HMS *Vichy* and HMS *Vivid II*, he then served on HMS *Woolwich*, HMS *Columbine* and HMS *Leander*. The role of these last three ships was to provide off-shore support, reequipping and maintaining the fighting ships of the Grand Fleet. After demobilisation, he set about building up the family business. Well-known and well-respected in the community as a businessman, William was also a successful club cricketer, playing for Bridgwater and described as a 'googly bowler'. He also represented West Buckland Past and Present. His one appearance for Somerset was not an auspicious one. He made 1 not out in his only innings and took no wickets for 34 runs.

In 1931 he was married in Bridgwater to Mary (née Bond) and, residing in Wembdon, they would have one daughter,

William Berry – 'loved by all with whom he came into contact'.

Bridget, born in 1933. By this time, William was already suffering from the debilitating effects of diabetes, about which he was at times understandably despondent. It would subsequently become apparent that it was the burden of his condition rather than business worries that would drive William to take his own life in Bridgwater on 24 April 1949 at the age of fifty-one. He had gone to the offices on Dampiet Street on that day – a Sunday – less than twenty-four hours ahead of a scheduled hospital appointment, his condition having deteriorated, despite the regular use of insulin injections. William appears to have been a very private man, reluctant to talk even to his wife about his 'attacks' as he and Mary termed them. The details are spelt out in the *Taunton Courier* in a report of the inquest:

> *Just before one o'clock on Sunday, his twin brother, Mr J. H. Berry, went to the offices of Berry & Co. and found him lying dead in a room filled with gas. The body was removed to the mortuary ... A member of Bridgwater Rotary Club, Mr Berry and his twin brother were well-known cricketers for the Bridgwater club some years ago and he had made one appearance for Somerset.*

As another report states, 'a verdict of death from coal-gas poisoning, self-administered while the balance of mind was disturbed was recorded'. The *Bridgwater Mercury* informs us that 'his cricket prowess was of a very high standard and he had the honour of playing for the county – and he was loved by all with whom he came into contact'. William left a considerable sum of money, though this will have been of little comfort to his grieving wife and daughter.

References in some cricketing sources to 'Wilfred Ernest Berry' are incorrect.

284
Cuthbert Blair Godwin
21 July 1926 v. Lancashire, Taunton

C. Blair Godwin.

Cuthbert Blair Godwin was born in Clevedon on 16 October 1891 and baptised at Clevedon All Saints church. His father, John Colthurst Godwin, was a stockbroker and would work at the Bristol stock exchange for upwards of 50 years until the time of his death in 1935. Cuthbert's Indian-born mother Amelia Clara Reynolds (née Blair) already had one son by her first marriage and in addition to a half-brother, Cuthbert would have a sister and a brother, Charles, who was killed in action in 1914 in the retreat from Mons.

Between 1905 and 1907 he attended Winchester College, being one of the eleven original members of Beloe's House, set up for boys who had arrived at the school late in their education. He was clearly an able pupil, with the school records confirming that he 'raised books' in the Summer Term of 1906, a reference to the fact that he had earned the right to be moved up a class ahead of time. He left in the spring of 1907, before having had a chance to earn selection for the First XI.

Cuthbert spent the First World War in the Army Service Corps initially joining as a private. Having arrived in France in November 1915, he was gassed the following April and returned to England in June 1916. He was awarded a commission as a second lieutenant in February 1917, although he would not return to active service but remained at the Grove Park Depot in Lewisham. The letter recommending his commission notes that he had attended Winchester College, that he was an able driver, and that his brother had been killed at Mons. He had risen to the rank of lieutenant by the time of his demobilisation.

Prior to the war, immediately on leaving school he had joined his father as a trainee stockbroker in their office in High Street, Bristol. His father had played for Bristol Optimists and, following in the paternal footsteps, Cuthbert proved a promising young cricketer, appearing for Clifton CC and later for Frenchay and Optimists. He was invited for a trial by Gloucestershire as a nineteen-year-old in 1911, but was not selected by the county.

C. B. Godwin – a Winchester schoolboy (top) who performed the double in Bristol club cricket in 1928.

He was married in 1918 to Florence Mavis Estelle Wells (known as Mavis) with whom he would have a daughter. On the basis of his performances in club cricket in the Bristol area, where his slow right-arm bowling yielded some fine results and where he was a capable batsman, he was selected twice by Somerset in 1926 but met with little success, taking one wicket at a cost of 72 runs and averaging only 2.00 with the bat. Back enjoying his club cricket in 1928, the *Sports Times* notes that, playing for Optimists and Frenchay, he was the first club player in the region to perform the double of 100 wickets and 1,000 runs that season.

Cuthbert would continue throughout his working life to act as a stockbroker, based at Albion Chambers in Bristol and enjoying the longevity that his father before him had. He celebrated his Golden Wedding Anniversary in 1968 but died the following year on 23 October 1969 in Clifton, shortly after his seventy-eighth birthday.

1927

*"Mr White has not a long list of players to select
from like some county captains."*

A. E. Newton (Committee Member and Former Player)

Championship Position: 14 of 17

Reverend Archie Wickham was appointed President for the year. An eccentric wicket-keeper from the Victorian age, perhaps he had been charged with praying for divine intervention. If so, his prayers were ignored. The takings were severely affected by the wet summer and the county made a loss of £1,515, despite having secured a further increase in membership. Jack White was appointed captain, John Daniell having made it clear he felt too old and careworn to continue. Whereas Daniell had exhorted his troops loudly, White was regarded as a cold fish, buttoned-up and unprepared to praise his men. In the new, more dour environment it seems appropriate that Box Case should have stepped up to the plate and ground out two centuries. It was left to Tom Young to add sparkle to the batting. Bill Greswell was back and among the wickets but it was of course Jack White who again claimed most victims.

In a changing world, there were fewer and fewer amateurs to call on. 1927 marked the retirement of the combative John Daniell and the elegant Randall Johnson. Recognising the need to build up a stronger core of professionals, the committee offered full-time contracts to Jack Lee and Wally Luckes. Among the new recruits the stand-out performer was Arthur Wellard, a pro who had forsaken his native Kent to give his all for Somerset, delighting the supporters over the years with his heroics. Dicky Burrough, an amateur who practised as a solicitor in Bath, made the occasional more sedate contribution to the cause.

The Somerset XI who played Worcestershire at Amblecote in 1927: Somerset won at a canter, with Bill Greswell at his devastating best, taking a combined total of 10 wickets for 43 runs.
STANDING: W. T. Luckes, A. Young, G. E. Hunt, J. W. Lee, F. G. Lee, A. E. S. Rippon.
SEATED: C. C. C. Case, G. F. Earle, J. C. White, W. T. Greswell, R. A. Ingle.

285
Horace Thomas Perry
11 May 1927 v. Lancashire, Old Trafford

Horace Perry was born in Bedminster on 29 November 1905, the son of Horace Frank, a railway clerk, and his wife Lillie Sophia (née Noble). Although he joined the Knowle CC Second XI as a fourteen-year-old, he failed to grab the headlines in the local press

until undertaking a prank-gone-wrong in 1926. Horace and two friends were apprehended following a very early example of joy riding, having purloined what they later claimed they believed to be a friend's Singer motor car. Fully intending to return the vehicle, they discovered that they were lost. To add to their woes, they discovered they had stolen the wrong car. The story was so far-fetched that the judge was inclined to believe them and showed leniency.

Engaged in the more wholesome pastime of cricket he met with success as an all-rounder, often opening the batting and described – in the context of club cricket – as a right-arm fast bowler, and by now established in a Knowle team coached by the old Somerset and Gloucestershire pro Wally Hale.

Horace was offered a trial in early May 1927 and although he achieved nothing of note in that match, he was not alone. The only decent performance with the bat by any of the triallists came

Horace Perry taking the field at Knowle.

from a nineteen-year-old wicket-keeping pro named H. J. (Joe) McReynolds from Beverley in Yorkshire, who surfaced with the Yorkshire Second XI the following season before disappearing from the cricketing radar. There were no issues over Somerset-born Horace's qualification and he was therefore asked to fill a vacuum for one match before being replaced by the returning John Daniell.

Part of a threadbare Somerset team thrashed by Lancashire at Old Trafford by an innings and 125 runs, Horace made scores of 9 and 0 and was not asked to bowl. Returning to club cricket at Knowle he met with rather more success with both bat and ball.

Horace worked, as his father before him had, in clerical roles. He left the local cricketing scene when he was married in 1937 in Hendon, Middlesex, to Lydia Davies, twenty-one at the time and ten years his junior. They would reside in Harrow. A son, Martin was born in 1939.

Horace Perry died on 25 December 1962 in Kingsdown, Bristol, aged fifty-seven. He was survived by Lydia, who was remarried in 1972.

Top: *H. T. Perry (left) and D. A. Wilkins (right) of Knowle CC and Somerset.* Above: *W. N. Bunce (left) and H. T. Perry (right) in a representative game for Somerset*

286
Donald Albert Wilkins
29 June 1927 v. Yorkshire, Bath

Don Wilkins was born in Brislington on 13 October 1903. His father, Albert, was a warehouse foreman for a provisions merchant, married to Laura (née Strange), who hailed from Keynsham. Don made a name for himself as a useful right-handed batsman at the Knowle club and joined his teammate Horace Perry at a trial match in early May 1927. Having performed indifferently at the trial, Don would have to wait nearly two months for a call-up. He might have wished that he had not accepted the offer. With Randall Johnson and Raymond Robertson-Glasgow unavailable, he and John Daniell came into the side. It was a miserable, rain-affected game against Yorkshire at Bath and in his only innings Don faced three balls, hitting two confident singles before offering

Don Wilkins – appeared in two miserable, rain-affected games.

The Wilkins Bakery & Tea Rooms on Keynsham High Street.

up a simple catch. No play was possible on the second and third days. A fortnight later, at Taunton, Somerset endured another drenching in a drawn game against Lancashire. Don Wilkins came away with a total of six runs at an average of 2.00. He returned, chastened, to the brighter, sunnier world of club cricket.

Don earned his living by running a bakery and confectionery shop at No 63 on Keynsham High Street, known to the locals as 'Wilkins Bakers' and already a well-established family concern. The tea rooms and gardens were a popular meeting point in the town. He continued to live four miles down the road at Knowle. In 1933 he was married to Beatrice Edna Brown and they would have a daughter, Anne Patricia, who would later farm with her husband in Wiltshire.

After his retirement, he moved to nearby Saltford where he died on 22 January 1972 at the age of sixty-eight, less than two years after the death of his wife.

287
Louis St Vincent Powell
13 July 1927 v. Lancashire, Taunton

Louis Powell – a well-known figure on the Bath sporting and business scene.

Louis St Vincent Powell was so named because his birth occurred in Kingstown, St Vincent, while a hurricane raged outside. The date was 13 November 1902. His father, Arthur Henry, married to Rosa Alice (née Purnell), had been dispatched there by Kew to dispense advice and had become curator of the Botanical Gardens. Having enjoyed his upbringing in the West Indies, young Louis and his brother were then taken to live in Nairobi before, in 1911, the family settled in Taunton, where he was educated at Huish's Grammar School.

Louis soon established a reputation as a fast bowler – very quick by club standards – playing for Taunton CC, whose home fixtures were at the County Ground. He would recall that his major influences were Sam Woods, still a ubiquitous presence at Somerset, dispensing useful advice to the youngsters, and Ernie Robson, whose 'smooth run-up and easy delivery' Louis tried to replicate. He was given his county debut as a twenty-four-year-old and often recounted the tale that as he padded up, the old pro Tom Young took one look at his pads and offered the loan of his own, informing the debutant that unless he took them, Lancashire's fiery paceman Ted MacDonald was likely to break his legs. The anecdote neatly encapsulates Tom Young's droll cussedness, masking a concern for others.

Louis Powell soon moved to Bath where over time he became a well-known estate agent and auctioneer, managing the firm of Louis Powell & Co., and a central figure in the Bath sporting scene. He was a member of Bath CC and of a strong Bath rugby team, playing for the Somerset XV on seventeen occasions. Between 1927 and 1938 he played ten first-class matches for Somerset CCC, averaging 10.92 with the bat, including one half-century, batting at number ten. He also took five wickets (three of those on his debut) at 75.20 apiece.

He was married in 1935 to Nora Pratten, the daughter of Frank Pratten, who ran a successful business constructing timber buildings and was a major employer in Midsomer Norton. They would have three daughters. Even after he had retired from playing, Louis remained active in sporting circles, setting up cricket and golf trophies in his adoptive city. He was also instrumental in inaugurating cricket commentaries on the Royal United Hospital radio in Bath, covering matches at the Recreation Ground in Bath along-side his irrepressible former Somerset teammate, Bill Andrews.

Louis Powell – represented Somerset at rugby and cricket.

In later life he was made an Honorary Life Member of Somerset CCC for his services to the club on the management committee and later the Bath area committee. His greatest contribution to the cause was perhaps his part (accompanying Len Creed to the West Indies) in completing the negotiations with a promising young player named Vivian Richards, whom the county were determined to sign before word spread of his prowess.

His daughter, Jean, says of Louis that 'he was a very happy man who loved people and adored sport of all kinds, always enjoying his trips in later life to The Rec to watch Bath RFC or to the County Ground at Taunton to see the cricket'. She adds that 'he had a real zest for life and went about everything - business or sport - in a wholehearted way'.

Louis Powell died in Bath on 6 June 1995 at the age of ninety-two.

288
Arthur William Wellard
6 August 1927 v. New Zealand at Weston-super-Mare

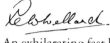

*Arthur Wellard – a whole-
hearted all-rounder who scored a
quarter of his runs in sixes.*

An exhilarating fast bowler and a batsman who scored a quarter of his runs in sixes, Arthur Wellard gave heart and soul, always with a wide smile. While he had bat or ball in hand, Somerset cricket was imbued with hope and the crowd would be afforded a flurry of excitement.

He was born in Southfleet, Kent, on 8 April 1902, the unplanned, third child of Ernest Arthur Wellard, an agricultural labourer. Ten years later, Ernest, exhausted by his work and approaching sixty, moved the family to Bexley, taking over the tenancy of a pub, The Black Horse. Unable or unprepared to settle down at school, Arthur regularly played truant and was actively involved in running the pub from an early age as his father's health deteriorated. He left school at fourteen and even at this age had an imposing physique. A natural sportsman, he played in goal for Bexley FC and the Kent X1. Some of his pub regulars were members of Bexley CC and they encouraged him to try cricket. He did so for the first time at the age of nineteen and was soon a first team regular, attracting the attention of the Kent authorities.

Bexley's 1926 fixture with Kent Club & Ground was Arthur's unofficial trial and Gerry Weigall, the autocratic Kent coach, was there to pass judgment. Arthur was called away during the lunch interval to help his mother, Amy, deal with some unruly customers. He was late back and Weigall marked him down as unreliable. Arthur was not engaged despite taking 5 wickets in the match and signed instead for Somerset. Kent had missed their opportunity. He

Arthur Wellard – made two Test appearances for England.

served his two-year residency qualification with Weston-super-Mare CC and lodged with the family of his future Somerset bowling partner, Bill Andrews.

In 1928, while guesting for Bexley in their annual fixture against the Kent XI, Arthur was approached by Gerry Weigall, and asked to reconsider his future and sign for Kent. A witness to the event – Bexley's scorer, George Lovegrove – overhead Wellard, normally the most taciturn of men, angrily telling Weigall to 'stuff your contract up your arse'. Later in the day, Wellard clean bowled Weigall with one of the fastest deliveries he had ever mustered.

He achieved the double of 1,000 runs and 100 wickets in 1933 and 1935, the latter achievement leading to his being named a *Wisden* Cricketer of the Year in 1936. Most commentators – *Wisden* included – thought him unfortunate not to have been given a Test place against South Africa. He had to wait until 1937 before being chosen for the Second Test against New Zealand at Old Trafford. At the end of that season he was invited to join Lord Tennyson's tour of India where in the Fifth Unofficial Test at the Brabourne Stadium in Bombay he hit a six out of the ground. A number of reliable witnesses, including Tennyson himself, claimed it was the biggest they had ever seen.

He would hit 561 sixes in a first-class career that spanned four decades from 1927 to 1950. The total included a mighty six in his second and last Test appearance for England versus Australia at Lord's in 1938. Twice he hit five sixes in an over, but he was technically sound, with a batting average for the county of 19.34, including two first-class centuries and 54 half-centuries. Bowling was, however, his defining skill. He took 1517 first-class wickets for Somerset at 24.32 apiece. Only Jack White has taken more. The war interrupted his career and denied him an MCC tour of India for which he had been chosen in 1939/40.

Having served with the Army in Italy, he was welcomed back to the Somerset fold and most supporters considered his release in 1950 to be premature, despite his advancing years. The committee would have believed him to be forty-eight, although Arthur had lied about his age throughout his career and was in reality approaching fifty. The normal rules concerning the ageing process never applied to him. Two productive seasons with Kidderminster and Lancaster made the point.

He returned to Sutton in Kent and to his longsuffering wife, Vera, known as 'Jack', whom he had married in 1928. They had spent more time apart than together and never had children. With the exception of a three-year period when they separated temporarily, Jack tolerated his absences and occupied herself with the running of a sweet shop in Sutton, an enterprise with which Arthur himself had few if any dealings. Throughout his career, he had lived a peripatetic lifestyle. Although built like an aurochs, he was almost childlike and otherwordly. Unable to drive, he relied on friends or public transport and, often out of pocket, he was dependent on offers of free accommodation. Somerset committee member Len Creed, in particular, would invite him for extended stays at his farm in Evercreech and here Arthur was able to indulge his passion for shooting and fishing. Calling on his skills as a gambler – no one knew more about horse or greyhound racing – Arthur was able to help Len in the setting up of a betting shop which became a successful enterprise.

After his first-class playing days were over, he took to coaching at the indoor school run by his longstanding friend Alf Gover. Later he coached at the Finchley Indoor School and Epsom College. He was still coaching well into his seventies and continued to play for anyone who asked, including Sutton CC, Putney Eccentrics and Gaieties CC. Playwright Harold Pinter, a Gaieties player, idolised Arthur and wrote a moving tribute to him after his death. Arthur ceased playing for the Gaieties in 1975 but still managed to turn out for Old Somerset at Clarence Park in his seventy-fourth year.

He retired eventually to Eastbourne, persuaded to do so by his wife, Jack. He died there on the 31st December 1980, aged seventy-eight. Bill Andrews, his bowling partner and lifetime friend, summed up Arthur's career by stating that 'he challenged fate blithely, even recklessly, and whether his gambles came off or not, the crowd loved him.'

289
Herbert Dickinson Burrough
27 August 1927 v. Glamorgan, Cardiff

He was known as 'Dickie' or 'Dicky', signing himself the latter way. Dicky Burrough was born in Wedmore on 6 February 1909, the son of William George Burrough, who had played on occasions for the county and had been a pacey club bowler in his youth, known as the 'Wedmore Express'. William Burrough was a man of boundless energy. While practising as a solicitor in Wedmore, he had set up an electrical supply company in order to bring power to the village. He had also served as the President or Chairman of more or less every club or society in the vicinity and had become the Coroner for North Somerset.

Dicky was educated at Brean House School in Weston-super-Mare and then at King's School, Bruton, before going up to St Catharine's College, Cambridge. Although an accomplished hockey player and cricketer, he failed to gain a blue in either sport. The former is perhaps more surprising, given that he would go on to play

three times for England at hockey. He retained his enthusiasm for the game, becoming President of the Bath Hockey Club in the 1960s. Indeed, Dicky approached most aspects of life with enthusiasm and is recalled with great fondness by those who knew him. An ebullient and sociable man, he had a wide circle of friends and his effervescence was apparent on a cricket field, where he was an energetic outfielder, happily chasing after the ball like a dog allowed off the leash, although, unlike a canine, he was also blessed with a safe pair of hands.

After graduating, he became a solicitor in Bath, working for the father of Somerset teammate Bunty Longrigg, before later going into partnership with Bunty in the firm of Longrigg & Burrough. He would remain there throughout his working life, playing his favoured sports for the city and the county. He would captain Bath CC in

Dicky Burrough – a Bath solicitor and England hockey international.

the late 1950s. He came from a sporting family and his brother was offered a trial by Somerset though he never played first-class cricket. A cousin, J. P. Burrough played for Gloucestershire and was, we are told, 'the tallest and reputedly the strongest of the Oxford [rowing] crew'.

Dicky was married in 1940 to Cecille Babbette Dickinson and they would have a daughter and son. During the Second World War, he served as an officer in the Somerset Light Infantry. After the cessation of hostilities he would make occasional appearances for Somerset. In all, between 1927 and 1947 he played in 171 matches and averaged 20.92, with four centuries and 23 half-centuries to his name. David Foot writes that 'he played most of his cricket off the front foot. He was happiest of all when being asked to go for his shots, but the various Somerset captains he played for didn't usually bother him too much with instructions.'

He retired to Padstow, Cornwall, where he died on 9 April 1994 at the age of eighty-five.

1928

"There is not much of interest to be said about the prospects of Somerset County Cricket Club for 1928."

Wells Journal

Championship Position: 14 of 17

Reggie Ingle began the season brightly with a century in both innings against Middlesex at Taunton, but the game was drawn and he was upstaged by J. W. Hearne with a knock of 223 not out followed by an unbeaten 97. Thereafter things never really got going. Ingle was well supported in the batting department by Tom Young. Jack White and the returning Bill Greswell took the honours with the ball. Too many catches were dropped, although the pro George Hunt who 'fielded brilliantly at short leg' showed how it should be done, taking five catches in one innings at Weston-super-Mare and thirty-one over the course of the season.

A knock-out competition was introduced for the Under 25s, in each case led by a more experienced player to guide the young hopefuls. It was designed to unearth new talent. Bath Area beat Taunton Area at a canter in the final in September. Six of the youngsters would go on to play for Somerset, although only Bertie Buse and John Cameron would do so with any frequency.

Among the season's new recruits, only the amateurs Laurie Hawkins and Michael Bennett would make any contributions of note, the latter on occasions as captain.

Bill Greswell, who played for Somerset intermittently from 1908 until 1930 and was an outstanding swing bowler: despite spending much of his prime as a cricketer in Ceylon (Sri Lanka) – where he managed the family's tea plantation – he still took 454 wickets for Somerset at 21.57 apiece.

290
Charles Thomas Worsfold Mayo
12 May 1928 v. Nottinghamshire, Trent Bridge

David Foot offers a brief, tantalising glimpse of Charlie Mayo's eccentricity in his history of Somerset cricket:

> Charlie ... lived opposite me in my village of East Coker and was the first county cricketer I ever met. He kept a pet raven which was apt to terrorise the neighbours; but he was a gentle man who was killed in the Second World War.

Killed, yes, but by a virus or bacterium and not in action. The record states that he 'died from illness contracted while on active service'. Charlie Mayo was born in Victoria, British Columbia, on 5 February 1903. His father, Henry Herbert Worsfold Mayo, was married to Florence Bartlett (née Fall). Describing himself on official documents as a 'gentleman', Charlie's father was essentially a landowner in possession of inherited wealth. Indeed, Charlie, following the example of his father, would generally file the word 'nil' against his occupation, seeing virtue in being too wealthy to endure anything other than a life of indolence.

Money must of course be begotten at some point and in Charlie's case he had reason to be thankful to ancestors who had made their fortune through the manufacture of gloves in Yeovil. While living at Nether Compton, the Mayos enjoyed fortuitous relationships, first in business – George Mayo Snr and John Ryall forming a company – and through marriage between the two families, with further wealth accruing from the Worsfold family. Within three generations they had earned their place as pillars of Yeovil society, with John Ryall Mayo (grandson of George Snr and great-grandfather of Charlie) being elected the first Mayor of Yeovil in 1854. The family appear to have built their fortune yet further by way of business loans and investment in agricultural land.

Henry Herbert had similarly invested in land, in Canada, but the family returned on a regular basis to the Yeovil area and Charlie would spend some of his upbringing at Devonshire Cottage in East Coker, a larger home than the name suggests, with thirteen rooms, a governess and two maids. The place was sold – along with some of the valuable

Charlie Mayo – a product of Eton who enjoyed only a brief first-class career.

C. T. W. Mayo – a gentleman of leisure who lost his life at forty in the Second World War.

contents – when Charlie's father downsized to Estate Cottage in 1913. It is not clear when Charlie's raven moved in to the new residence.

Educated at Eton, Charlie would soon be making a name for himself in the local papers. Whereas his father, Henry, was an upstanding citizen and chairman of a number of committees, his efforts culminating in an OBE, Charlie exhibited some of the characteristics of Mr Toad of *The Wind in the Willows*. At sixteen, he had his first brush with the law, hauled before the courts for driving his motor-cycle without a licence. He was had up again in 1922 for driving in his Mercedes with no functioning rear light. By 1927 a pattern was emerging. This time he was done for driving recklessly through the crowded streets of Seaton, with women apparently fleeing to safety. Charlie, with some of the chutzpa that Eton had bred into him, declared it all a storm in a teacup, insisting that the loud engine created an illusion of speed. Witnesses refuted this, noting that the he was driving 'at such a speed that it was impossible to take his number' and that the 'hind wheels jumped off the ground'. Not that identification was necessary. Everyone, it seems was aware of Charlie. Another witness noted that 'it was the same when he had his motor-cycle; they used to say he was driving too fast'. Charlie was fined £2. Shortly thereafter he spent time in Australia. Perhaps his father had thought it desirable to despatch his son to foreign climes where out of sight was out of mind.

Charlie seems never to have shown much interest either in the idea of work or marriage and would enjoy himself by playing cricket and proving a useful club batsman for East Coker (as his father had been before him). He played for Somerset on six occasions in 1928. Quick off the starting grid, he scored 35 and 60 on his debut and notched up score of 48 in his second game but thereafter he ran out of gas and stuttered across the finishing line with a batting average of 21.44.

Charlie was then despatched to Quebec for a short while before returning home.

His father, Henry, died in 1938 and Charlie continued to reside at Estate Cottage. When he joined the North Somerset Yeomanry Royal Armoured Corp as a sergeant, he might have perhaps finally found a purpose in life but he was struck down by illness and died near Alexandria in Egypt on 10 April 1943 at the age of forty. He left his estate to his sister, Lallie, by then Mrs Thompson and a widow, residing with her mother-in-law at the family home in East Coker. Perhaps Charlie's raven was there, too, missing his erstwhile companion. Charlie's body lies at the Hadra War Memorial Cemetery.

291
Reginald Bert Marsh
16 May 1928 v. Warwickshire, Edgbaston

R. B. Marsh – 'brilliant batting, splendid fielding and energetic fast bowling'.

Reginald Marsh was born in Street on 11 August 1897, one of eleven children of Edwin and Jane Marsh. The parents and most of their offspring would earn a living as outworkers, making shoes at their home on the town's High Street for the famous Clarks company.

Married in 1918 to Florence Lily (née Parsons), Reginald proved a successful club cricketer for Frenchay in the Bristol area. An outstanding fast-medium bowler and a consistently good batsman at club level, he regularly topped the averages for both disciplines and would continue to do so at various clubs until the late 1940s.

He would be invited to play twice for Somerset in 1928 and a further two times in 1934, averaging 10.50 with the bat and taking 2 wickets at an expensive 98.50 apiece. In the intervening period he would play as a professional for Aberdeenshire. His appointment in Scotland was confirmed in November 1929, after he had earlier taken part in a post-season trial at the club's Mannofield ground. The local West Country newspapers reported that Frenchay would feel the loss keenly. Given that he had scored two centuries in the preceding season and taken a hatful of wickets, including a 10 for 32 in one game, this response is unsurprising. Reginald remained at Aberdeenshire from 1930 until 1933. His four seasons were deemed a success, with the *Aberdeen Journal* declaring on 5 August 1933 that:

Today will have a mournful interest to many inasmuch as it is R. B. Marsh's last home county match for Aberdeenshire. Marsh's brilliant batting, splendid fielding and energetic fast bowling have endeared him to spectators, just as his cheerfulness and good sportsmanship have made him a first class favourite with his fellow players.

The old Frenchay cricket ground where R. B. Marsh 'spent so many, many happy hours' and where he requested that his ashes be scattered.

Reginald returned to Bristol in order to work as a clerk within the Ministry of Labour. He would find time to play his club cricket for the Bristol Civil Service team and was a key member of the national Civil Service side, playing for them every year from 1935 until 1939 inclusive in the annual fixture against MCC at Lord's. During the Second World War he played for Gloucestershire Services against their Somerset counterparts.

In later life, as his and his wife's health deteriorated, their daughter, Vera, acted as their carer and the presence of a grand-daughter, Celia, brought joy. After a more interesting and varied life than that enjoyed by the majority of his family who had spent their days as shoe makers in Street, Reginald died at the age of seventy-one on 25 April 1969 in Frenchay Hospital, near Bristol. As requested in his will, his ashes were scattered on Frenchay Common, where, in his words, he had 'spent so many, many happy hours on the cricket field'.

292
Wyndham Rowland Thomas
19 May 1928 v. Derbyshire, Chesterfield

Wyndham Thomas was born in Bedford on 1 June 1911. His father, Hedley Vicars Thomas worked as a travelling salesman for an oil importing company and his mother, Winifred Nina (née Rowland) came from Pill, in Somerset, where Wyndy, as he came to be known, was raised along with three older brothers. He went to Cotham Secondary School and benefitted from the encouragement offered by Lodway CC, who allowed free membership to the local schoolboys in the hope of unearthing talent. They succeeded, with a number of young players going on to represent the county – including the Hunt brothers (George and Hubert), Wilde, Hambling and Bunce.

Wyndy impressed the Somerset committee at a county trial match. According to a report in the *County Herald*, 'his style was free, a good pick-up and a follow-through being combined with executive skill that made his shots delightful. Those who have seen him at the nets expect much of him.' His promising innings in the trial was cut short when he made the mistake of hitting out at the wily swing bowling of Bill Greswell and was caught at cover.

His debut managed to combine the entirely startling with the utterly mundane. Seen as a useful stand-in for J. C. White, given the similarities – a left-arm bowler and capable right-handed batsman – he was given his chance while Jack White was away playing for MCC. Wyndham Thomas was still only sixteen at the time of his debut, making him the youngest professional in the Championship and inspiring great hope for the future. In the event, there was no play for the first two days. Having been listed as the number five batsman and 'a left-arm change bowler', he neither batted nor bowled on the third day. That was the sum total of his first-class career. Jack White returned to the fold. Wyndy was blown out of the water.

W. R. Thomas – selected as a sixteen-year-old, he neither batted nor bowled in his only first-class game.

He worked as a bank clerk for the Midland Bank and would rise to become a branch manager. An excellent rugby player, he appeared for Portishead and also in 1934 for Newton Abbott, when his work took him briefly to south Devon, though he soon returned and starred for a strong Clifton side in the mid-1930s as a three-quarter, praised as a regular try-scorer until his career was curtailed by injury. His brother, Eric, played rugby for Bristol. Wyndy served in the Second World War as a corporal. He was married immediately after the war on 5 December 1945 to Evelyn Ann Caird (née Gibb) from Bristol. The couple would have no children.

He continued to combine his career as a bank manager with his club cricket. He is described in the history of the club as 'an elegant batsman and a cover point whose speedy and accurate returns to the wicket were feared by all opposing bats'. He was also called upon to bring opposing innings to a close in a less-than-orthodox manner. In *Game for Anything* author David Foot admits to having been a victim of Wyndy's wiles. The orientation of the old Lodway ground meant that the sun would set adjacent to The Anchor pub, behind the bowler's arm. As late-summer fixtures drew to a close,

the cry would come up 'Give it to Wyndy' and he would duly toss the ball up high, directly in the line of the sun and with uncanny accuracy, bowling many a temporarily blinded tail-ender. He apparently bought a pint of ale for those he had dismissed, by way of an apology. He captained the First XI for ten years and was Chairman for a while. Mike Lovell, a stalwart of Lodway CC and the club's historian says: 'Wyndy always found time to encourage young players, patiently sharing his knowledge of the game and helping us to fulfil our potential.'

He retired to Weston-super-Mare, where he died of heart failure at the age of eighty on 29 January 1992.

Wyndy Thomas – an elegant batsman and brilliant cover point.

293
John Charles Pengelley Madden (or Madden-Gaskell)
26 May 1928 v. Kent, Taunton

J.C.P. Madden-Gaskell.

Born in Llangibby (Llangybi), Monmouthshire, on 1 March 1896, John was the second of four children of Andrew Charles Madden and his wife Winifred Alice. His father had attended St John's College, Cambridge, and after serving as a deacon in Llandaff was ordained in 1894. He was then a priest at a number of churches, culminating in a spell between 1903 and 1905 at St George the Martyr in Southwark. A noted breeder of bulldogs, Rev. Andrew Madden was, it transpired, not suited to the priesthood and eloped to Buenos Aires with a girl named Maud Addems, who was in her twentieth year when the couple set sail for a new life. The former priest carved a new career first raising cattle and then as a vet, with spells in Canada and the United States. Evidence that Andrew and Maud were ever married has proved elusive, although if they were, their union would have been bigamous. They did, however, have a son named Andrew Addems Madden. Andrew Snr died in Chicago in 1928 and Maud was later married and became a boarding house owner in County Orange, California, living to the age of nearly a hundred.

What of Andrew's wife, Winifred? She continued to raise her youngest child, Edith, but the three remaining children were placed with other families, very probably in 1901. John was adopted by his mother's sister, Kathleen, and her husband, John's uncle, John Gaskell, a brewery manager in Newport. Although John Jnr's name appears never to have officially been changed to Madden-Gaskell, he was known as such. He was subsequently sent to Haileybury, where he proved a useful rugby player and also appeared for the college's cricket First XI in 1913.

He served with the 2nd Battalion of the Welsh Regiment for the duration of the First World War, commissioned as a second lieutenant in October 1914 and promoted to lieutenant in 1915, involved in training and logistics. He was later given command of a Provisional Brigade, charged with coastal defence. It appears that he never served overseas and was not involved in any direct conflict.

He was married in 1920 to Frances Hope Lacey, the daughter of the Rev. Lacey of Exmouth and Budleigh Salterton. They would have a son and daughter. Having played club cricket in Penarth, John Madden-Gaskell appeared once for Glamorgan in 1922 but then moved to Somerset, living at Court Blethyn in Ruishton and going into partnership with A. Garraway to form the company Gaskell and

John Madden-Gaskell in serious pose (top) and enjoying post-match celebrations in a photo booth (bottom. left) with Algy Bligh (right).

Garraway Ltd. Based in Bridge Street, Taunton, they were described as 'electrical and refrigerating engineers' although the bulk of their transactions were centred around the wireless. The business was a successful one, remaining in operation for many years and including the sale and repair of wirelesses as well as the hiring out of public announcement systems for events. They also oversaw a network of travelling salesmen who offered their wirelesses for sale or hire purchase, one of their reps being taken to court when he attempted to defraud the two men by cooking the books.

John Madden-Gaskell played a prominent role in Taunton's sporting scene. An accomplished outside centre, he played for Taunton RFC, becoming Club Secretary in 1929 and he was also elected Secretary of the Somerset Stragglers cricket team, credited with injecting new life into the organisation, substantially increasing the fixture list, membership and funds over a five-year period. With regard to his skills as a player,

H. J. Channon, writing in the *Taunton Courier*, informs us that:

> *John Madden-Gaskell was the gay cavalier of local cricket. To him slow cricket was an abomination. My scrapbook records a match for Somerset Stragglers in which his batting was simply dazzling.*

Between 1928 and 1930 he played nine times for Somerset, beginning in a blaze of glory. A half-century against Kent was followed by scores of 42 and 63 against

J. C. P. Madden-Gaskell.

Nottinghamshire, with their feared attack of Larwood and Voce. Thereafter, his form fell away sharply and he averaged 15.35 for the county. Peter Roebuck asserts that 'when facing Bill Voce, Madden-Gaskell, who batted in glasses, was much put out to find one ball whistling past his nose, whereupon he called to the opposing captain that Voce was dangerous and should be taken off.' We should perhaps treat this anecdote with caution, given the author's tendency to give well-crafted phraseology precedence over mere facts.

After the death of John's biological father in 1928, his mother, Winifred, was free to marry a man named Alistair MacLachlan the following year. Her son had therefore garnered the trinity of a biological father, an adoptive father and a stepfather.

The business – Gaskell and Garraway Ltd – was wound up in 1938. Mobilised at the start of the Second World War in 1939, John was appointed Staff Captain Headquarters Eastern Command (based in Hounslow) in1942 and promoted to Deputy Assistant Quartermaster-General in 1945. He was awarded the MBE in 1947 (by now listed as Major Madden-Gaskell of the Royal Artillery) on the basis that he had been 'heavily involved in provisioning, preparing and despatching troops for Overlord [D-Day]'. After his retirement from the Army in 1954, he received the OBE in 1955 for 'outstanding service' in two wars, including the organisation of the HQ cricket team. It appears that the Army had valued his organisational skills highly.

In 1952 he was married for a second time, his partner being Mary Rose Lowerton Dawson, and he would have four further children by this marriage. Deciding that their two sons might benefit from the Madden name which had long been associated with the military (although it had admittedly been tainted in ecclesiastical circles by the exploits of his black sheep of a father), Rose suggested that her husband should confirm his and their names as Madden by deed poll. This he did in 1962.

He died on 4 February 1975 at Anvower House in Helston, Cornwall, at the age of seventy-eight.

294
William Gordon Lock
7 July 1928 v. Essex, Chelmsford

W. G. Lock.

In another case of mistaken identity, William Gordon Lock's limited achievements as a first-class cricketer have for a number of years been attributed to the wrong man. Born in Taunton on 11 October 1907, he was known to his teammates as 'Pad Lock'

William Gordon Lock – 'always a source of worry to the opposing batsmen'.

or 'Paddy', but was generally referred to as Gordon. His parents, William Henry and Ethel May (née Gregory), lived above their bakery and confectionery shop in Bridge Street. William Henry was one in a long line of bakers, his grandfather, John, a master baker, having set up in the same street (although in different premises) by the early

172

1850s. The business had then passed down the generations until Gordon qualified as a master baker and took over after initially working for his father.

He became active on the Taunton social scene and a leading bowler for Taunton CC. Wrting in the *Taunton Courier*, H. J. Channon states that:

W. G. Lock ... was a good medium-paced bowler, with clever variations in flight and pace. "Paddy" was a fine forcing batsman, and very safe and agile in the field.

As a press report recounts, 'Somerset called on a new man in W. G. Lock of the Taunton club' for the game at Chelmsford in 1928. He was a last-minute replacement after Tom Young suffered from a thigh strain. With four regular bowlers already in the side, Gordon was not asked to bowl by Jack White – a captain never moved by sentiment or inclined to take risks with the newjoins – and, batting at number nine, scored 2 in his only innings. Owing to some inspired batting by Dar Lyon and a sustained period of steady bowling from the Somerset quartet, who shared the wickets, Somerset won by nine wickets. Gordon Lock was not called on again.

He was married in 1935 to Alice Emma Lucy Summerhayes, a farmer's daughter from Curry Rivel. The couple would have no children.

After the Second World War, he captained Taunton CC and headed the bowling averages. A report of the 1946 season informs us that 'skipper Gordon Lock ... captured most wickets. Turning the ball both ways, Lock was always a source of worry to the opposing batsmen.'

In later years he became a prominent member of the Pickeridge Golf Club near Taunton, for many years as club captain and later as a trustee and a Vice-President. He was also listed as a director of Hawkes & Sons, suppliers of agricultural equipment.

He died in Taunton on 10 March 1980 at the age of seventy-two, survived for a further nine years by his wife, Alice.

References in some sources to 'Walter George Lock' are erroneous.

295
Laurence Cyril Hawkins
18 July 1928 v. Nottinghamshire, Taunton

Born in Acocks Green (in the district of Solihull) on 15 May 1907, he was the son of Herbert and Nellie Hawkins, who ran a jewellery and watch chain manufacturing business together before moving to Weston-super-Mare. Laurie followed his father

into the jewellery business but found time to indulge his passion for cricket with the Weston-super-Mare team for whom he was captain for many years. He also played for the YMCA football team in the the town. A right-handed batsman and leg-break bowler, he was a genuine all-rounder capable of match-winning performances on a regular basis at club level and some highly creditable performances at first-class level. His best form with the bat came in 1934 when he made his highest score of 96 at Lord's and took a courageous 82 off the fearsome Nottinghamshire duo of Larwood and Voce, who had many amateurs quaking in their boots. He also twice took 4 for 39. In all, over forty-six matches between 1928 and 1937 he averaged 17.15 with the bat and took 22 wickets at 48.50 apiece. A well-built man, he was not

Laurie Hawkins – an all-rounder who made useful contributions with bat and ball.

always the most energetic of cricketers. Frank Lee recounts in his autobiography a match at Old Trafford where Somerset found themselves needing to hold out for a draw. Having been unexpectedly promoted to opener, Laurie repeatedly turned down calls for a single. When challenged, he informed Frank that there was no hurry, given that they had more than a day to cling on. Laurie had no intention of tiring himself out in the process. Arguably his greatest service to Somerset cricket was to incur an injury shortly before the match with Essex at Frome in 1935. John Daniell took Laurie's call and, so the folklore has it, noticing that a young triallist, just rejected by the county, was leaving, called out to him to ask if he would be able to make it to Frome. Harold Gimblett went on to score one of the most talked-about debut innings in cricket history, and one that launched the career of a Somerset legend.

Unlike a number of the amateurs, Laurie was at ease in the company of the pros and was indeed on friendly terms with fellow Weston teammate and Somerset professional Bill Andrews, with whom he reputedly kept fit by going on thirty-mile walks on Sundays. He shared some of Bill's concerns over the shoddy treatment of the pros

L. C. Hawkins (left) and R. A. Ingle (right) of Somerset CCC.

and no doubt this was a subject of conversation on their walks, though Laurie would have done well to get a word in edgeways. In particular, he was critical of Jack White's approach to captaincy claiming that he was 'a rotten captain. He was very sullen and only spoke to his contemporaries.'

He was married in 1945 to Hazel Rita Huxley, known as Rita. They would have three daughters together. Laurie retired to Cornwall where he became an enthusiastic golfer and captain of his local club. He was predeceased by Rita and died in his home in Padstow on 4 October 2003 at the age of ninety-six. Former teammate Trevor Jones had visited him days

Laurie Hawkins – enjoyed a long and happy association with Weston-super-Mare CC.

earlier and noted that 'he was as mentally sharp as ever and was ready to talk cricket all day long.'

296
Geoffrey Michael Bennett
18 August 1928 v. Essex, Bristol

g. m. Bennett.

Michael Bennett was born on 17 December 1909 in Bruton, Somerset. His father, Philip, married to Evelyn (née Davenport), was a land agent based in the town and was the brother of former Somerset cricketer Charles Oatley Bennett. Michael attended King's School, Bruton, where he proved an outstanding sportsman. A highly successful schoolboy athlete, hockey and rugby player and, above all else cricketer, he was drafted into the King's School First XI as a thirteen-year-old by his mentors – Somerset cricketers P. W. Vasey and C. J. Bowring – and remained an important member of the team as a batsman and fast bowler for five years. On leaving school, he joined his father in the firm of Bennett & Co, learning the ropes of the land agency business.

Philip was liberal in allowing his son to indulge his passion for cricket, including appearances for the likes of Free Foresters, Somerset Stragglers and Men o' Mendip, for whom Michael acted for a while as Club Secretary. A popular figure, he was invited to make his debut for Somerset as an eighteen-year-old and would represent Somerset 109 times over a twelve-year period, on seven occasions as captain. He led the side with an air of calm assurance, which contrasted with the relentless enthusiasm of Bunty Longrigg, whom he replaced in those fixtures. Michael's batting average was 15.32. As with so many amateurs, his outstanding promise was never quite fulfilled, although he made some telling contributions, including his scores of 71 and 73 against Gloucestershire at Bath in 1934, when he led a fightback but to no avail. With insufficient support offered by the other batsmen, Somerset lost by 10 wickets. With a tendency to attack the bowling and to be too easily bored by defensive cricket, he often gave up his wicket too cheaply when he looked ready to build a big score. He was not alone in this. Indeed, it might be said to have been endemic among the ranks of the Somerset amateurs.

He was also an occasional bowler with 14 wickets at 32.00 runs apiece and a best bowling performance of 4 for 39. Peter Roebuck writes of Michael that he 'made his mark as an attractive batsman whose best moments were memorable, as a brilliant fieldsman, and as an immaculately dressed and invariably debonair fellow'. Indeed, he was a dashing figure, whose good looks, charm and athleticism ensured that he was a frequent guest at country house parties where he was a popular choice as a partner in

Michael Bennett – born in Bruton, he captained Somerset seven times.

G. M. Bennett – an attractive batsman and brilliant fielder.

games of mixed doubles tennis, with some suitors eager to ensnare the eligible bachelor. Certainly he bowled more maidens over than he ever bowled maiden overs.

He joined up with the Devonshire Regiment at the start of the Second World War and found life in the military more to his liking than land agency, opting to continue serving until the early 1960s. He was married in 1949 to Monique Nugent, whom he had met in Cairo and who was half-Irish and half-French. After having retired from the Devonshires with the rank of major, Michael emigrated with his wife and children to Canada, with Monique having been offered work in teaching, where she would be able to utilise her bilingual skills. The family remained there as permanent residents, living in Toronto, where Michael died on 26 July 1982 at the age of seventy-two.

1929

"They had really good spasms which did much to
counterbalance a number of serious deficiencies …
On a number of occasions there were signs of a devastating
rot and the batsmen would file back to the pavilion
in a dismal procession."

Western Daily Press

Championship Position: 15 of 17

Wins for the team were few and far between with the *Western Daily Press* observing that 'several games were thrown away when victory appeared to be well within their grasp'. Somerset were at least able to retain their proud 'boast' that they had never propped up the table since the dark days before the First World War.

The talk was all of Jack White. Announced as a *Wisden* Cricketer of the Year in 1929, he had spent the winter as vice-captain of the England team Down Under and had come back a national hero, his finest moment being the capturing of thirteen Australian wickets in England's 12-run victory in the searing heat of Adelaide. He then bagged 168 first-class and Test wickets during the English summer and made 1,179 runs – the first time he had achieved the double.

Tom Young, Bunty Longrigg and Box Case also topped 1,000 runs and Arthur Wellard began to show his worth with well over 100 wickets, approximately half of his victims clean bowled. Perhaps Jack White had advised him to bowl at the stumps, given the side's ability to spill more catches than they held.

The pick of the debutants were Frank Lee, Horace Hazell and Bertie Buse, all of whom would give sterling service the county for many years.

Lionel Palairet, thought by many to be the most elegant batsman of his era, was appointed club President. He was one in a run of highly-regarded former players to be appointed to the role.

Jack White was the most taciturn of men. Year after year he was Somerset's leading wicket-taker. In 1929 he returned from Australia a national hero after his astonishing feats of endurance, bowling in oppressive heat. His success continued unabated over the English summer and he was named a Wisden Cricketer of the Year. *The team as a whole struggled throughout the 1929 season. The above cartoon appeared in* Sports Times, *entitled* ANOTHER ONE TO KEEP HIM COMPANY. *Drawn by F. G. Lewin, it shows 'Farmer' White celebrating a rare win for his county team.*

297
Frank Stanley Lee
11 May 1929 v. Worcestershire, Bath

Born on 24 July 1905 in St John's Wood, Middlesex, close to the Lord's cricket ground, Frank was the youngest of three cricketing brothers. They all played for Middlesex but while the eldest, Harry, stayed at Lord's, Frank followed Jack down to Somerset to further his first-class career. He was employed as a coach at Kingswood School in Bath and also played for Lansdown while he qualified for Somerset. Later he would

Somerset pros (left to right): W. T. Luckes, F. S. Lee, H. L. Hazell and A. W. Wellard.

transfer his allegiance to Bath CC.

A left-handed opening batsman, he was at times a dour figure as he held his ground at the crease, though this was often precisely what was required as wickets tumbled around him. There is no better example of his stubborn resistance than a match against Worcestershire when he carried his bat in the first innings and fell just short of the same achievement when he was the last man out in the second innings. Between 1929 and 1947 he would play 328 first-class matches for Somerset, averaging 27.96 and compiling twenty-three centuries in that time. He made more than 1,000 runs in each of the seven seasons leading up to the Second World War and again in 1946. He often opened with his brother Jack, although when he was partnered in later years with Harold Gimblett – as cavalier as Frank was cautious – the contrast in styles could not have been more marked.

Frank's most prolific season was 1938 when he became the first Somerset man to score over 2,000 runs in a season. A versatile player, he took 23 wickets (bowling right-handed) at 32.56, including one five-wicket haul against Warwickshire in 1933. He also stood in as wicket-keeper on a number of occasions when first-choice keeper Wally Luckes was unavailable.

He was married in 1932 to Ruby Tanner, the sister of his friend, Jim Tanner, a Bath rugby forward, who encouraged Frank to take up the sport, which he did with only limited success. He achieved more turning out at football, for clubs such as Warminster FC. Frank and Ruby were shaken by the untimely death of their daughter,

Susan, at the age of thirteen, but within a year of her death, two boys – Jonathan and Marcus – had been born, perhaps offering some comfort to the grieving couple. These were difficult times for Frank who had also lost his brother, Jack, in the war, killed in action in Normandy.

In 1947, the year of his retirement, Frank was given a benefit year in which over £4,000 was raised, the Somerset supporters grateful for his contribution over so long a period. His eldest brother, Harry, had enjoyed a spell as a first-class umpire (although he subsequently went on to become the cricket coach at Downside School). Frank would go one better, officiating in 484 first-class matches and, between 1949 and 1962, in 29 Test Matches as well as the first ever Gillette Cup Final in 1963.

Widely respected, Frank gained fame (or infamy, depending on one's standpoint) for no-balling South Africa's Geoff Griffin eleven times in the Second Test (at Lord's) in 1960. Griffin's unusual action was due in part to a bent arm that resulted from an accident in childhood. The decision was not without controversy and was certainly coura-geous on Frank Lee's part. To add fuel to the fire, when a limited overs match was hastily arranged after the test finished early,

Frank Lee – a left-handed opening batsman who completed twenty-three centuries.

Griffin opted to bowl underarm but was no-balled once more when he failed to notify the umpire of his intention to do so. A techni-cally correct decision, although arguably an overly-officious one in an exhibition match.

Frank was certainly well versed in the technicalities of the game. His book *The Umpire's Decision*, published in 1955, was long regarded by many as the oracle on the art and science of umpiring. Having clearly developed a taste for writing, Frank saw his auto-biography *Cricket, Lovely Cricket* published in 1960.

He retired to London and lived a short walk from Lord's in a flat in Bronwen Court. He died of heart failure at St Mary's Hospital in Westminster on 30 March 1982 at the age of seventy-six.

F. S. Lee – enjoyed a second career as a leading umpire.

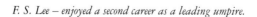

298
Walter Stanley Wilde
11 May 1929 v. Worcestershire, Bath

Known in adult life as 'Tich' or Stanley, he was born in the village of Pill on 27 February 1908, one of eight children of a mason's labourer, Christopher Wilde, and his wife, Elizabeth. In a letter to the *Western Daily Press*, Frank C. Cox writes of a serendipitous coming together of young talent in the village of Pill:

> At one period a few years before the war, the Lodway club included eight {county} players, seven of whom had assisted Somerset and one who played for Gloucestershire.
>
> There were the brothers George and Hubert Hunt, both good all-rounders: Wyndham Thomas, Newman Bunce and Monty Hambling, all attractive batsmen: Stanley (Tich) Wilde, a clever young wicket keeper at that period: Bob Draper and Jack Beasant, both fast bowlers and hard hitters. All are products of the village of Pill, excepting Draper who resided at Portishead.
>
> As boys they used to assemble each evening on 'Batch Green', a piece of waste land at the centre of the village where they often attracted the attention of passers-by.

Tich Wilde – a nimble wicket-keeper and club opening batsman at Lodway CC.

We are left with an image of carefree summer evenings with the boys no doubt dreaming that they would one day represent their chosen county and Tich Wilde, the smallest of the group, hoping that he might one day be orchestrating proceedings from behind the stumps.

He was in fact a very nimble keeper and a useful club batsman for Lodway CC. For many years he opened the batting for the club and we are informed that 'his eyes and feet were so quick that he was banging anything a bit short to the square leg boundary long before the shine was off the ball'.

He was invited to play for Somerset on seven occasions, all during May and June of 1929. Over thirteen innings, he averaged 5.62 with a highest score of 21. He also claimed ten victims – nine caught and one stumped. After his services were dispensed with, Somerset turned for a while to a number of occasional part-time amateur keepers to fill the wicket-keeping slot.

Tich worked as a plumber, following the work wherever it took him around the West Country. For example, at the time of his marriage, in September 1933 he was working in Poole. He was married to Maggie Amos at Doynton parish church near Bristol and the couple would have a daughter.

He continued to be employed as a plumber throughout his working life and died at the age of sixty in Clevedon on 21 August 1968.

299
Reginald Philip Northway
8 June 1929 v. Gloucestershire, Taunton

The cousin of fellow Somerset cricketer E. G. 'Ned' Northway (and not his brother, as is sometimes stated), Reg Northway was born in Ceylon on 14 August 1906, the son of Charles Louis Northway, a rubber plantation owner. He was educated at The Oratory School in Woodcote, near Reading. Arriving as a young man in Bath, where his uncle and cousins lived, he worked initially at the Guildhall in the city as a surveyor and quickly immersed himself in the sporting scene, playing cricket for Bath CC and occasionally for Lansdown. He was regarded as a technically sound batsman, prone to caution and only likely to attack the bowling when the circumstances demanded it. Also an enthusiastic rugby player, he was only ever on the fringes of the Bath XV.

Reg Northway – 'a sound opening bat'.

He was invited to play for Somerset as an amateur at the age of twenty-two, a local report describing him as having 'a wonderful defence' and adding that 'he is a splendid opening batsman'. In seventeen matches between 1929 and 1933 he would average 14.50 with a highest score of 75 not out. In short, he was regarded at first-class level as a man who could usually be relied on to take the shine off the new ball, without achieving any spectacular success.

Having been offered a job with a Bath engineering firm he subsequently moved in 1932 to Grafton Regis in Northamptonshire, continuing work as a road surveyor. He would go on to play for Northamptonshire on seventeen occasions. By 1936 he was clearly adopting a more positive batting style. A local report on the new recruit to the Northants team states that he had 'won a great reputation as a forcing bat in club cricket while playing for Northamptonshire Amateurs'.

But then, in a tragic irony, the road surveyor died in a motor accident near Kibworth, in Leicestershire on 26 August 1936 as he drove back from an away fixture against Derbyshire at Chesterfield. In a drawn match, Reg had struggled, scoring 1 run in each innings. His opening partner A. H. (Fred) Bakewell had done rather better with an unbeaten 241 in the second innings. An England international and former *Wisden* Player of the Year, Fred Bakewell's methods were as unorthodox as Reg Northway's were correct.

Reg was driving the two of them back, following behind J. E. Timms, who was more familiar with the route. Noticing headlights no longer in his rear mirror, Timms went back and found the two flung from the car. Reg North-way was lying in a ditch with multiple head injuries. He had died instantly. Fred Bakewell was lying on the verge with a fractured skull and was going in and out of consciousness. A driver was flagged down and asked to summon an ambulance. Rushed to hospital, Bakewell would survive the crash although his cricketing career was finished by the tragedy. The death sparked much discussion about the pressures players were under with a crowded itinerary. A week later, Gloucestershire's captain, D. A. C. Page, suffered a similar fate.

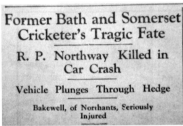

Former Bath and Somerset Cricketer's Tragic Fate

R. P. Northway Killed in Car Crash

Vehicle Plunges Through Hedge

Bakewell, of Northants, Seriously Injured

R. P. Northway – he hit the headlines when killed in a motor accident in 1936.

One obituary describes Reg Northway as 'a sound opening bat who could always be relied on to stay there' and 'a splendid outfield' who did 'brilliant work on the boundary'. Yet another report describes him as 'a brilliant man in the outfield with a fine turn of speed and a sure hand and eye'. It seems that his batting, though sound, was never likely to elicit superlatives.

He was thirty years old at the time of his death and unmarried. At the funeral, his Northamptonshire captain, Geoff Cuthbertson, had written a message on a card attached to a bunch of red carnations: 'To a great little sportsman.'

300
Horace Leslie Hazell
8 June 1929 v. Gloucestershire, Taunton

H. L. Hazell.

H. L. Hazell –
'trundling in from a
short run' he took 957
first-class wickets.

The incomparable John Arlott once joked that Horace Hazell was the only bowler slow enough to keep wicket to his own bowling. Born in Brislington, Bristol, on 30 September 1909, Horace was the son of George Hazell, a brewery clerk, and his wife, Matilda. The last of four children, he arrived on the scene when his mother was already in her late thirties. As a child he was dogged by ill-health – in particular from double pneumonia and pleurisy. The resultant absences from school caused his education to suffer. Peter Roebuck suggests that as a result of this he had a continuing inferiority complex that led him to retreat from the limelight, relaxing completely only when with his teammates. He would develop a public persona as a joker, and was not beyond stunts such as reputedly ordering a pint at every stop on the train journey from Taunton to Brislington after a match. His japes extended to the changing room where he was appointed the rain prophet by his teammates and – perhaps having secretly already consulted forecasts – would invoke rain by dancing around a bowl of water with a towel over his head, aided and abetted by his partner in crime, Bill Andrews. According to Frank Lee, Andrews and Hazell also insisted on leading a song they had penned to the tune of *Three Black Crows* in order to ensure victory in the following fixture. It normally failed to have the desired effect but this did not quell the pair's enthusiasm for the superstition.

As a boy, Horace grew up in the shadow of his older brothers. Cliff was a talented cricketer and Billy a county footballer. Horace would spend hour after hour bowling in the nets at the local Brislington club, encouraged by his father, who saw signs of promise. The club pushed his case. Rejected by Gloucestershire, Horace was then recommended to Somerset who agreed to fund a trip to a London indoor cricket school.

The report came back that he was 'too slow a bowler' to succeed in first-class cricket but it was conceded that he bowled an accurate line and length. H. J. Channon reports an exchange where an elderly lady, watching Somerset but not versed in the subtleties of cricket, looked up from her knitting and commented: 'Isn't Hazell a good bowler. He hits the bat with every ball.' Coming in off seven or eight short paces, he certainly bowled a fine length and tended to pitch the ball on leg stump, moving to off, varying his flight and pace. As a result of his accuracy, nearly a third of the overs he ever bowled were maidens. In a tribute in the *Daily Telegraph* to his boyhood hero, Christopher Brooker observes of Horace that 'trundling in from a short run, Hazell scarcely looked like a professional sportsman'. He goes on to cite two extraordinary feats that stuck in his memory. This first was the occasion during Horace's benefit year of 1949 when he took eight Gloucester wickets for only 27 runs – and this against a team that included four internationals. The most extraordinary element of the feat was that he had completed 105 balls over two hours without conceding a single run. The other unexpected moment of glory came when in 1936, against Hedley Verity, generally regarded as the foremost left-arm spinner of the day, Horace, an avowed tail-ender, called on his

Horace Hazell – the team joker and an unlikely hero.

knowhow as a bowler of similar style to plunder 28 runs (including four sixes) off one Verity over. This last feat was particularly unexpected, given that Horace had a reputation for keeping a cool head when either hanging on for a draw or attempting to steer the team past the winning post.

Despite taking 250 wickets in club cricket in the 1930 season, he was not called upon on a regular basis until Jack White began to appear less frequently from 1932. Thereafter, Horace was regularly at or near the top of the county's bowling averages and twice took more than 100 wickets in a season. Over the course of 350 matches he took 957 wickets at 23.97 apiece. During the 1952 season he took 63 wickets, including a best return of 6 for 16. It therefore came as a shock to most observers that his contract was not renewed, though less of a surprise that Somerset's fortunes nose-dived for a number of seasons as they sought to find a replacement.

Somerset's loss was Mitchells and Butlers Limited's gain as they took him on as a pro. He later returned to the Somerset set-up as a coach, instilling the need for accuracy in young bowlers by placing a plate on a length and consistently landing the ball on it, to show what could be done.

Essentially a shy man behind his jovial façade, he was never married and continued to live in the house in Brislington in which he had been born. He died there on 31 March 1990, aged eighty.

301
Leslie Hugh Bean
22 June 1929 v. Essex, Chelmsford

Sometimes referred to as Hugh, Leslie Bean was born on 2 February 1906 in Berrow, near Burnham-on-Sea. His parents, Percival Frederick and Emily Gertrude were sufficiently wealthy to need no employment. Percival's father had made his fortune as a stationery wholesaler in Beckenham and Emily (née Palmer) was the daughter of an auctioneer from Axbridge. Leslie was sent to Sherborne School in Dorset, his parents having purchased a property in the Dorset town. He featured in the school cricket XI, opening the batting in his final year of 1923.

As an only child of wealthy parents, he could have perhaps enjoyed a leisurely existence but chose to join the military. A report headed 'Success at Sandhurst' informs us that he had 'passed out of Sandhurst with distinct credit. He was head of the Champion Company at Sandhurst last year, and he has now passed out top.'

He was commissioned as a second lieutenant in the Somerset Light Infantry in 1926 and would progress inexorably through the ranks. In 1929 he was made a lieutenant and then in 1933 was seconded to the Sierra Leone Battalion of the Royal West African Frontier Force, set up in 1900 to protect British interests in the region, primarily against the threat of French expansionism rather than any local uprising.

In the meantime, Leslie had enjoyed his leisure time as a keen golfer and a cricketer. He would play three times for Somerset during the 1929 season, coming away with a batting average of 5.83 and taking 1 wicket for 24 runs, bowling leg-breaks. He had more success in Minor Counties cricket for Dorset, whom he represented on occasions between 1928 and 1939. Thinly built, he relied on timing and athleticism rather than brute force.

By 1938, his military career still progressing well, he was formally confirmed as a captain and would be promoted to the rank of major in 1943. When he retired from the Army in 1948, the year in which his mother died, he was awarded an OBE for his service to king and country and was afforded the honorary rank of colonel.

He was appointed General Manager of the Ghana Chamber of Mines shortly thereafter, calling on his vast experience of the region (if not necessarily of business matters). He made regular trips between Takoradi in Ghana and the family home in Sherborne and, perhaps planning for his retirement, invested in a property in Eastbourne. In the event, on the death of his father in 1962, he inherited 'Woodstock' in Sherborne. Never married, he led a quiet existence and was for many years a member of the Association of Cricket Statisticians.

He died on 13 January 1988 in Accra, Ghana, aged eighty-one, perhaps on a nostalgic return to the region where he had spent so much of his working life.

L. H. Bean of Sherborne School (top) – he took only one wicket for Somerset but enjoyed more success in Minor Counties cricket.

302
Michael Vyvyan Spurway
3 July 1929 v. Leicestershire, Taunton

Michael Spurway enjoyed a long life and lived it to the full. The son of the rector of Heathfield in Somerset, former Somerset cricketer Edward Popham Spurway, Michael and his twin sister, Rachel, were born on January 24 1909. His father died when Michael was six, and three of his brothers were killed in the First World War, leaving his mother, Gertrude, to bring up her three remaining children. After attending St Edward's School, Oxford, Michael went on to Christ Church, Oxford, where he read

History, played cricket and hockey for his college and learned to fly with the University Air Squadron.

He was invited to represent Somerset as a wicket-keeper batsman during the summer vacation while a twenty-year-old undergraduate, thus following in the footsteps of his father, Edward, and brother, Francis. His first-class career proved short-lived. He made three appearances during the month of July 1929, averaging 7.33 with the bat, holding four catches and managing one stumping. He blamed his short career on the fact that Jack MacBryan had plied him with whisky while the amateurs were staying at the Grand Pump Room Hotel in Bath and he subsequently took to the field hung-over and dropped two catches, but the statistics suggest that he might have struggled to make his mark with or without his being led astray by a seasoned player who should have known better. As an aside, Michael would later report that he was left open-mouthed with astonishment at the way the amateurs were cosseted with first-class travel and luxurious accommodation provided free of charge while the hard-up pros were obliged to find their own way to the ground and source their own cheap lodgings. It remains an irony that amateurs were often rewarded far more generously than the pros.

After graduating in 1931, Michael joined the Colonial Service, initially spending eight years in Nigeria as assistant to a succession of senior civil servants. He was married in 1937 to Margaret Plowden-Wardlaw. In 1939 he was posted to Cyprus where, in addition to his administrative duties, he became Adjutant of the Cyprus Defence Force. The follow-

M. V. Spurway – played three times as an amateur wicket-keeper while at Oxford before he joined the Colonial Service.

190

ing year he joined the RAF. Considered too old to fly in active service, he became an instructor on Tiger Moths. He was subsequently involved in helping with the delivery and reassembly of crated Spitfires. Demonstrating admirable versatility, he became the CO of the Middle East Photographic Interpretation Unit in Cairo, involved in reconnaissance, before moving to a similar role in Italy. By the end of the war he had been made a wing commander, involved in the resettlement of refugees. He was awarded an OBE for his services to king and country.

After the war he returned to the Colonial Services, rising to become an acting Colonial Secretary in Cyprus. There followed spells in London involved in the implementation of the Marshall Plan followed by time in Malaya and Singapore until his retirement from the Civil Service in 1953.

With an unquenchable thirst for life, he then became a partner in a firm of management consultants – Urwick Orr – whose areas of expertise included the airline, steel and brewing industries. As a result of this he joined United Breweries as a director in 1963 and went on to be offered a string of non-executive directorships, mostly connected with the drinks trade or steel production.

Throughout his career he had continued to play cricket and hockey and had also enjoyed success at polo and tennis, adding a substantial collection of big game trophies for good measure.

In 1976 he finally retired and returned to the West Country. A year earlier, following the death of his first wife, he had been married to Jennifer ('Jenna') Halliday. His hobbies in what we might loosely call retirement included fishing and shooting and one of his proud boasts was that he once bagged 250 pheasants at a single stand. He also began to make cider and wine from his own orchards and vineyard and, showing no signs of taking things easily, made regular fishing trips to Scotland and Ireland.

In his nineties, he went on a trip to Sri Lanka, flew over the Quantocks in a hot-air balloon and could still be seen driving around in his beloved Aston Martin.

He died at Corfe, near Taunton, on 7 July 2007 at the age of ninety-eight.

303
Herbert Francis Thomas Buse
17 July 1929 v. Surrey, Kennington Oval

He was generally referred to as Bertie. Punctilious, possessed of an air of serenity, and with a run-up that suggested a man carrying a tray of drinks, he was dubbed 'The

Butler' by John Arlott. In many ways he was a natural successor to a very similar character, Ernie Robson, a journeyman all-rounder who had also won the hearts of the Somerset supporters.

Bertie was born in Bristol on 5 August 1910, the son of a self-employed provisions broker, Francis Buse, and his wife, Edith. Educated at the City of Bath School, he was an outstanding young sportsman. Although not naturally athletic in his movements he excelled as a cricketer, hockey player and rugby full-back, also proving outstanding at billiards, table-tennis (at which he was once West of England champion) and, we are informed, shove ha'penny. Working as a clerk in a solicitor's office and already making waves at Bath RFC and with Bath CC, he was invited to play for Somerset as an eighteen-year-old amateur. He would also represent the county at rugby.

At The Oval, he was thrown in at the deep end when handed the new ball against Hobbs and Sandham, against whom he made no inroads. But this heralded a long career with the county in which he would play 304 times, averaging 22.69 with the bat and taking 657 wickets at 28.77 apiece. From the late 1930s he had given up his amateur status and played as a professional, once he had decided the life as a conveyancing clerk was not for him. He supplemented his meagre professional's allowance with some journalist work for the *Bath Chronicle*. He was married in 1940 to Elsa Nash and they would have two sons together.

Bertie Buse – his benefit match against Lancashire in 1953 was over in less than a day.

As a batsman, Bertie had an unusual style – 'all bat and bum', he called it – where he would crouch with his head low as he took guard. His batting was decidedly one-paced and he played along the ground, rarely going for a lofted shot and relying heavily on 'Bertie's dab', a cut played well away from the body. Although unorthodox, he was good enough to score seven centuries. His bowling was equally unique. He would carefully fold his county cap (awarded in 1934), before handing it to the umpire. His run-up began with a short walk that looked more like a Sunday afternoon stroll, followed by a few hops and an increase in speed with the ball clasped in both hands and his chest turned away from the batsman until the last moment. He never rose above medium pace but he swung the ball and was very accurate. H. J. Channon, the Taunton-based journalist, stated that 'he is the embodiment of steadiness, thoroughness and modesty'. If he beat the batsman and narrowly missed the stumps, he smiled and never snarled. When he

H. F. T. Buse – dubbed 'The Butler' by John Arlott.

Bertie Buse – 'he is the embodiment of steadiness, thoroughness and modesty'.

dismissed an opponent, the smile turned into a broad beam of delight.

His benefit match against Lancashire at Bath in 1953, his final year of first-class cricket, was a disaster. Over in five and a half hours, Lancashire's total of 158 on an unplayable track was enough to win comfortably by an innings, with Somerset mustering 55 and 79. It would have been little consolation to Bertie that he came away with bowling figures of 6 for 41.

In 1953 he was offered the chance to become the rugby and cricket coach at King Edward's School in Johannesburg. The school was home to 1,500 boys and so Bertie's role was a demanding one. He would remain there until returning in 1963 to work within the brewery industry where his line manager was G. E. S. Woodhouse, who had captained Somerset after the war. Woodhouse offered Bertie the role of landlord of the St Peter's Finger pub in Lychett Minster, Dorset, and he remained there for a number of years until his retirement. Here Bertie was able to demonstrate his skills not just as a host but in games of darts or shove ha'penny, where he had apparently lost none of the skills manifest in his youth. There is a certain irony in Bertie's having become a publican, given his reputed aversion to ever buying a round. It is said that he would even pretend to doze as his turn to buy drinks approached, rousing himself as the next in line reached the bar. His teammates invariably forgave him his parsimony.

A hugely popular figure whom it was impossible for anyone to dislike, he returned to his beloved Bath and died at the Royal United Hospital on 23 February 1992 at the age of eighty-one.

1930

"There cannot be any doubt that White, Longrigg
and Young carried the team along."

Western Daily Press

Championship Position: 13= of 17

This was Tom Young's benefit year. He had served the county well since making his debut in 1911, his continuing ill-health never having been allowed to dampen his fighting spirit. Initially used as a batsman, he had been encouraged by Jack White to develop his skills as an off-spinner and had thus become a useful all-rounder. In 1930 he hit 1,219 runs and took 71 wickets. Sadly, his chosen benefit match (against Sussex at Bath) proved a wash-out but £750 was nevertheless raised for a much-loved veteran.

Jack White continued to be the rock on which the team was built and again completed the double of 100 wickets and 1,000 runs. Indicative of Somerset's hand-to-mouth existence is the away fixture versus Yorkshire. Somerset arrived at Bradford with eleven men, only for their captain, Jack White, to be summoned for Test duty. A telegram was sent to Bill Andrews to head north, the captaincy was handed over to Reg Ingle and White fielded until Andrews's arrival. Perhaps White's mind was elsewhere when he dropped Frank Dennis three times in quick succession off the bowling of Jack Lee.

The season's principal run-maker was Bunty Longrigg, whose opening partnership with Young was working well. One press report touts him as worthy of consideration as an England player, praising his temperament and noting that 'he can take the edge off the bowling without being perturbed about getting runs'. His four centuries included a 205 against Leicester that set up a successful run chase for victory with two minutes to spare. Dar Lyon chipped in with a wonderful double-century against Gloucestershire but he could only manage a handful of appearances. And lurching from the sublime to the ridiculous, at Taunton in the match against Notts, with Voce terrorising the batsmen, George's Hunt's novel solution was to switch to a left-hand guard. Box Case, less dextrous than Hunt, fell onto his wicket and in his confusion set off towards the pavilion with a stump instead of his bat.

304
Eustace John Hewitt Hart
7 May 1930 v. Warwickshire, Edgbaston

E. J. H. Hart – a chartered accountant and an occasional first-class cricketer.

He made his debut in the same match as Bill Andrews but his career would be considerably the more shortlived of the two. Although born in India, Eustace would in fact spend much of his life ensconced in the city of Bath. He was born on 14 November 1907 in Poona (Pune), Maharashtra. His father, Henry Eustace was Secretary of the Bombay Port Trust and married to Hilda Isabel (née Poole). Both parents were of landed Irish stock, Eustace's paternal grandfather having been born at Doe Castle in Donegal.

The Harts relocated from India to England (perhaps as a result of the death of Eustace's grandfather in 1914) and resided at 'Solsbury End' in the village of Upper Swainswick, close to Bath. Eustace attended Monkton Combe School from 1919, entering the senior school in 1922 and playing for the First XI for four years in succession. On leaving in 1925, he qualified as a chartered accountant, practising for a while in Bath before becoming a partner in the firm of Tribe, Clark & Co. in Bristol.

He was a regular in the Bath CC side and on occasions for Lansdown, piecing together some successful innings. He played three times for Somerset in 1930, averaging only 9.00 with the bat, and might have played at least once more, given a press report in which we are informed that 'E. J. Hart of Bath was invited to play [against Northants] but was obliged to refuse on account of a professional examination for which he is sitting'.

He was married in September 1931 to Mary Sanforth Jefferies, who lived in nearby Long Ashton. As with Eustace, she had Irish connections. The couple would have one daughter and would continue to live with Eustace's mother, Hilda, in 'Solsbury End', his father having died in 1927. Hilda appears to have been a feisty woman, Honorary Secretary of the Bath Eye Infirmary and fiercely proud of her Irish ancestry. Her patriotism is evidenced in a letter in 1940 to the *Bath Chronicle* in which she expresses her outrage at Churchill's 'acid references to Southern Ireland'.

For his part, Eustace would play an active part in village life, acting as billeting officer and an auxiliary fireman in addition to his work as an accountant. A press report of the Swainswick Home Guard Christmas Dinner of December 1940 informs us that 'Platoon-Commander Hart presided' and that 'much amateur talent was revealed and a cheerful selection of music was provided at the piano'. Perhaps conscious that details of all that merriment might have undermined the public's confidence, the reporter ends by

Platoon-Commander Hart of the Swainswick Home Guard.

adding by way of reassurance that 'the Home Guard Platoon boasts many excellent shots'.

After the war, things having returned to some sort of normality, Eustace and Mary would continue to reside at the same family home, with their only child, Jennifer, until her marriage. Eustace died in Upper Swainswick on 4 February 1972 at the age of sixty-four.

305
William Harry Russell Andrews
7 May 1930 v. Warwickshire, Edgbaston

- WHRAndrews

Few cricketers could have given more to the county Bill Andrews served for five decades. He was a gangly, gregarious individual who on first acquaintance would invite you to 'shake the hand that bowled Bradman'. The recipient of the crushing handshake would then be informed that Bradman had been on 202 at the time. The greeting provided the title for his autobiography, published with author David Foot's patient assistance.

Bill was born on 14 April 1908 in Swindon where his father, William Snr, was a publican. The family moved to Weston-super-Mare when Bill was twelve. Here, he was introduced to cricket by a teacher, former Somerset player Harry Saunders. Bill's association with Somerset began in 1922 when he sold scorecards and worked the scoreboard at the Weston Festival. He was playing in the Weston-super-Mare CC First XI by the age of sixteen.

W. H. R. Andrews –
twice completed the
double of 100 wickets
and 1,000 runs.

His fine copperplate handwriting stood him in good stead for his first taste of employment in a solicitor's office but the job made him restive. He left to join East Coker CC as their professional, persuading them to take his brother as his replacement, when Somerset came calling in 1930. Jack, a wicket-keeper, later played for Hampshire. Bill joined his great friend Arthur Wellard, in what would become a hugely successful opening bowling partnership. Arthur had lodged with the Andrews family while he qualified for Somerset by residence and Bill would later recount that: 'I only had one real complaint with Arthur all the time I knew him. He always had the choice of ends and would bowl with the wind behind him. And even if there was half a gale, he'd look at me and say there was nothing between the two ends.' He had three disappointing seasons with Somerset

before experiencing the first of his four well-documented sackings. Two successful seasons for Forfarshire were to follow before he returned to the fold in 1935.

He was an important member of the team during the five seasons leading up to the Second World War and twice completed the double of 100 wickets and 1,000 runs. His crowning achievement was in 1937 against Surrey at the Oval when he took 8 for 12 including a hat-trick and a dropped catch off his bowling that went for six.

Bill Andrews – complemented Arthur Wellard in a successful opening bowling attack.

He had been married in 1933 to Joan Ambler and a son, Michael, was born in 1937. The war interrupted his first-class career but he spent time in the Army playing cricket for Blackpool, the British Empire X1 and Glamorgan. His marriage to Joan was over by the time he resumed playing for Somerset in 1946. His performances tailed off and by the end of the 1947 season he was out of favour and out of contract. He had played 226 matches, taken 750 wickets at a respectable average of 23.38 and averaged 15.59 with the bat.

In 1947 he was married again, this time to Ennyd Williams and they had a son, Mark, and a daughter, Sara. He remained in Weston-super-Mare, running a small sports equipment business, coaching at local schools, writing a newspaper column and plying his trade as a professional player and coach with Stourbridge, in the Birmingham League. A clash with Arthur Wellard's Kidderminster side took place during the last of his three seasons there and brought the best out of both of them. His bowling figures of 7 for 57 were trumped by Arthur's 10 for 33.

Bill continued to badger the Somerset authorities, offering his services as player and coach or recommending promising youngsters. Throughout the 1950s and 1960s he wrote a weekly article for the *Green 'Un* – the sports newspaper issued by the *Bristol Evening Post* – maintaining a high profile and occasionally using the column to challenge the authorities. He was elected by public vote onto the Somerset Committee, giving him a platform for further lobbying, and his persistence was rewarded with his appointment as coach in 1955. His third spell with Somerset was shortlived. His reinstatement in 1958 was even briefer, lasting only months before George Lambert was preferred in 1959.

He remained on the committee, as opinionated and vociferous as ever. His last paid employment with Somerset commenced in 1965, when he was made Second X1 Coach, but he soon wormed his way onto the Management and Selection Committees. This all came to an end in 1969 when Brian Langford convinced the committee that senior players had lost confidence in Bill's coaching. Bill had often been the architect of his own downfall. Never inclined to diplomacy, his impetuous outbursts made enemies of those in power.

His outgoing personality masked a lack of self-confidence not helped by a tendency to stutter that dogged him throughout his life. He also resented many of the amateurs their money and influence. He held many grievances, such as blaming Wally Hammond for the fact that he never received a Test call-up. Above all else he battled all his life with clinical depression. He had good cause to worry, given that it ran in the family. His father had spent time in an asylum and his first son, Michael, had died from drowning, following a spell in hospital suffering from the affliction. Bill retreated into himself during his final years, declining the many invitations to attend functions. He would also refuse to meet visitors to his house in Worlebury where he died on 9 January 1989, aged eighty. One newspaper headline read: *End of Somerset Legend*. An unabashed self-publicist, Bill could not have put it better himself.

306
Ernest Gerald Holt
17 May 1930 v. Surrey, Taunton

E. G. Holt was known in adult life as Gerald. Born on 2 July 1904 at The Hall in Burnham-on-Sea, he was the third child of Thomas Holt and his wife Margaret Jane. The family owned the Burnham Brewery in Burnham-on-Sea and had done so since Gerald's grandfather and great uncle had combined their resources in 1878, to buy the business, which had originally been founded in 1771. After purchasing the enterprise, the Holt family invested in improving the premises whilst also building up a roster of more than sixty pubs in the surrounding area. The family also built the Brean Down Hotel and met with some resistance when a licence

The Holt family owned the Burnham Brewery.

was initially denied them, though their persistence paid off in the end. The firm passed into Gerald's hands when his father died in 1929 and would subsequently be amalgamated with Starkey, Knight and Ford before being taken over by Whitbread. The shares in the company had by then been spread among a number of family members but the takeover ensured that Gerald would be comfortably well off.

The 1911 census shows him residing at The Hall with his mother and father, six servants and one guest: a certain Samuel Moses James Woods, listed as a 'cigarette manufacturer', though supporting evidence for the Somerset cricketing legend's claimed business is hard to find. The entry is possibly a jocular reference to his deftness at rolling a cigarette. Sam was in fact godfather to Gerald and would often take him along to Taunton to watch the county play. He was protective of his young charge, whose two brothers were killed in the First World War. Gerald would recount the tale of one occasion when, travelling on the bus together, Sam bellowed to the driver to stop, having seen a ewe on her back and despatched Gerald to get the animal back on her feet, before allowing the bus to continue.

In another connection with Somerset cricketers of a bygone era, Gerald was married in 1931 to Blanche Frances Hill, the daughter of Vernon Hill and sister of Somerset cricketers Mervyn and Evelyn. Gerald and Blanche would name their son Vernon Thomas. They also had a daughter, Gwynedd (or Guinea), named after her maternal

Gerald Holt as a promising young sportsman (top) and on his wedding day in 1931 (above).

grandmother.

Gerald was a keen sportsman who played golf, tennis, hockey and squash for Somerset. As for cricket, although he enjoyed some success as an all-rounder, playing for Brent Knoll and Burnham as well as prestigious sides such as Free Foresters, Somerset Stragglers and Men o' Mendip (who included other Somerset players in their ranks), he would only be a peripheral figure in the first-class game. His two appearances in 1930 yielded a batting average of 4.00 and he took no wickets, conceding 15 runs in six overs. He would be offered a place in a further trial match in 1933 but was not invited to play again, although he did join the MCC tour of the Netherlands in that year, appearing in a match deemed first-class which the Dutch won at a canter. His interests beyond the world of brewing were many and various, including the presidency of the Highbridge and District Skittles League, reflecting his commitment as a regular member of the brewery skittles team.

Gerald was a successful breeder of racing pigeons and was very actively involved in efforts at avian conservation. A member of the ornithological branch of the Somerset Archaeological and Natural History Society, he was a leading light in efforts to stop egg collecting and the shooting of rare birds in his part of the county. As Chairman of the Wild Birds Protection Committee, he called upon the help of Captain Cochrane of West Monkton in the training of the local constabulary. In an unintentionally comical cameo, Capt Cochrane pleaded with the Committee to come up with a less arcane set of rules. It was noted that 'of the six constables, only two had been brought up in the country and their knowledge of birds was very sketchy indeed'. The identification charts they had been supplied with had failed to solve the problem. The 'poor policemen' needed a simpler set of rules about which birds were or were not protected.

A member of the Burnham and Berrow Golf Club, founded by a group of men who included his father, Gerald turned increasingly to the sport and met with some success, often partnering his wife, Blanche, herself a keen golfer. He was also a very good shot, spending the latter part of the Second World War training new recruits how to use a rifle.

His daughter Guinea reveals that 'although he disliked public speaking, he had a great sense of public duty. He was modest and reserved, but he had a good sense of fun and had many friends and was a wonderful father.' His sense of duty is reflected in his time as a county councillor. He died on 27 August 1970 at The Croft in Brent Knoll, aged sixty-six.

307
Alec George Gordon Cunningham
4 June 1930 v. Cambridge University, Cambridge

Alec Cunningham was born in Knowle on 15 July 1905, one of five children. His parents were John Edward, a tailor and outfitting dealer from Knutsford, and Annie Emily (née George), who hailed from nearby Bedminster. As with so many others in the area, he went on to work for the Imperial Tobacco Company, a major corporation which had begun life in 1901 with the merger of W.D. and H. O. Wills of Bristol and twelve other cigarette manufacturers. Imperial's sporting facilities were outstanding. Their cricket ground at Knowle would play host to nine Somerset first-class fixtures between 1957 and 1966, and eight one-day county matches. In the years before the First World War they had employed a

Alec Cunningham – kept wicket for many years at Imperial but only twice for Somerset.

succession of pros, paying the wages of some – such as Percy Hardy and Bertie Francis Morgan – while they qualified for Somerset by residency. Regrettably, this particular pair had shared common traits of rich promise blunted by a fondness for alcohol. In 1988, another rebel was offered a contract. Joining them as an unknown, Shane Warne would prove a popular addition to the Imperial team and retained his affection for the club, even after achieving worldwide fame. Sadly, the club was wound up in 1998 and the locals benefitted in a different way when a housing estate was built on the old ground.

Alec Cunningham was a bona fide employee of Imperial but also a valued member of the cricket team, playing as a wicket-keeper batsman for many years while working in the administrative sections of the business and rising to the level of Senior Clerk and later Private Secretary to the Deputy Chairman.

A local press report confirms that 'Cunningham the Bristol Imperial "stumper" deputises for Luckes, who is still receiving medical treatment'. In two games for the county he averaged 10.00 with the bat and effected four dismissals. Unavailable on a more regular basis owing to his work commitments, he was thereafter replaced by Seymour Clark, a fine keeper but one who would have longed for a batting average that stretched into double figures.

Alec was married in 1930 to Annie Grace Maddicks, from nearby Keynsham. The couple resided at Courtenay House in the Wellsway district of Keynsham. They had no children. Committed to the community as well as to Imperial Tobacco,

A. G. G. Cunningham of the Imperial Tobacco Company.

he offered his services as an ARP first aider at the onset of the Second World War.

Alec Cunningham died on 21 July 1981 in Keynsham, having just turned seventy-six: a man who had remained rooted in one place, had worked throughout his adult life for one company and had been a loyal servant of one cricket club. Annie had predeceased him and in his will the beneficiaries were his relatives, the local Baptist church, the PDSA and RSPCA, bequests that speak of a caring and gentle man.

308
Arthur Henry Seymour Clark
21 June 1930 v. Derbyshire, Chesterfield

A. H. S. Clark

Somerset have all too often been on the receiving end of record-breaking achievements – landmark performances from batsmen such as W. G. Grace, Archie MacLaren or Jack Hobbs or noteworthy feats from opposing bowlers. It is rarer for them to claim records of their own. How unfortunate, then, that Seymour Clark goes down in the record books as having batted on a record nine occasions without ever having troubled the scorers.

Born on 26 March 1902 in Weston-super-Mare and known from the outset as Seymour, although friends and teammates often referred to him as 'Nobby', he was the son of Arthur Clark, a carpenter employed in the building industry and married to Laura. Seymour's first job on leaving school was as an office junior in a local solicitor's office but he left in May 1918 when an opportunity arose to join the Great Western Railway. Initially employed as an engine cleaner and then, from 1920, as a fireman, he subsequently became an engine driver. Not exposed to the game of cricket as a boy, he played for the first time in 1927 when, aged twenty-five, he agreed to keep wicket for a local GWR team.

Seymour Clark – the least successful batsman in the history of first-class cricket.

To everyone's surprise he took to it like a duck to water. Standing up even to Weston's quicker bowlers with naïve fearlessness and crouching in an unorthodox way, he demonstrated wonderful reflexes combined with a safe pair of hands. He was spotted by Wally Hale, a Somerset and Gloucestershire stalwart from an earlier era. Somerset were at the time struggling to find a regular replacement for Wally Luckes, who was being rested owing to a heart condition. Invited to a county trial at Yeovil, Seymour impressed observers.

During his debut, the perils of standing up to all bowlers became apparent when Archie Slater of Derbyshire accidently connected with Seymour's head when completing a hook. No permanent damage was done and Archie inflicted rather more mental scarring with his 14 wickets in the match for a total of 48 runs. He twice dismissed Seymour, who made his customary pair.

The Somerset folklore has it that Seymour was a brilliant keeper but the facts suggest that although clearly a competent replacement for Luckes, he was not outstanding at first-class level. The first Northamptonshire innings at Kettering in

June 1930 paints two contrasting images. Seymour held on to five catches, but the Northants total of 275 included 23 byes and 8 leg byes. Appearing in five games in all, he completed 8 catches and, perhaps reflecting the fact that he was unschooled in the art of wicket-keeping, he failed to complete a stumping. For the record, he conceded a total of 86 byes. This is noted not to decry his creditable efforts for his county but simply to impart some perspective.

It is his record as a batsman that catches the eye. It is said that bowlers attempted valiantly to gift Seymour with a first-class run. Peter Smith of Essex helpfully sent down a long hop but having bounced twice it removed Seymour's bails. In Seymour's final game, Albert Thomas of Northants promised to get him off the mark and sent down a succession of slow full tosses and long hops before inadvertently foxing him with a straight half volley. To the amusement of his teammates, Seymour grumbled that he had been hoodwinked by Thomas.

Seymour had shown sufficient promise for Somerset to offer him a contract where he would receive £10 for each away game and £6 for home games. Expenses such as hotel bills would be borne by him. Having considered the proposal, he declined, and, opting for the life of a railway engine driver, would remain with the GWR for the rest of his working life.

He had been married in 1928 to a local Weston-super-Mare girl who had grown up with him. Eileen Stower was the daughter of a local plumber. They would have no children. Able to offer unstinting service to the town's cricket club, he is said to have appeared for them on 250 occasions, although his batting failed to show any improvement. The reports that he failed ever to reach double figures are likely to be true. But his exploits behind the stumps – such as his 'remarkable catch high and wide on the leg side' in one game – merited approving reports in the local papers.

He was promoted to a supervisory role based in Hereford in 1944, but after six years he requested a return to engine driving, perhaps in part because he missed his home town. He retired from the GWR at the age of sixty-three and from then on he devoted his energies to his beloved vegetable garden, also finding time for games of bowls. A description of him in old age has him as 'a dapper little man in a white suit'. He was hopefully not tending his vegetable garden at the time.

Seymour died in Weston-super-Mare on 17 March 1995 at the age of ninety-two. He was the subject of a small volume by Irving Rosenwater, entitled *Seymour Clark of Somerset: An Appreciation* and published in the year of Seymour's death. His story remains a quirky and treasured part of Somerset's cricketing folklore.

309
Frederick Lewis Pratten
19 July 1930 v. Leicestershire, Leicester

7. 4. Pratten

Fred Pratten was born on 13 February 1904 in Midsomer Norton. His father, Theophilus, was a labourer who tried his hand at everything from agricultural work to coal mining and whose longsuffering wife, Eliza, had given birth to a succession of children, Fred being the tenth. By the time of the 1911 census, Eliza had borne eleven offspring into the world and they were all still single and living at home. Theophilus was either relaxed over the matter of his son's name or semi-literate, referring to him as 'Fredrick Louis'. Alternatively he was struggling to recall the burgeoning list of offspring.

Although the Prattens of Midsomer Norton (Frank Pratten & Co. Ltd) were famed for their range of affordable pre-fabricated timber agricultural and garden buildings and a major employer in the town between the two wars, this was in fact a very distantly related branch of the family.

Fred worked in a printer's warehouse. Purnell and Sons were a large concern with production facilities in Paulton, two miles from Midsomer Norton, and retail outlets in some of the local small towns. Most of Fred's siblings were boot makers, employed by Ashman Bros, who specialised in industrial footwear, and, like Purnell's, were based down the road at Paulton.

Fred was married in 1930 to Gladys Stephens and together they would have three sons and a daughter. He enjoyed success both as a footballer – playing at outside right for Welton Rovers FC and Somerset – and as a wicket-keeper batsman for Midsomer Norton. The *Wells Journal* announces his elevation to county cricket by stating that 'besides

F. L. Pratten of Midsomer Norton CC and Somerset.

Fred Pratten – 'besides being a splendid wicket-keeper he is a good batsman'.

being a splendid wicket keeper [he] is a good batsman'. Alas not a good enough batsman to excel in the first-class game. He would play twelve times for Somerset during the 1930 and 1931 seasons, averaging 7.88 and effecting eleven dismissals.

He died on 23 February 1967 in his home town of Midsomer Norton at the age of sixty-three.

310
Patrick Hassell Frederick Mermagen
6 August 1930 v. Essex, Weston-super-Mare

Patrick Mermagen was born in Colyton, Devon, on 8 May 1911. His father, Lothar Hugo Mermagen, was headmaster of Colyton Grammar School and was married to Marie Lucie. Patrick was their third child. Sent to Sherborne School, he proved a star pupil. In the First XI for three years, he captained them for his final two seasons. He took more than 100 wickets for the school, scored 1,349 runs and also made appearances for The Rest versus Lord's Public Schools (i.e. those schools, such as Harrow or Haileybury who enjoyed an annual fixture at the Lord's ground). He also played for The Public Schools against The Army. A description of him speaks of 'a vigorous right-handed batsman, an accurate right-arm fast medium bowler and a brilliant cover'. In addition, he was captain of the school rugby XV and head boy. To cap it all he won an open scholarship to study Mathematics at Pembroke College, Cambridge. Little wonder, then, that he was spoken of as one of the school's finest products.

Drafted in to the Somerset team as a nineteen-year-old school leaver, he appeared for the county on eight occasions, all in 1930, but never managed to make his mark. Given every encouragement with the bat, he slowly slipped down the batting order and ended with an average of 11.40. After proving expensive in his initial bowling spell, either he or his captain, Jack White, lost confidence in his powers: he took no wickets in a career total of five overs. Although he captained the Pembroke College XI, he failed to gain his cricketing blue.

On graduating from Cambridge University, he opted for a career in teaching. Initially an assistant schoolmaster at Loretto School in Scotland, he found time to play cricket at The Grange in Edinburgh. The ground has long had links with Somerset. In

Patrick Mermagen as captain of the Sherborne School XI: behind him stands the school cricket coach, E. J. Freeman, formerly of Essex.

the early part of the Nineteenth Century, the county's first recorded professional, John Sparkes (sometimes spelt as Sparks) of Lansdown, had gone on to become the groundsman at The Grange for many years. Later, prior to the First World War, George Jupp of Somerset had lit up the ground with many an exhilarating innings.

Patrick Mermagen was married in 1934 to Neva Sonia (née James), known as Sonia, the daughter of a company director who lived in Chard. They would have three sons together. He would retain his links with the county, regularly appearing for Somerset Stragglers over the summer months.

During the Second World War he served with the Royal Berkshire Regiment. He then took up an appointment as a teacher at Radley College. His final appointment was as headmaster at Ipswich School from 1950 until 1972. He retained his enthusiasm for the game of cricket and instigated summer coaching classes, co-opting the Northants cricketer Vincent Broderick as his fellow coach. In 1953, his wife, Sonia, died and it was not until 1965 that he was married again, this time to Inge (née Schutt), with whom, by now in his fifties, he would have a son and daughter

Patrick Mermagen died in hospital in Ipswich on 20 December 1984, aged seventy-three.

P. H. F. Mermagen – he became a headmaster but retained his links with the county, often appearing for Somerset Stragglers.

1931

"It would be a thousand pities if the present difficult financial times ... necessitated the retirement of a county which has such splendid traditions as Somerset."

Bath Chronicle

Across the board, attendances at first-class fixtures were hit by the awful weather. Somerset suffered particularly when the takings were disastrously down at the Weston-super-Mare and Bath Festivals – in good years an excellent source of income. With the county now running an overdraft of nearly £2,500, the new President, Major A. G. Barratt, launched an appeal for donations from 'all those interested in cricket and indeed any others who may feel disposed to help'.

It was a season of solid but unspectacular performances. Tom Young was the only man to top 1,000 runs although Jack Lee fell only six short of the target and Box Case, having ground out two excruciating centuries in his first three games, fell just nine short of the milestone. Jack White was the only bowler to take more than 100 wickets and had indeed done so in every season since the end of the First World War, the only amateur able to make that claim. He was well supported by Arthur Wellard who had rediscovered his form and claimed 86 victims.

In late August, Jack White announced that he would no longer be able to continue as captain owing to pressures of work on his farm. Later, it was confirmed that George Hunt's contract would not be renewed, but with Bill Andrews having arrived on the scene, a core of reliable pros was emerging. The veteran Tom Young had now been joined by a group who included Andrews, Wellard, the Lee brothers and Horace Hazell. There were only two debutants. The pro, Keith Linney, was never afforded the opportunity to shine and the amateur 'Mandy' Mitchell-Innes, although precociously talented and an England international, would be able to play only infrequently, owing to his work in the Sudan.

In December, A. F. Davey announced that he would be leaving the club to become Secretary of Surrey. His energy, ideas and efficiency would all be missed.

311
Charles Keith Linney
6 May 1931 v. Hampshire, Taunton

Born in Hobart, Tasmania, on 26 August 1912, Keith Linney was the son of George Frederick Linney, a prominent Quaker and a headmaster who played one game for Tasmania as a wicket-keeper. Keith arrived at a young age in England and was educated in the Quaker tradition. Separate reports indicate that he attended both Sidcot School in Somerset and Stramongate, a Quaker secondary school in Kendal (subsequently closed). He certainly starred as a useful all-rounder with some devastating bowling returns for Old Stramonians in 1931. With his parents now based in Somerset, he was snapped up by the county and offered a professional contract in 1931. As a technically correct left-handed batsman and a medium-paced left-arm bowler, he was regarded as a potentially important asset. And yet Somerset squandered the opportunity. With amateurs given precedence, Keith was generally deployed as at best a tail-ender and at worst as twelfth man and the bag carrier. He played on nineteen occasions in 1931

C. K. Linney – treated shoddily by the amateurs who called the shots at Somerset.

and a further seven times in 1932, after which his contract was terminated. Generally batting at No 9, he managed scores of 60 and 43 but was rarely able to build an innings. He also bowled on an infrequent basis.

Fellow professional Bill Andrews refers to Keith Linney in sympathetic terms in his autobiography:

Typical of the professionals' frustration was the case of Keith Linney ... He seemed to me a very talented young player with a lot of potential. Yet he ... was put in either at No. 9 or 10 – as a batsman. What chance did he have?

Keith continued to play until 1934 for Weston-super-Mare, where his parents lived, before transferring his allegiance to Wells City CC. He spent a brief period as a teacher or coach at Dunstable School from 1935 before returning to Somerset, working as a chief cashier in the leather industry, in all probability, for Clarks. As a prominent Quaker, his father would have been known to the Clark family. He was married in 1937 to Dorothy Margaret Gibbs Barrett of Winscombe, a shorthand typist and work colleague. They would have no children. Living in Glastonbury until the outbreak of war, he continued to play for Wells CC. He also returned to the first-class fold, making occasional appearances for the county who had treated him so shoddily. Perhaps his grounding as a Quaker had taught him the merits of infinite patience. In thirty-two appearances for the county he averaged 14.40 with the bat

Keith Linney (right) with fellow pro Arthur Wellard (left).

and, bowled only sparingly, he took two wickets at 59.50 apiece.

After the Second World War, he was appointed to a role overseeing the movement of displaced people and was then seconded to the United Nations as the Director of Shipping for the international refugee operation. In the next phase of his career he acted as a consultant on shipping and ship valuation for a number of governments around the world. How insignificant the world of Somerset cricket must have now seemed to him, hidebound as it was by outdated notions of the virtues of amateurism.

Keith Linney died on 12 October 1992 in Tunbridge Wells, Kent, at the age of eighty.

312
Norman Stewart Mitchell-Innes
29 August 1931 v. Warwickshire, Taunton

He was known as 'Mandy', a diminutive version of the name Norman inherited – according to Mitchell-Innes's own account – from his father, who, with the forenames

N. S. Mitchell-Innes – a natural gift for cricket and golf.

Norman D., was unable to escape the moniker. The Mitchell-Innes family were for many generations prominent in Scottish society. Mandy Jnr's grandfather, Gilbert, for example, had been a successful golfer who was one of the individuals who had proposed the idea of a British Open and had helped to fund the purchase of the famous claret jug.

Born in Calcutta on 7 September 1914, Mandy Jnr was five when his father retired to Minehead. He later won a scholarship to his father's alma mater, Sedbergh School in Cumbria, where he proved an outstanding sportsman. Captaining the side in both 1932 and 1933, he averaged over 100 in the latter year. The *Sunday Post* talks about him in glowing terms, headlining an article as *Mitchell-Innes Will Go Right To The Top* and predicting (inaccurately, as it happened) that the 'Calcutta-born Scot' was likely to play rugby for Scotland in the future and noting, a propos his cricket, that 'he stands the right way at the crease. Natural – it was never taught him. He moves about his job the right way. That, too, was never the result of coaching. It was born in him.' As a twenty-year-old, Mandy Mitchell-Innes was seen as representing the future of English cricket: an exceptional talent.

He was in Glasgow, a spectator at a schoolboy golf tournament from which he had just been eliminated when a telegraph boy arrived with the message that Somerset required his services. He took the overnight train to Taunton, where his gardener was waiting with his flannels. Exhausted, he took to the field but was fit enough to take two Warwickshire wickets bowling at a fast-medium pace.

He had already been offered a place at Brasenose College, Oxford, and would go on to gain a blue in four successive years, captaining the team in his final year whilst also captaining the golf team in the Varsity match. His performances for the University side were impressive: a batting average of 47.41 in forty-three matches and 50 wickets at 33.10 apiece. In only his second year at Oxford, he was fast-tracked into the England team after having caught the eye with a superb century for Oxford University against the South Africans. He played in the First Test against the tourists in 1935. Although he scored only 5 in his one innings, he was earmarked for further international caps but had to withdraw from the Second Test owing to a severe attack of hay fever – a problem that would dog him over the years. He would also be selected for the MCC tour of Australia and New Zealand in 1935/36 (with hay fever affecting him in Australia but proving less of a curse in New Zealand).

Mandy was offered a post in the Civil Service, working in Sudan as a magistrate – and part of an elite sometimes described as 'Blues ruling Blacks' – and this would seriously limit his appearances for Somerset. In sixty-nine matches between 1931 and 1949 he averaged 24.23 with the bat (including three centuries) and took 31 wickets at 35.67. During the 1948 season he shared captaincy duties with a bewildering number of other players as the Somerset Committee clung blindly to the belief that only amateurs were capable of being leaders of men.

Married in 1944 to Patricia (née Rossiter) he would have one son and one daughter. After retiring from the Civil Service in 1954, he joined the world of business, becoming Company Secretary of Vaux and Associated Breweries Ltd, whose operations were based in Sunderland. He would remain in that role for twenty-five years.

Mandy is described as an unassuming, good-natured man whom most pros had regarded as a thoughtful and caring captain, although some interpreted an

Mandy Mitchell-Innes – his England career was cut short by hay fever after only one Test Match appearance.

economy with words as aloofness. After having retired to Llangarron, near Ross-on-Wye, he spent his final years in the care of his daughter, Penelope, in Llantilio Crosseny, a village between Monmouth and Abergavenny. In later life he endured his status as the country's oldest surviving Test Match player with great forbearance, politely responding to the endless requests from autograph hunters. He died at the Monnow Vale Hospital in Monmouth on 28 December 2006 at the age of ninety-two.

1932

"R. A. Ingle … undertook his duties with commendable zeal and, playing in every match, managed the team with marked ability."

The Cricketer

Championship Position: 7 of 17

There were reasons to feel optimistic. Under the leadership of new captain Reggie Ingle, the side won more games than they lost for only the fourth time in their history. True, there were no outstanding performances but most players had chipped in at one point or another. Despite scoring three of the nine centuries registered, Ingle failed to reach 1,000 runs. Indeed, not a single batsman achieved the milestone, although one bright spot was when the Lee brothers – Jack and Frank – put on 234 for the first wicket against Essex at Leyton. Somerset won the game by an innings and 74 runs after Horace Hazell claimed twelve victims. Only Jack White – preferred to Hazell when available – secured 100 wickets.

The Appeal Fund, combined with a Car Competition, had helped to clear much of the overdraft. The Committee might have had misgivings about the competition, regarding it as a tawdry descent into gambling and declaring in the Year Book that they were 'reluctant to employ these methods of raising funds', but the crowds loved it. Asked to guess the attendance at a chosen three-day match, the winner with the best estimate stood to win a 'Standard "Little Nine" complete with sliding roof and hide upholstery: List Price £174'.

DOWNSIDE'S JOY NIGHT

MENDIP CLUBS' EFFORT FOR SOMERSET CRICKET

OVER 1,000 DANCERS

If Reggie Ingle was to be congratulated on his performance as captain, he also merited praise for his tireless and successful efforts raising funds off the field, offering his services as Master of Ceremonies at functions and helping to organise the successful ball at Downside School where revelry descended on the Roman Catholic institution strictly for one night only.

The club announced the death of an old favourite, Vernon Hill, a hard-hitting left-hander from the Golden Age and more recently the club's President, described as 'a cheery optimist, capable administrator and staunch supporter and friend'. There were fewer plaudits for the irrepressible Bill Andrews, released for the first of a number of occasions after a mediocre season.

Among the debutants, Jake Seamer was a decent player who would later captain the club and John Cameron is notable less for his performances for Somerset than for the fact that he would later be appointed Vice-Captain of the West Indies.

The Somerset XI at New Road, Worcester in 1932.
STANDING: F. S. Lee, H. L. Hazell, W. H. R. Andrews, A. W. Wellard, J. W. Lee, A. Young.
SEATED: G. M. Bennett, E. F. Longrigg, R. A. Ingle, C. C. C. Case, R. P. Northway.

313
Richard Ashley
1 June 1932 v. Leicestershire, Leicester

Top: *Richard Ashley at the time of his Somerset debut.*
Above: *Richard Ashley (in the foreground) with his Wiltshire Regiment cricket teammates.*

Born a twin (with a brother named George) on 27 October 1902 in Weston-super-Mare, Richard Ashley was the son of Martin Ashley (a surgeon who later became a Medical School inspector) and his wife, Edith. He was sent to Clifton College and on leaving school went up to Sandhurst before embarking on a career in the military. He joined the Wiltshire Regiment as a lieutenant in 1925 and between 1927 and 1929 acted as Aide de Camp to Sir C. A. Innes, the Governor of Burma.

On returning to England in 1930 he became an active member of the Wiltshire Regiment cricket team, often opening the batting and regularly among the wickets as a pace bowler. Invited to play for Somerset on two occasions in 1932, he averaged 12.50 with the bat and his all-too-brief cameo as a bowler reads impressively as 1 wicket for 0 runs in two unblemished overs. He also played in two first-class fixtures in India, where again his performances with the ball were more impressive than his batting exploits. He was married in 1935 to Patience Gedge, a medical practitioner's daughter from Pewsey, with whom he would have two children, Nigel Richard, born in 1937, and Jennifer Jane, born in 1940, in both cases in India. In 1936 he served for a brief period in Palestine and before and during the Second World War was a staff captain in India, commanding the 7th Battalion of the Wiltshire Regiment. After the war he was made OC (Officer Commanding) of the Training Corps in Devises, Wiltshire. There followed staff appointments in Germany and the UK.

After leaving the Army in 1956 with the rank of lieutenant colonel, he retired initially to Milford-on-Sea in Hampshire, although any plans for a long and happy stay there were disrupted when his wife, Patience, died in 1957. He resided for a while at Selsey, Sussex, in all probability to be near his daughter, but died at the age of seventy-one at the Nyecroft Nursing Home in Bognor Regis following a coronary thrombosis on 7 August 1974.

314
Alastair MacDonald Watson
18 June 1932 v. Surrey, Taunton

Alastair MacDonald Watson — a fast left-arm bowler who starred for Bristol University and Knowle.

The name is sometimes hyphenated but not in any official documentation or in his correspondence with Somerset, where his surname is given as Watson. Born on 29 January 1909 in Wallington, Surrey (and not nearby Croydon as sometimes stated), he was the son of a dentist, Alexander Macdonald Watson, and his wife, Louisa. Soon after Alastair's birth, the family moved to Bristol, where his father ran a dental practice from their home on Redcliffe Parade West. Alexander was a Quaker and often undertook work on a pro bono basis for those struggling financially.

After attending Sidcot School in Bath, where he was the senior prefect, Alastair went to Bristol University to study Medicine, specialising in Dentistry. While there, he gained a reputation as a very fast left-arm bowler whose efforts led Bristol to the University Cup, beating Nottingham University in the final.

He played his club cricket for Knowle and made his first appearance for Somerset in a non-first-class fixture for Gentlemen of Somerset against the touring South Americans in June 1932, impressing with a five-wicket haul in the first innings. He would play in four first-class matches for the county over the 1933 and 1934 seasons, taking 8 wickets at 27.37 apiece, including a best bowling performance of 5 for 27 against Derbyshire at Ilkeston. His batting was less impressive: he mustered an average of 0.40, only ever scoring 2 runs.

On graduating he elected to join the Royal Navy where he deployed his dentistry skills, becoming a surgeon captain and finding time to represent the Royal Navy at cricket, with appearances in the annual fixtures against the RAF and the Army, at Lord's. He also made appearances for Incogniti and I Zingari, among others.

Known to his colleagues as 'Toothy', the 1939 census confirms him as working on

The wedding of Alastair MacDonald Watson and Betty Thompson in 1940.

A. M. Watson – played four games for Somerset and later became the Queen's Honorary Dental Surgeon.

HMS *Victory* and a year later he was married to Berta Elenar (née Thompson) who was born in La Paz, Bolivia, and whose name was sometimes anglicised to Bertha Eleanor, though Alastair always referred to her as Betty. They would have two sons, one of whom enjoyed a distinguished career as a commander in the Royal Navy and, later, as a director of the English Civil War Society and the other as a chartered secretary.

A later listing confirms Alastair Watson as a 'Surgeon Captain and Senior Specialist in Dental Surgery'. He was awarded the OBE in 1958 for his service to king (and queen) and country, and the dental health and hygiene of many a sailor. He was also appointed the Queen's Honorary Dental Surgeon. He continued to be a keen follower of cricket and enjoyed visits to Lord's, having been elected an MCC member immediately after the war.

His younger son, Robert, recalls the occasion in 1963 when Alastair turned out for the Fathers XI against the King's College Choir School First XI and, even at that age, 'bowled so fast that we hardly saw a ball, though he deliberately bowled short of a length so as not to take our wickets. The keeper had to move half way back to the boundary.' Robert describes his father as 'a very modest man who cared deeply for people'. Alastair's Quaker upbringing had instilled a sense of compassion.

After retiring from the Royal Navy he served for many years as a Hampshire county councillor. He died on 19 November 1987 in Alverstoke, Hampshire, at the age of seventy-eight.

315
Kenneth Charles Kinnersley
6 August 1932 v. Essex, Weston-super-Mare

Ken Kinnersley's grandfathers had both been in the grocery business, one as a 'produce broker' working as a wholesaler in Bristol and the other a 'produce merchant'. The business conducted between the two men was perhaps the reason his parents had met. Conrad Joseph Kinnersley had opted not to go into the family business but to become a Theology student and he and his wife, Ethel (née Slade), would work as missionaries in Samoa under the auspices of the Congregational Church. Their son, Ken, was born in Apia, Upolu, Samoa on 13 March 1914. In 1916, Ethel returned to Bristol with her first two children as guests of her father-in-law. It must have been a perilous journey with the ever-present threat of attack by U-Boats. Conrad followed them home

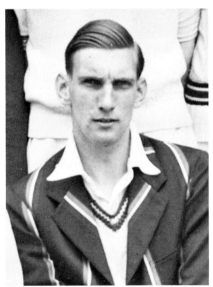

in 1917 but after the war they returned for a while to Samoa, in order to continue their work. He later became for many years the minister at the Congregational Church in Wellington, Somerset.

Ken was educated at Clifton College and proved a talented sportsman. Excelling at rugby and cricket, he played in the First XI for four seasons from 1929 until 1932. He was selected to play for the Lord's Schools v. The Rest in 1932, when he would be one of the future Somerset player John Cameron's ten victims, in his case lulled into a stumping. Somerset turned to him immediately on his leaving school and he would play for the county in ten matches between 1932 and 1938. A tall, rangy man, he was regarded as an all-

Ken Kinnersley – 'a forcing, right-handed batsman'.

K. C. Kinnersley – businessman, thespian, cricketer and an England rugby triallist.

rounder. The *Somerset Year Book* describes him as 'a forcing, right-handed batsman, strong on the off-side and with an untiring defence' and elsewhere he is described as 'patient'. But he averaged only 9.53 in first-class fixtures and his slow right-arm bowling yielded 17 wickets at 25.64 runs apiece.

He also played as a rugby full-back for Bristol and Somerset and took part in three England trials without ever being awarded an international cap. He was forced to retire from the game owing to injury in 1935.

No blushing violet, he was keen on amateur dramatics. He was married in 1940 to Evelyn Bertha Cox, who had carved out a successful career as a secretary in the Programme Department at BBC Bristol. Perhaps his talents as a part-time thespian had come to her attention. Their wedding reception was apparently held in Clifton Zoo, though hopefully in the restaurant. A daughter was born in 1949, when Evelyn was forty. For his part, Ken worked for E. S. & A. Robinson, a large printing business in Bristol, which later became part of the Dickinson Robinson Group Ltd. The Robinson dynasty were noted for their annual fixtures in which they fielded eleven members of the family, once taking on W. G. Grace and ten of his relatives. The Robinsons had produced first-class players in the late Nineteenth Century, including Theo and Crescens, both of Somerset.

Ken Kinnersley would spend time at the company's headquarters in Bristol but even more of his career based elsewhere overseeing sales, first in South Devon and then in Leicester and Luton. It would appear that he combined his parents' missionary zeal with his grandparents' commercial acumen in persuading buyers of the benefits of Robinson's card and paper products. While living in Topsham, Devon, between 1946 and 1955, he played on a number of occasions for Devon in Minor Counties cricket. He would return to Bristol in the latter part of his career, before retiring in 1978.

He became an enthusiastic member of the Somerset Former Players' Association, regularly attending their annual dinners. He died on 30 June 1984 in Clifton, Bristol, at the age of seventy.

316
John Wemyss Seamer
24 August 1932 v. Derbyshire, Taunton

[signature]

Jake Seamer had something of the look of a gangly and bookish parson about him. His father, Charles Ernest Seamer, was indeed a clergyman, married in Kent in 1912 to Katherine (née Anson). By the time of their son's birth, on 23 June 1913, they had moved to Shapwick in Somerset. Jake was educated at Marlborough College where he played for two years in the First XI and also appeared in the hockey and rugby teams. He followed his father to Brasenose College, Oxford, where he won blues at hockey and cricket. During his final year he captained the hockey side. He would play cricket alongside fellow Brasenose undergraduate N.S. Mitchell-Innes. In a career mirroring that of 'Mandy', he would also go on to work as a government official in Sudan, though not before he remained at Oxford to complete a course in Arabic to prepare him for his career.

Although he showed great promise when playing for Oxford University, scoring four centuries in twenty-one games, his record for Somerset was more modest, with an average of only 15.61 in 59 matches. Bowling leg breaks, he took 4 wickets for Oxford University at 24.00 apiece but took no wickets for his county.

As a young man he had been an avid fan of Somerset and so his call-up fulfilled one childhood ambition. His other great hope as a boy was that he would become an actor, though it is said that the nearest he ever came to a stage career was taking part in the annual pantomime staged in Sudan, where he regularly starred as the dame. He did, however, have a captive audience in the Somerset changing room where he would entertain his teammates, speaking in a broad West Country accent or donning a fake beard and an old MCC cap and impersonating W. G. Grace with humor-

Jake Seamer – capatain of the Marlborough College XI and an Oxford blue.

ous monologues.

J. W. Seamer – returned to Marlborough College as a teacher.

For an intelligent man he was surprisingly prone to superstition. It is perhaps best not to dwell on how such ill-logic might have impacted his work in maintaining the rule of law in Sudan. In *Cricket, Lovely Cricket*, teammate Frank Lee recounts that Jake 'always carried around in his cricket bag an old train destination board 'To Tonbridge' – he felt that it helped to improve Somerset's fortunes.' One would have thought that more net practice and the influx of more professionals might have proved a little more effective.

He was married in 1947 to Lettice Dorothy (née Lee). Sadly, their first daughter, Katherine, died in infancy, but they had a second daughter, Mary. Jake's career as a civil servant culminated with his holding the position of Deputy Commissioner for Khartoum North. After retiring from the Civil Service in 1950 he returned to Marlborough College to teach Latin, English and History and to act as a housemaster until his retirement in 1973. He helped with the coaching of the school's Second XI and was persuaded to play for Wiltshire during the 1956 season. There followed two directorships but his energies were also focussed on public service with Jake being twice elected mayor of Marlborough and undertaking duties as a JP.

Following a heart attack in 1999, he lived at the Merlin Court Nursing Home in the town of Marlborough, dying there on 16 April 2006 at the age of ninety-two.

317
John Hemsley Cameron
27 August 1932 v. Warwickshire, Taunton

John Cameron was born on 8 April 1914 in Kingston, Jamaica, the son of John Joseph Cameron, who had studied Medicine in England and had played for Jamaica and the West Indies on their 1906 tour. John Jnr's brother, Francis James, would also represent Jamaica and the West Indies.

Educated at Taunton School, John Jnr showed precocious talent as a schoolboy leg-spinner, playing for the First XI from the age of thirteen and also representing the school at rugby (though association football was his preferred code). Having turned in some outstanding performances, he was invited to play for The Rest v. Lord's Public

J. H. Cameron – Vice-Captain on the West Indies tour of England in 1939.

Schools at Lord's in 1932 and bamboozled his opponents with his leg-spin, taking 10 for 49 in the first innings. The only man who had held out was Jake Seamer. John Cameron then went on to represent the Public Schools side against The Army and enjoyed further success.

He was offered a place at St Catharine's College, Cambridge, where he played for the University XI from 1934 and won blues in three seasons between 1935 and 1937. After leaving school, he had found that his bowling skills – largely uncoached – had deserted him and his father, aware of John's outstanding talent, had funded coaching sessions in London with the likes of Tich Freeman and Wilfred Rhodes. John put his loss of control down to the fact that he had used his fingers and not his wrists and that as he matured and his fingers thickened, he lost the knack, no longer hearing the click of his finger joints as the ball left his hand. Reinvented as an off-break bowler, he met with some success, but never as much as he had enjoyed as a schoolboy prodigy.

His bowling figures for Somerset, for whom he would play on forty-eight occasions, make less impressive reading than his performances for other teams. He took 45 wickets at 43.66 apiece. His batting, described as sound rather than spectacular, improved over time and he was capable enough to complete three centuries while aver-

John Cameron in 1955, flanked by Bertie Clarke (left) and Sir Frank Worrell (right).

aging 18.55. His career with the county would in fact come in two separate spells: first as an undergraduate and later, after the Second World War, when he had returned to England.

After graduating in 1937, he was married to Kathleen Cecilia Jones in London, before the couple left for Jamaica to begin his career as a teacher. Within two years he was back, asked to tour with the West Indies in 1939 as their Vice-Captain. Although not considered one of their stand-out performers, he was a sound choice: articulate and very familiar with the English game. A description of him in the Official Souvenir of the tour reads:

Although short of stature he delivers the ball well up with unusual spin and decep-tion, has plenty of stamina and patience. He is also a good reliable batsman and a very alert field.

After appearing in the first two Tests and performing reasonably well – taking the wicket of Harold Gimblett with his very first over in international cricket – he subse-quently split his hand badly whilst fielding, ironically, against Somerset and was obliged to miss the third and final Test.

He would return to Somerset in 1946 when offered a job as a teacher at Millfield by the school's maverick headmaster R. J. O. Meyer. By this time, he and Kathleen had a son, Geoffrey, who would predecease them in 1994. While back in the county, John played for Somerset on three occasions in August 1947. After leaving Millfield he went on to teach in Chigwell, Essex.

He had a sunny disposition and was popular among amateurs and pros alike. A victim of his times he was on the receiving end of the racism inherent in most walks of life, reflected in his monikers of 'Monkey' and 'Snowball'. There were rumours that his colour was an issue when the Somerset committee were struggling to find an amateur captain and – still teaching at the time at Millfield – he offered his services, only to be declined. Although he bore it all with good humour he was, according to David Foot, who conversed with him about his career, worn down at times and suscep-tible to depression. A quiet man, in later life he was happy to be surrounded by his collection of cricket books, listening to Classical or Big Band music.

John Cameron died at the age of eighty-five on 13 February 2000 in Chichester, Sussex. His wife Kathleen died two years later at the age of ninety.

1933

"Seldom a day went past without Wellard achieving
something of note, either with bat or ball, or both; while,
if the rest of the fieldsmen had held their chances as surely
as the big-hearted all-rounder himself, he would have
had an even more impressive haul of wickets."
Ron Roberts in Sixty Years of Somerset Cricket

Championship Position: 11 of 17

1933 was the breakthrough year for all-rounder Arthur Wellard, who performed the double of 100 wickets and 1,000 runs. It was also the year when, at the age of forty-two, Jack White's form finally began to fall away. In addition to Wellard, four other batsmen - the Lee brothers, Case and Burrough – each compiled 1,000 runs. Tom Young offered important support for Wellard as a bowler, with 90 wickets.

Former Secretary A. F. Davey had done his best to convince the county of the need for a business plan that embraced professionalism. With Major A. G. Barratt as President and former captain John Daniell as Secretary, there was a lurch back towards amateurism. Barratt had announced prior to the season that 'people like to see amateurs play lively cricket, rather than watch a dull game. We make a game of it and not a profession. This is the way the game should be played.' Ill-health meant that he had to stand down ahead of the start of the season. Not so John Daniell, who regarded professionals as a blight and who would retain his position until 1936.

None of the debutants made any noteworthy contributions.

318
John Russell Watson
17 May 1933 v. Derbyshire, Ilkeston

Generally referred to as Jack, he was born on 22 August 1910 at Manor Farm in Purse Caundle, Dorset, a small village where among very few claims to fame is the myth that a pack of deceased hounds – defying the laws of physics, chemistry and biology as any self-respecting ghosts must – are said to haunt the manor grounds. His father was a wealthy farmer and the son would follow in time in his footsteps. Jack was educated at Stowe School in Buckinghamshire and his family had by then moved to Manor Farm in North Cadbury. A fine sportsman, he played rugby for Yeovil and was indeed captain for a while before standing down in 1937. His performances in club cricket – where he played as an all-rounder – were strong enough for him to receive an invitation from Somerset to appear as an amateur. He had by then signed up with the North Somerset Yeomanry as a second lieutenant and according to a press report 'obtained leave from Budleigh Salterton where he was in camp with the yeomanry'.

As appeared to be the case in far too many instances for Somerset's comfort, his outstanding performance came on his debut. Enjoying a stand with Michael Bennett when Somerset had been reeling at 75 for 7, he 'relied exclusively on the pull shot to begin with, but afterwards, like his partner, employed a variety of strokes, and … scored 56 without giving a chance'. This would remain Jack Watson's highest score in nineteen appearances for the county and he would come away with an average of 12.09.

He was married in 1935 to Laura Cecil Willett, whose father, Major Kingsley Willett MC, lived at nearby South Cadbury, having retired from the Royal Artillery. Both parties will have approved of a happy union of nearby land-owning families. Laura and Jack would proudly announce the birth of their three children

J. R. Watson – rugby player, cricketer and noted cattle breeder.

– Henry, Gillian and John – in the local papers, although another announcement followed hot on the heels of the birth of their daughter. Jack Watson's dog had gone walkabout, perhaps having taken umbrage at the presence of a new arrival. A generous £5 reward was offered for 'a black and tan dachshund (with a grey muzzle)' who answered to the name of 'Roddy'. The advert in the *Western Gazette* informs us that Jack and his family (and indeed Roddy) were now based in Poyntington, a small village near Sherborne.

By the start of the Second World War, Jack had been promoted to lieutenant and he would rise to the rank of major, a title he would retain in civilian life. After the war he played Minor Counties cricket for Dorset and also became a noted cattle breeder and a leading light in the South Western Guernsey Breeders Association, acting as a respected judge at agricultural shows. He also acted as an agent for the sale of cattle, working from an estate office in Sherborne.

He died in Queen Camel, near Yeovil on 7 March 1980 at the age of sixty-nine.

Jack Watson was included in the Somerset XI who played Worcestershire at Amblecote in 1933. Box Case was asked to captain the side. Somerset won a low-scoring game with ease, Tom Young taking a total of ten wickets.
STANDING: A. Young, W. T. Luckes, A. W. Wellard, F. S. Lee, J. W. Lee, H. L. Hazell.
SEATED: J. R. Watson, H. D. Burrough, C. C. C. Case, G. M. Bennett, A. M. Watson.

319
James Priddy
7 June 1933 v. West Indies, Taunton

J. Priddy.

Known as Jim or Jock, he was one of eight children of Charles and Lily Priddy. The Priddy family had farmed for at least two generations at Combe St Nicholas, but Charles and Lily left for the USA in October 1892, intending to settle in California on a permanent basis. They had a change of heart and returned to South Somerset after the birth of their first two children. By the time of Jim's birth on 3 December 1909, they were ensconced at Parsonage Farm, Crewkerne.

Jim Priddy of Weston-super-Mare CC and Somerset.

His parents sold the farm when Jim was sixteen years old and the family moved to Weston-super-Mare. His brothers left for America, but Jim remained in Weston. He would become actively involved in the local business and sporting scene, playing hockey and cricket for the town. In the 1930s, he opened a sports shop at 48 Regent Street in Weston. This was followed by the opening of a number of electrical appliance stores which he built up into a chain of six. A man of considerable energy, he added a further *Radio Relays* outlet and – happy to find any means to grow his burgeoning business empire – he rented the flat above. In addition he bought a shop named *Coulstings*, a well-established gift and toy store with a cafeteria on the first floor. This last enterprise was run by his wife. Jim also had the drive to manage an electrical contracting business, calling on the services of a combined total of eighty electricians and plumbers, taking on major contracts such as a reported example of wiring 118 new council houses being built in the Weston area. Jim was by now a leading business figure in the town and became President of the local Chamber of Trade. He was instrumental in the introduction of Christmas lights on Weston-super-Mare High Street.

Back in the days of his arrival on the scene, he had quickly gained a reputation as a fine medium-paced swing bowler who formed a devastating club partnership with Somerset's Jim Bridges. Jim Priddy's away-swing was a useful counterbalance to Jim Bridges's in-swing. A profile in the local press talks of 'a thoroughgoing sportsman' and gifted ball-player, suggesting that he was also accomplished at lawn tennis and

Jim Priddy – 'a thoroughgoing sportsman'.

'real hot stuff at table tennis'. For many years, he captained the Weston Sunday XI, while fellow Somerset cricketer Laurie Hawkins took charge of the Saturday XI. According to Peter Roebuck, writing in his history of Somerset cricket, Jim was competitive by nature and at times combustible on the field of play. Certainly a press report of a clash between Jim and a competitor on the hockey field in 1939 suggests an uncompromising approach to sporting combat: both men were rushed to hospital after a collision that resulted in stitches for deep wounds above their eyes.

J. Priddy – President of the Weston-super-Mare Chamber of Trade.

He was married in 1933 to Iris Eva Hockey and together they would have three children. He played twice for Somerset in 1933 and on a further five occasions in 1939, averaging 13.00 with the bat and taking 4 wickets at 60.25 apiece.

He continued to play club cricket for some years for his home town and after hanging up his boots, he often helped in the preparation of the wickets at Clarence Park, although, never one to sit back and relax, he continued to oversee his businesses and also mastered the game of golf. He died in Weston-super-Mare on 12 July 1994 at the age of eighty-four. One report states that 'were he not so incurably modest, it would be possible to say more about him'. It is hard to imagine what else he could have packed into his busy, successful career.

320
Hallam Newton Egerton Alston
26 July 1933 v. Surrey, Kennington Oval

Hallam Alston earned the sobriquet 'Granny' as a result of his marked fondness for cups of tea. A tall and heavily-built man, he took to his incongruous moniker. Which was just as well, given that it remained with him throughout adulthood. A larger than life character, he was never likely to walk into a room or grace a cricket ground without his presence being noted.

Born in Cheltenham on 10 June 1908, he was the son of Hallam Newton Alston Snr, a solicitor in the town, and Mary (née Hodgson). Sent to Cheltenham College, initially as a boarder but later as a day boy, Granny was a successful schoolboy cricketer,

Granny Alston – amassed over 30,000 runs and 3,700 wickets in club cricket but played only once for Somerset.

appearing in the school First XI from 1925 until 1927. It remained a source of frustration to him that as the school's pace bowler, he was asked to bat lower down the order than he felt – with some justification – his abilities merited. He would later state that his love affair with the game blossomed during the summer holidays when he decamped to the family's holiday home in Guernsey. Here he starred with bat and ball. He would recount – although it is, of course, hard to substantiate the claim – that he scored the first ever century on the tiny Channel Island of Alderney.

His thirst for club cricket was as unrelenting as his partiality for a cup of tea. He played wherever and whenever he could and it is said that he amassed over 30,000 runs over the course of his career at an average of approximately 31 and took 3,700 wickets at fewer than 15 runs apiece. Initially a pace bowler, he turned to off-breaks as his weight increased and his fitness diminished. We know this because Granny kept detailed records of his appearances and copies of his copious correspondence, which he left in his will to the Cricket Society, though his collection has now been broken up. He turned out for at least twenty different clubs, including sides such as Somerset Stragglers, Nomads and the Sou'Westers, of whom he was President from 1974 until 1985. He would carry on playing the game until the age of seventy-five. He was also a successful (hard) racquets player as a schoolboy and would go on to represent Somerset at the similar game of squash between 1935 and 1939. Granny Alston's primary interest beyond his work and sport was Natural History and particularly Entomology.

He forged a career as a food salesman and was a member of the Incorporated Sales Managers' Association, living for a period in Bristol where it appears that he supplemented his earnings by renting out rooms to lodgers. His career was interrupted by the Second World War, when he was commissioned as a second lieutenant in the Somerset Light Infantry, ultimately rising to the rank of captain.

It is perhaps surprising that he was not invited to play for Somerset on more than one occasion. His club record was certainly better than some of the other men who turned out for the county. He would also claim the prized wicket of Jack Hobbs, as he would be keen to remind people over the years. Bowling seven overs, including three maidens, he had taken 1 for 6. John Daniell and Jack White – the two most influential men at the club - must have had their reasons for not asking Granny to appear again. Perhaps he had complained about the volume of tea he was served.

Never married, Granny Alston died in Gloucester on 19 October 1985 at the age of seventy-seven, having not long since retired from club cricket. His generous bequests in his will reflect his many and various interests with beneficiaries including, among others, Sou'Westers CC and the Somerset Stragglers alongside the Wood Green Animal Shelter and Save the Children.

321
Anthony George Pelham
26 July 1933 v. Surrey, Kennington Oval

Anthony Pelham's family included the Earls of Chichester. Tall and aristocratic, he was able – as were a disproportionate number of Somerset's amateur cricketers – to claim descent from William the Conqueror, although he was not one to trumpet the fact. Modest, gentlemanly and correct, there was no pomposity to him. Born on 4 September 1911 in Minehead, where his maternal grandparents lived, he was the son of Hon. Henry George Godolphin Pelham and his first wife, Agnes Lee (née Ollerhead). Henry Pelham oversaw the running of the Sudan Government Railways.

Anthony attended Eton College and in the fixture with Harrow at Lord's in 1930 took 7 wickets for 21, bowling right-arm medium pace. He would go up to King's College, Cambridge, that same year and would play thirty-five first-class fixtures, most frequently for Cambridge University but also ten times for Sussex and twice in 1933 for Somerset, whilst still an undergraduate. His link with Sussex was that his father by then resided in Ringmer and his connection with Somerset was through birth. He averaged 13.50 in his four innings for Somerset and took 4 wickets at 54.00, his form proving better for Cambridge University. He had in fact played for the Varsity side on an intermittent basis with some success but failed to gain his blue until 1934, when *The Times* bemoaned the fact that, having taken 2 for 6 in nine overs, he was not called on again until the final stages of Oxford's second innings, by which stage the impetus had entirely slipped away from Cambridge.

After little more than a flirtation with first-class cricket he embarked on a career as a junior political officer in Sudan, working as a magistrate, having first undertaken a course in Arabic and Law to prepare him. This posting was as shortlived as his first-

Anthony George Pelham: painting by Nellie M. Hepburn Edmunds.

class cricket career. He left in order to be married in Boras, Sweden, to Ann Margret Bergengren in 1938. The couple had met in Cambridge, Ann having come over to develop her command of English. They had become engaged but junior political officers were barred from being accompanied by wives in Sudan. As a result, Anthony – valuing their relationship more highly than his career – had resigned his position and returned to England. He had found employment working for the Gabbitas & Thring Educational Agency in London. His wife, Ann (whose second name is often anglicised to Margaret), was the daughter of a successful businessman named Axel. She and Anthony would have three children together.

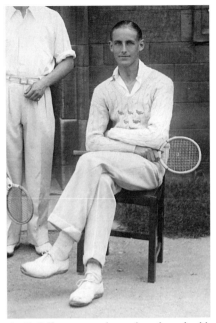

A. G. Pelham – a modest and gentlemanly old Etonian.

During the Blitz, Anthony served with the Royal Artillery as a second lieutenant in the 38th Anti-Aircraft Brigade Headquarters. In July 1942 he was posted to Aden where, able to speak Arabic, he played a key role in training the local gunners. In July 1944 he was made the commanding officer (OC) of the island of Socotra (now under the jurisdiction of Yemen) where he oversaw the airbase from which submarine hunts were coordinated. Mentioned in despatches, he had risen to the rank of major.

Returning to civilian life, he was reunited with his wife and two children – a third would be born in 1952 – and lived in Putney, working once more in consultancy for Gabbitas & Thring and becoming a director. In 1949 he decided to pursue his own business interests although his first venture failed. Worldwide Publications (London) Ltd was set up to produce quality magazines but the company had to be sold to a newspaper group at a large personal loss.

A subsequent partnership with a friend, Denys Wrey, who owned an antiques shop on Sloane Street, proved both prosperous and a source of great pleasure. Anthony set up and managed an antique repair service and undertook buying trips around the country. After the birth of their third child, the family moved to Dorking. Based here he continued his commitment to his antiques business whilst also developing an extensive garden in the lee of Box Hill, planting a large number of fine trees – a legacy that

A. G. Pelham of Cambridge University, Sussex and Somerset.

is still inching towards maturity. He died at the age of fifty-seven on 10 March 1969 at the General Hospital in Redhill, Surrey. His son, Richard, describes him as 'a man with a fine sense of humour, who could rub along with anyone, regardless of their background', whose one vice was that 'unfortunately he smoked too much'. Modest to the last, Anthony Pelham requested in his will that no memorial stone or tablet should be erected after his death. He was more interested in the idea that the children he had raised and the trees he had planted should continue to flourish. His infamous ancestor, William the Conqueror, had possessed a rather less phlegmatic character.

1934

"They have finished almost at the bottom of the County Championship table. This undignified position can partially be attributed to the bad play of the team in the field, for several matches have been thrown away by dropped catches."

Taunton Courier

Championship Position: 15 of 17

There was a setback before the season had begun when Tom Young, for years a mainstay of the team, was stricken by illness and obliged to retire. Were it not for the sterling efforts of the Lee brothers, Somerset would very probably have propped up the table. Opening the batting, Jack and Frank scored more than 3,000 runs between them, including seven centuries. Box Case was the only other man to exceed 1,000 runs. Given that the three leading batsmen were prone to slow scoring, it was left to Arthur Wellard to inject brief excitement into the batting. Jack Lee was also the leading wicket-taker with 75 victims although the generally poor bowling analyses owed much to the sheer quantity of spilled catches. Perhaps the biggest disappointment was the performance of the Varsity boys, who arrived at the start of the summer vacation. Mandy Mitchell-Innes, Jake Seamer and John Cameron had been expected to give Somerset's season a much-needed shot in the arm. They promised much but delivered little.

Reggie Ingle persuaded the head-

Brothers Frank (left) and Jack Lee open the Somerset innings at Trent Bridge.

master and governors of Downside School to play host to a three-day game. It was a one-off that proved a commercial success and helped Somerset to nibble away at their overdraft. Given the event's popularity, the committee agreed that fixtures would be held at Wells and Yeovil the following season in order to spread the gospel of Somerset cricket. Yeovil, in particular, was felt to be a neglected part of the county, with historically low levels of interest or membership.

None of the three debutants made lasting contributions to the first-class game, although Phil Davey, a local boy and Cambridge undergraduate, had his moment of glory with a scarcely believable – and never to be repeated – return of 6 for 9 against Worcestershire.

The Somerset XI who played Worcestershire at New Road in 1934.
STANDING: H. L. Hazell, F. S. Lee, R. B. Marsh, A. W. Wellard, W. T. Luckes, J. W. Lee.
SEATED: G. M. Bennett, L. C. Hawkins, R. A. Ingle, C. C. C. Case, P. J. Davey.

Harold Percival Fear
30 May 1934 v. Sussex, Taunton

Harold Fear was born in Finchley on 16 April 1908. While
he was still an infant, his father, Charles, who had been born
in Old Cleeve, Somerset, and his mother, Susanna (née
Lowe), moved to Taunton, where Charles set up in business
as a baker and flour merchant, running the Norton Mills
Bakery in Norton Fitzwarren.

Harold attended Taunton School before leaving to enter
the family firm. He was a fine schoolboy and club cricketer,
playing regularly for Taunton CC. In one particularly purple
patch in 1939, he scored four centuries in successive innings,
two of them unbeaten. For good measure he followed up
with two half-centuries. In six consecutive innings he had
scored 619 runs at an average of 154.75. Most club batsmen
can only dream of such glories. Writing in the *Taunton
Courier*, H. J. Channon says that:

> *Harold Fear was a great all-rounder. The fielding side gave
> a sigh of relief when they got him out for a small total. He took
> risks in the early overs, but if he stayed his innings sparkled
> with skill, artistry and terrific power.*

Harold Fear – 'the field-
ing side breathed a sigh of
relief when they got him
out for a small total'.

Elsewhere, Channon writes concerning Harold's off-drive
that 'of the local cricketers I have known, none executed this
stroke more gracefully and correctly than the late Harold
Fear'. His skills as a club player did not transfer to the first-class arena, with a batting
average of 9.33 in his two matches, both in 1934. He also bowled three expensive
overs, taking no wickets but conceding 29 runs. His skills as a baker, on the other
hand, stood up to close scrutiny.

Married in Taunton in 1933 to Molly Eileen (née Dike), they would move to
Bishops Hull, christening their home with the quaint portmanteau name of 'Harmol'.
Harold took over the Norton Mills Bakery from his father and would oversee a substan-
tial business. They milled flour, baked bread and delivered their goods far and wide.
Their delivery men were perhaps at times hard pressed to meet demand, with a news-

*An advertisement for Norton Mills bread and flour (left) and one of
their fleet of delivery vans (right).*

paper report in 1942 of one of his bread roundsmen, Albert Shattock, in such a tearing hurry that his delivery van forced a motor car off the road, causing injury to the occupants.

Their woes were as nought compared to Harold's. He was by then seriously ill and was diagnosed with Hodgkin's Disease. He died on 13 May 1943, aged only thirty-five, the event certified by fellow Somerset cricketer Dr Leslie Marshall. Harold had been serving at the time in the Bishops Hull platoon of the Home Guard and was a member of the local Rural Food Control Committee, set up to oversee rationing. He lies buried in the churchyard of St John the Evangelist in Staplegrove, Taunton. With no children from his marriage, he left Molly well provided for. She remarried in 1951 and died in 2003, sixty years after cancer had claimed Harold.

323
Philip John Davey
16 June 1934 v. Surrey, Kennington Oval

He was known as Phil among the cricketing fraternity but always Philip in the context of his teaching career. Here he is referred to as Phil. Although most reports suggest that Phil Davey was born on 10 August, he in fact arrived on 11 August 1913 according to his birth certificate. His parents, John and Bessie, owned Westmoor Farm in Bishops Hull, now swallowed up by the town of Taunton.

Educated at nearby Queen's College, he was already playing for the Bishops Hull cricket XI as a twelve-year-old. An adaptable player, he could bowl medium pace and

spin – both leg- and off-breaks – and skit-
tled out opposing school teams at Queen's
with great regularity. He took 53 wickets
at an average of 5.90 in his final year before
going up to Trinity Hall, Cambridge, to
study Modern Languages. He was also a
capable batsman. In his history of the
school, H. J. Channon notes that 'we felt
sure he was a future Somerset player'. Elsewhere, in a newspaper article, Channon
would write:

*Phil was a natural cricketer and one could
believe that he was born with a cricket ball in
his hand. He had a wonderful control over it …
At school Davey was a brilliant hitter but when
he changed his style in county cricket, he met with
little success.*

He appeared for Somerset as a twenty-
year-old amateur in 1934 and made an immediate impact.
His first wicket was that of Jack Hobbs and in the match
against Worcestershire at Frome, on a peach of a wicket
where Somerset had amassed 522 runs, he returned the
astonishing bowling figures of 6 for 9 in 9.2 overs. He was
never again so successful. On one occasion, having been hit
for five successive fours by Emrys Davies of Glamorgan, he
was surprised when the umpire, E. J. 'Tiger' Smith,
suggested that he try a long-hop. Davies played, missed and
was bowled. Over the course of sixteen games, Phil would
take 22 wickets at 28.18 apiece and average 10.21 with the
bat. A fine slip fielder, he would also take ten catches.

*Phil Davey – 'one could
believe that he was born
with a cricket ball in his
hand'.*

After graduating, he taught briefly in St Albans before taking up a teaching post
at the Nautical College at Pangbourne, where he would remain throughout his
working life, his thirty-eight years of service only interrupted by the Second World
War when he served in the Fleet Air Arm, stationed near Inverness. He taught French
at the Nautical College, apparently 'in a highly individualistic fashion' and coached
the school cricket team for over twenty years, adopting a relaxed regime about fitness
but dispensing advice from his position at first slip during practice sessions and enter-

P.J. Davey (left) seen at the time of his retirement with his successor as Nautical College cricket team coach, Lionel Stephens.

taining the boys with withering remarks. His extra-curricular activities included the vice-presidency of the local Working Men's Club and his avid support for Reading FC. Less of a positive example to his pupils was his fondness for a regular flutter on the horses.

He would continue to play club cricket and, interviewed in later life by the journalist Richard Walsh, revealed that he was still in possession of a mounted ball with which he had taken ten wickets in an innings for Nautical College. 'You have to have a lot of luck for that', he is quoted as saying. Luck, yes, but skill and application, too.

He was married in 1941 to Eleanor Harris, known as Nora, a Taunton girl who worked in a ladies' outfitters store. Having joined Phil in the village of Pangbourne, Nora would become active in local politics and was for a while Chairwoman of the Parish Council.

Having retired from teaching in 1974, Phil returned to Taunton and became an enthusiastic follower of the Somerset cricket team, delighting in any successes. Nora died in 1992, leaving Phil to 'reminisce with anyone who would listen about the game of cricket he loved so much'. He died in Taunton on 8 December 2000 at the age of eighty-seven. In an obituary, Lionel Stephens, who replaced him as the first team coach at the Nautical College, quotes an earlier reference, asserting that 'Philip's main cricketing weapons were a skilfully-flighted off-break and a devastating finger-spun leg-break that only happened once every two overs and always caused havoc'. He also observes that Phil was 'always elegantly attired' and that 'genial and rubicund, he enjoyed life to the full'.

324
Peter Jeofry Searle Courtenay
30 June 1934 v. Derbyshire, Chesterfield

Peter Jeofry Searle Courtenay

Peter Courtenay was born in Weymouth on 11 March 1914, the son of Percy Donald Athon Courtenay and his wife, Ethel Florence (née Donne). Percy was an England international at hockey and had taken over the watchmaking and jewellery business in the town from his own father. Although also a fine outside-left at hockey, Peter was never quite able to reach the heights his father Percy had, although he would gain blues at the sport as well as representing Somerset and The West of England.

Educated at Marlborough College, Peter played for the cricket First XI and captained the school hockey First XI before going up to Pembroke College, Cambridge. On graduating, he left the country to work for the Bombay Burmah [sic] Trade Corporation, founded in 1863 in order to oversee the development of the teak exporting business from Burma (now Myanmar). By the time of Peter Courtenay's arrival in 1927, the company's main business was in the growing and processing of tea. He would remain with them only until 1932 when he opted for a prolonged sabbatical in which he presumably resided with his father, now a widower and living in Burnham-on-Sea. Here he indulged his passion for hockey as a member of the Weston-super-Mare club but also found time for tennis and golf. There is little to suggest that he was an outstanding cricketer. Indeed, this was borne out by the recollections of Dicky Burrough:

> *In the evening prior to a match, Somerset discovered they only had ten men and so began the search for another player. Rumour reached the captain that one Peter Courtenay was a particularly fine player and he was duly summoned. Unfortunately the captain had not been told that although Courtenay was, indeed, a player of international standard, it was at hockey not cricket. Needless to say his county cricket career was decidedly shortlived.*

Burrough was no doubt indulging in slight exaggeration and there is no mystery over the so-called 'rumour': the recommendation would almost certainly have come from Somerset's Jake Seamer, who knew Courtenay well from their time together at Marlborough College. Peter had in fact been drafted in along with Horace Hazell, owing to the unavailability of Jack White and Reggie Ingle, the latter through injury. Over the course of two consecutive games, he mustered a batting average of 3.75. An appearance for Somerset Stragglers followed before he left to join the Burmese Army

Jake Seamer (left) and Peter Courtenay (right) in 1932.

in 1936. At the time of his marriage in Weston-super-Mare in 1940 to Doris Helen Woods, he was a major. She is described as a nursing governess. The couple would have two daughters and Peter would rise to the rank of lieutenant colonel by the time of his retirement from the Burmese military in 1945.

The Courtenay family lived for a number of years in Burnham-on-Sea but he moved to Dorset to become Secretary of the Broadstone Golf Club. The clubhouse was attached to his and Helen's lodgings and they acted as steward and stewardess. While Peter oversaw administrative matters, Helen took charge of catering. By early January 1959 his behaviour had become erratic and the Chairman of the club insisted that the couple should take a week's holiday and that if his problems persisted, he should seek advice from Dr Beadles, a member of the club. Although it was not fully understood at the time, Peter was suffering from severe depression. Beadles would later confirm that 'Mr Courtenay either would not or could not make clear to him the cause'. It was also reported that he would be 'on top of the world one moment and ... incapable of work at another.' Peter Courtenay put a gun to his head in the Broadstone clubhouse and took his own life on 3 April 1959 (and not 7 April as sometimes stated) at the age of only forty-five. It was made clear at his inquest that there was no question of impropriety, financial or otherwise. He was praised as a 'very successful and popular Secretary'. His wife, Doris, continued to manage the clubhouse until June, but then stepped down. She was made an Honorary Life Member of the club as a sign of appreciation and support and survived her husband by nearly half a century, dying in Cornwall in 2006.

P. J. S. Courtenay – a fine sportsman who succumbed to depression and took his own life.

Peter's younger brother, Geof Courtenay, a schoolmaster, would play cricket both for Somerset and Scotland.

1935

"The forceful cricket played by the county has
put them well into the limelight."
Taunton Courier

Championship Position: 14 of 17

Arthur Wellard was in wonderful form, completing the double and smiting 64 sixes
in the process. Bill Andrews was back from Forfarshire and together they formed
an excellent bowling attack with Andrews also topping 100 wickets. Jack Lee played a
useful supporting role with his off-spin but was released at the end of the season when
he brandished the offer of a coaching post at Mill Hill as a bargaining chip. He was put
in his place by John Daniell, who took exception to being held to ransom, as he saw it,
by any of the pros. Daniell had earlier dismissed approaches by George Emmett and
Harold Gimblett who both expressed the wish to play for Somerset as professionals. The
two young men – who would go on to amass nearly 50,000 runs and 87 centuries
between them – were dismissed as surplus to requirements. Emmett went on to play

Somerset take the field at Weston-super-Mare in 1935.
LEFT TO RIGHT: *H. D. Burrough, J. W. Lee (partially obscured), W. T. Luckes, F. S. Lee, A. W.
Wellard, N. S. Mitchell-Innes, W. H. R. Andrews, R. A. Ingle, J. H. Cameron, H. Gimblett, J. C.
White.*

for Gloucestershire and Gimblett would have been as great a loss, had it not been for a stroke of good fortune that had him drafted into the Somerset side at Frome, where he would steal the national headlines by blasting the fastest century of the season on his debut. John Daniell is to be praised for the energy he brought to the role of Secretary, as well as for the fact that he worked on a pro bono basis to save the club money, but his lack of judgement was matched only by his arrogance.

Mandy Mitchell-Innes topped the batting averages but his appearances were limited and Jack White, when available, gave backbone to the batting, with two centuries. Although he was no longer the force of old with the ball, he had his moments, including a couple of 5-wicket hauls.

Among the debutants, Harold Gimblett, destined to become a folk hero, was the only player of note.

The committee were saddened by the death of their President, Sir Dennis Boles, and of long-term servant of the club, the eccentric Rev. Archie Wickham. On a more cheery note, the bank balance was in credit for the first time in many a year, the share of the 1934 Test Match receipts having aided the cause.

The Somerset XI who played Worcestershire at Dudley in 1935.
STANDING: W. T. Luckes, H. Gimblett, W. H. R. Andrews, H. L. Hazell, H. F. T. Buse, F. S. Lee. SEATED: A. W. Wellard, J. W. Lee, R. A. Ingle, H. D. Burrough, R. A. Gerrard.

325

Harold Gimblett

18 May 1935 v. Essex, Frome

[signature: H G Gimblett]

David Foot gave his moving biography of Harold Gimblett the subtitle *Tormented Genius*, neatly encapsulating the essence of the man. An exhilarating batsman who was dogged by depression, an introvert whose genius obliged him to bear the price of fame, he bore the raucous banter of the changing room with stoicism and looked on as a number of his teammates gambled. He was a gambler of a different sort, prepared to back his eagle-eye and his yeoman's strength against a bowler of any reputation. A contradictory figure, he was assailed by self-doubt in quiet moments and yet fearlessness at the crease brought him a record-breaking number of runs and a number of avoidable dismissals. Some – particularly the England selectors – saw him as reckless.

He was born in Bicknoller on 19 October 1914. His father, Percy, ran the family farm, aided by Harold's mother, Louise. Blake's Farm sits in a beautiful but remote spot and Harold, the third of three sons, was happy to be isolated. From the outset he avoided company and would walk alone, find a place to lie on the grass, recovering from the migraines that troubled him or meditating on life. He learned his cricket in the farm's orchard with his brother Dennis, who later became a clergyman. They would use the trunk of an apple tree and bowl fallen apples. From the outset, Harold had the eye and the strength of upper body and wrist to hit a ball or indeed an apple an astonishing distance. Sent, as were his brothers, to West Buckland School, where one of his first duties was to fag for 'a big chap called Gale, one of the honey family', he was drafted into the First XI by the age of thirteen and was informed as a fifteen-year-old that he had been appointed captain. Terrified at the thought of having to issue orders to older boys, he begged to be excused the responsibility. His request was denied.

On leaving school, he was persuaded to try his luck in London, working in an office-bound job in the grocery trade. He hated it and soon returned to help out on the farm at Bicknoller. His father, recognising that Harold had an exceptional talent, allowed him to take every opportunity to play for Watchet CC. He was sensational, tearing opposition bowling attacks apart at will. Everyone, including Watchet's influential sponsor, W. G. Penny, believed him to be a shoo-in to the Somerset side. Everyone that is except for the one man who mattered: John Daniell. Harold's rejection by Daniell when he came to the County Ground for a trial, the last-minute call up when

Harold Gimblett at Old Trafford in 1936.

Harold Gimblett – fearless in his treatment of bowlers but tormented by depression.

Laurie Hawkins cried off, the astonishing debut at Frome when he blasted a century in 63 minutes are all well-documented. In defence of John Daniell, Harold Gimblett was a one-off: he played the game like a village cricketer who happened to be world-class.

His century at Frome won him the Lawrence Trophy, awarded for the fastest first-class century of the season. It came with 100 guineas to spend in a London store – an extraordinary payday for a twenty-year-old, who was being paid on a match-by-match basis. By the time of the award, his form had in fact fallen away and *Wisden* were unconvinced, observing that 'he appeared to pay little heed to defence'.

The following season, more equipped for the rigours of the three-day game and given a full-time contract, he proved his doubters wrong with a scintillating start to the season. Fast-tracked into the England team, he dug his side out of a hole, ensuring victory against India with a brutal assault on their attack. He had struggled in the first innings, grafting his way to 11 runs, but between innings Jack Hobbs, using his umbrella in lieu of a bat, had explained to him how to play in-swing. He had put Hobbs's theory to the test with devastating effect. Harold learned his trade on the hoof. Herbert Sutcliffe told him how to minimise the risks when hooking. Wally Hammond showed him how to play leg-spin and combat a googly. No one in the Somerset set-up knew the answers to his questions.

He played 329 times for his county, scoring over 21,000 runs at 36.96, including forty-nine centuries. An occasional bowler, he took 41 wickets at 50.09. He played only three times for England, averaging 32.35. He could have won more caps, but for the conservatism of the selectors, his own fear that he would be a village cricketer exposed at the highest level and an untimely and much written-about carbuncle that caused his withdrawal. Throughout his career and beyond he lived with the constant spectre of depression. It made him unpredictable. The man who could light up a cricket ground could plunge a changing room into darkness as he flung his bat against the wall.

He was married in 1938 to Marguerita Burgess, known as Rita, a local girl who understood the ways of the introverted country boy. They would have one son. Rita accepted Harold's sudden changes of mood, sometimes brought on by the cocktail of drugs he took to ward off his depression or his migraines or any other ailment he complained of. She knew she was married to a flawed genius. His career interrupted by the Second World War, Harold applied to join the RAF but was declined, presumably on the basis of his medical history, and was assigned duties as a firefighter, which he undertook with great bravery in places as far apart as Bristol and Plymouth. He was shaken by the suffering and death he witnessed.

He showed infinite patience and curt irascibility in equal measure. But the truth is he had reasons to feel aggrieved. He was treated appallingly by the Somerset hierarchy. When Arthur Wellard ventured to suggest a bonus after Harold scored the first triple century by a Somerset batsman, he was informed that Gimblett had been paid to make 300 runs. When he was forced to walk away after depression had finally defeated him and he felt he could bat no more, he eventually summoned the courage to return to the County Ground, but on being spotted by the Club Secretary, Air Vice Marshall Taylor, was promptly ejected for having let them down. Let them down? He had scored more runs for them than any other player and had kept the supporters flocking to their games. Like any outsider with the strength of character to swim against the tide, he spoke up for the dispossessed without fear. He had done so too often.

After leaving the first-class game he worked for a spell at the Ebbw Vale steel works, his contract linked to appearances and coaching duties for the cricket team, but he could not bear working in a factory for long. Jack Meyer came to his rescue and Harold worked for twenty years in varying roles from coach to shop manager at Millfield School. A year playing for Dorset brought an average of nearly fifty and much pleasure to spectators, although he left on a point of principle when the authorities decreed that all first-class and Minor Counties cricketers were obliged to sign away their right to any book deals unless the contents had been vetted by them. The ruling had followed a row sparked by Jim Laker's memoirs.

After leaving Millfield, no longer able to work, crippled by arthritis and over-whelmed by worries, Harold moved with Rita to a mobile home in Verwood, Dorset. His problems refused to disappear. Drugs could only manage rather than cure his depression. He regarded death as the only way of conquering it. He described it as 'living in a tunnel with no end and no light'. Despondent, even though he was fondly remembered by Somerset supporters and loved by his longsuffering wife, he took an overdose and died on 30 March 1978. At the age of sixty-three he could bear life no more.

Raymond Robertson-Glasgow – another who took his own life – wrote that Harold Gimblett was in every way 'too daring for those who have never known what it is to dare in cricket'. Daring enough to plunder sixes off the first ball of an innings and courageous enough to end his own life.

326
Thomas Ronald Garnett
5 June 1935 v. Cambridge University, Cambridge

BY KIND PERMISSION OF MARLBOROUGH COLLEGE

T. R. Garnett – a 'liberal, but disciplined and rigorous' headmaster.

Tommy Garnett was born on 1 January 1915 in Marple, Cheshire. At the age of thirteen, he won a junior scholarship to Charterhouse. A gifted young sportsman, he opened the batting for The Rest against Lord's Public Schools along with the precocious Mandy Mitchell-Innes. He would also win the national Eton Fives championship at doubles. He was awarded a scholarship to Magdalene College, Cambridge, to read Classics but failed to gain a cricketing blue.

Mitchell-Innes perhaps facilitated the invitation for Tommy Garnett to play for Somerset as an undergraduate in 1935. According to *Wisden*, Somerset were obliged to bat 'in a gale of wind that upset the sight screens and blew leaves on the pitch'. Tommy would play on a further four occasions in 1939. He would later recount the tale of how at Lord's, with Somerset facing defeat, Jack Meyer had suggested that each batsman should appeal for bad light on arriving at the crease, and that Frank Chester – a no-nonsense umpire who possessed only one arm – had dismissed his appeal with something approaching scorn. In his five outings, Tommy, a right-handed batsman, averaged 20.12.

He was also approached by Glamorgan and had agreed to appear for them while he was living for a brief while at Merioneth, although a telegram arrived on the morning of his planned departure to say that the MCC had barred Glamorgan's request.

On graduating, he had become an assistant master at Westminster School before returning to Charterhouse in 1938 in order to teach Classics. During the Second World War he served with the RAF. Having joined up in 1941, he was deemed unfit for flying (probably as a result of a congenital hearing defect known as high tone deafness)

but he served in Bengal and Burma. Promoted to the rank of squadron leader in 1944 he was involved in the advance on Rangoon in the latter stages of the conflict.

In 1946 he was married to Penelope Agnes Marion (née Frere) with whom he would have two sons and two daughters. He returned to Charterhouse where among other duties he managed the school's sixty-acre farm. Indeed, he claimed that he was contemplating trying his hand at farming as a career when in 1952, while carrying a pail of milk home in the evening, he was greeted with the news that he had been offered the headmastership of Marlborough College. Although he sometimes appeared aloof, this may have resulted from an inherent shyness. Tommy is described as 'short, tousle-haired …. a liberal, but disciplined and rigorous … unfazed by the youthful peccadilloes of the day'. Indeed he was a genuine innovator, embracing change. As an example, he redeployed the cadet force in building a new music department (headed by former Somerset cricketer Bruce Hylton Stewart) rather than undertaking drill practice.

In 1953, he played cricket for Wiltshire and in a letter written not long before he died, Tommy Garnett revealed to Barry Phillips:

I was disappointed that Somerset made no attempt to get in touch with me after the war. But I made a lot of runs for club sides – mostly the Sou'Westers and the Charterhouse Friars.

Believing that headmasters are in danger of becoming set in their ways after a decade in situ, he left in 1961 to become principal of the prestigious Geelong

Grammar School in Australia. Although some of his ideas were initially viewed with suspicion, he won his hosts over and under his tutelage, a young Prince Charles, miserable at Gordonstoun where he was said to be 'lacking in science or sport', spent two terms at Timberstop, the school's outback offshoot. The first in line to the throne came away inspired by the experience.

Tommy Garnett – innovative headmaster turned passionate gardener.

Tommy retired at fifty-nine to pursue his passion for the natural world. For many years he had taken his family on tours of the far reaches of the continent with a Land Rover and a decrepit caravan in tow, accompanied by another car loaded up with his family. A keen ornithologist and for many years the secretary of Birds Australia, he cited the desire to explore the flora and fauna of Australia as a major reason for having applied for the job at Geelong Grammar. In 1974 he purchased a stone cottage in the Victorian scrub and set about converting it into a garden paradise with ten acres of daffodils and over 3,000 different native plant species. In 1980, he opened the gardens to the public and throughout the 1980s he acted as gardening editor for *The Age* in Melbourne. He was awarded the Medal of the Order of Australia (OAM) in 1996 for services to horticulture.

He died in Castlemaine, Victoria, on 22 September 2006 at the age of ninety-one. Surely few men have achieved more in their lives.

327
Richard Vivian Macaulay Stanbury
5 June 1935 v. Cambridge University, Cambridge

Known as Dick, he was born in Madras (now Chennai) on 5 February 1916. At the time, his father was head of the police training garrison at Vellore in Tamil Nadu. As an eight-year-old, Dick was sent to a preparatory school, along with his brother, Ralph. The two of them would see neither of their parents for five years. Dick went on to Shrewsbury School in 1929 and would gain an Exhibition in Classics at Magdalene College, Cambridge. He was never selected to play for the Varsity XI, but it was while an undergraduate that he played his two games for Somerset as a wicket-keeper and lower order right-handed batsman, first at Fenner's against Cambridge University and then, the following year, against Essex at Colchester. His average was 10.33 and he took two catches.

After graduating he was offered a job with the Sudan Political Service in 1937, spending thirteen years as the District Commissioner in various regions of the country. In the last ten of those years he suffered the debilitating effects of malaria and repeated bouts of dysentery, finally returning to Somerset in 1950 for a period of recuperation. The West Country air worked its magic and he returned two years later to a more deskbound role with the Foreign Service, based initially in Egypt. It was here that he met the woman who would become his wife. Dick and Geraldine (née Grant) were married in London in 1953. They would have a son and daughter.

R. V. M. Stanbury – one in a long line of occasional Somerset wicket-keepers.

Meanwhile, he continued to play cricket, keeping wicket for the Gezira Sporting Club in Cairo, including a fixture in 1954 against a Pakistan team featuring the great Hanif Mohammad, where Dick came in at number three and scored 13 unbeaten runs in a paltry total of 52.

In the late 1950s he transferred to the British Embassy in Bahrain before a final spell as mentor and advisor to the British Ambassador. After retiring from diplomatic service, he farmed peaches and strawberries in Portugal for a number of years before settling in East Sussex, where he and his wife, Geraldine, imported and sold Portuguese pottery. In later life he remained an active member of the Somerset Former Players' Association until his death on 29 June 2008 in Peasemarsh, East Sussex, at the age of ninety-two.

328
Ernest Hugo Meggeson Hood
5 June 1935 v. Cambridge University, Cambridge

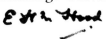

Hugo Hood was born in Burnby, Yorkshire, on 27 August 1915. His mother, Alice Annie (née Pottage) was already carrying him at the time of her marriage early in 1915 to Hugo's father, Ernest William Hood, a sergeant in the 12th Northumberland Fusiliers and prior to that a steel works manager. Killed in action a mere thirteen days after Hugo's birth, Ernest never saw his son. His mother remarried – becoming Mrs Williams – in 1932. Her son retained the surname Hood.

Hugo Hood – struck fear into the hearts of the Japanese in Burma. His bowling against the Cambridge University XI at Fenner's induced less terror.

He was educated first at the Southcliffe School in Filey and then between 1929 and 1933 at Wellington College in Berkshire, where he opened the bowling for the First XI and often batted at number eleven. For a year he worked as an assistant schoolmaster before going up to Emmanuel College, Cambridge, to study French, Spanish and Divinity. He was invited by Somerset to play against the Varsity side, coming away with a batting average of 3.00 and taking no wickets for 43 runs. A friend of Hugo has stated his belief that a member of staff at Wellington College had recommended the undergraduate to Somerset.

Hugo Hood – born and bred in Yorkshire and a Yorkshireman through to his very bones – would only ever play for Somerset on one occasion. He moved to the county to teach from 1937 but enlisted immediately with the Somerset Light Infantry as a second lieutenant in the reservists. This consumed much of his leisure time and called for two months of manoeuvres each summer. First-class cricket was out of the question.

During the Second World War, he would prove to be a 'Boy's Own' hero, who would win the DSO and Croix de Guerre for his actions. Having been posted to Gibraltar, he had risen to the rank of captain in 1942. Officially, he was transferred to the 3rd Battalion of the South Dorsetshire Regiment, but this was a smokescreen. Hugo had been chosen to become a member of the Special Operations Executive (SOE), parachuted behind enemy lines. His first involvement was to be in the Balkans but the plan was aborted when political agreement could not be reached. His enthusiasm unabated, he was chosen for a mission in France. Selected as part of the elite Jedburgh team on the basis not just of his personal qualities but his fluency in French, he was parachuted into the country, near Dijon. He broke his nose on landing and would bear the scars and misalignment for the remainder of his life, though this in no way diminished his commitment to the mission. The SOE teams acted in small groups, combining their skills to conduct guerrilla warfare and pave the way for an Allied advance. He would take part in three further missions in Burma (Myanmar), commanding Operations Cheetah, Zebra and Mongoose. In the first of these, when he was dropped into the Thurawaddy district of Burma, he led his troops through 120 miles of jungle. In his DSO citation of May 1945 it is noted that over a two month period he inflicted 616 casualties on the enemy, whilst losing only five of his own men and he was able to provide invaluable intelligence. When he met up with the advancing troops he had been suffering from severe dysentery combined with a cocktail of tropical diseases and was encountered 'complete with ginger beard, tattered shirt, native skirt and feet bound in rags'. His further missions were punctuated by spells in hospital recovering. He would return from the war a lieutenant colonel, retaining his title until his retirement from the reserve list on the grounds of age in 1965.

After the war he had applied to join a Control Commission for Austria or Germany, overseeing the rebuilding of the country's infrastructure. His application was declined owing to his health issues after his time in Burma and he settled for life as a schoolmaster. As well as teaching French and Geography, and coaching hockey and cricket teams, he was Commander of the Cadet Force for two years before stepping down for a prolonged period but taking up the post again in the 1960s. He served the school for the remainder of his working life, becoming something of an institution. Known affectionately as 'Scratters' on account of the way he repeatedly scratched at his war wound, his methods were not always orthodox. One former pupil, John Isles, recalls the time he was offered a Player's cigarette by his coach for having scored a half-century. Another pupil, John Hobson,

E. H. M. Hood – an eccentric schoolmaster, knocked down and killed by a passing car while walking to Scarborough College.

who later became a teacher at Scarborough College, paints a vivid picture of a man who came alive when overseeing the Cadets. He recalls Hugo's pride when his boys were banned from interacting with the Cadet Forces of the other schools because of their 'over-exuberance' on a combined exercise in the Brecon Beacons. With a day to themselves, Hugo replicated his days in the Burmese jungle when he and four hand-picked boys played the role of guerrillas parachuted behind enemy lines. John also recalls hockey practice where Hugo, who invariably played in goal, was 'dressed in the most extraordinary ancient leather hockey gear and would charge out of the goal with a blood-curdling scream to take possession of the ball'.

For many years Hugo played cricket for Scarborough although increasingly he turned to fishing as his favoured leisure pursuit. He never forgot his wartime colleagues and worked tirelessly for the British Legion, organising the Poppy Day collections.

He was married in 1960 – having announced that his headmaster had instructed him to find a wife – to Iona Maude Baker, who, like Hugo, was already in her forties. She worked at the time as a clerk for the Scarborough Rural District Council. A close friend, Owen Parnell, says of Hugo that 'he was a quiet, unassuming man with an oddball sense of humour' and that together they 'consumed many a pint, while he puffed on his pipe and quietly observed the people, often rendering a service song or two before the evening was out'.

On 11 July 1968, Hugo Hood was knocked down by a car whilst crossing the road near Scarborough College, suffering multiple injuries. He fought for his life but died in hospital in Scarborough on 1 August 1968 at the age of only fifty-two. His death certificate cites hypostatic bronchopneumonia and his many injuries as the causes. Crossing the Filey Road had done for the man who had survived the Burmese jungle and the Japanese Army. An inquest was held and a verdict of accidental death was passed. It had been a sad and untimely end for a man whose life had begun in tragic circumstances and whose story of quiet service to one school masked an extraordinary spell as a war hero and three rather less exhilarating days as a county cricketer. The Hugo Hood Memorial Fund was launched by the college's Old Boys Association, raising money to contribute towards the building of a new sports hall, completed in 1981. A plaque has been placed there in his memory.

Iona Hood remained an active, campaigning figure in the town of Scarborough for a number of years before retiring to Burnham-on-Sea, offering one final link between Hugo and the county of Somerset. She died there at the age of eighty-four.

329
Charles John Patrick Barnwell
12 June 1935 v. Gloucestershire, Bristol

John Barnwell was born in Stoke-on-Trent on 23 June 1914. His paternal grandfather was a clergyman and his father, Frederick Arthur Lowry Barnwell, was an engineer in the Public Works Department, married to Grace Winifred (née Laughton). He was educated at Repton and his parents had retired to Hinton St George, near Crewkerne, by the time he left school. He would live with them until 1939 when he was offered a commission with the 7th Battalion of the Somerset Light Infantry as a second lieutenant. By the end of the Second World War, he had risen to the rank of major. He was married in 1942 to Elizabeth Mary Shore, known as Betty, the daughter of Lord and Lady Teignmouth. Betty's parents owned properties in Clevedon in Somerset and in Kilkenny, Ireland. Sadly from John's perspective, she had two younger brothers who were ahead of her in the queue for titles and possessions. He and Betty would have two sons, one of whom died in Curry Rivel in 1970 at the age of only seventeen.

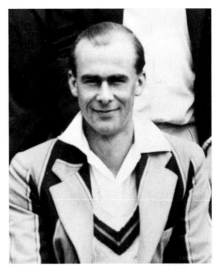

An accomplished schoolboy cricketer – seen then as an all-rounder – John Barnwell was regarded primarily as a batsman at club level, frequently appearing for Somerset Stragglers. Although he would play for Somerset in sixty-nine first-class fixtures, the step up in class proved a challenge. An obituary in the *Somerset Year Book* notes that 'he played correctly', having been well coached at Repton, but that he was 'occasionally found out at Championship level'. He would average 15.16 between 1935 and 1948 but also made useful contributions as a fit and adept outfielder. His brightest innings was his 83 against Hampshire in 1939, part of a fifth-wicket stand with F. M. 'Peter' McRae, who made a century. His commanding demeanour – he was a tall man – and his time as a major had certainly made him a natural choice to step in on occasions as captain of the county side. In 1946 his captaincy proved too decisive during the

C. J. P. Barnwell – lost his hair and acquired a fur farm.

fixture with Glamorgan at Pontypridd when he and Johnny Clay agreed on a contrived declaration in order to allow for the possibility of a result. The crowd, having paid their entrance money, were delighted to witness a well-fought contest rather than a limp draw. The authorities were apoplectic and the incident elicited a change in the laws of the game: captains were henceforth banned from discussing the detail of a contrived declaration together. Bunty Longrigg, whom Barnwell had replaced, remained outspoken in support of his stand-in's decision. Asked by one journalist if the action was excusable he is quoted as replying: 'Yes, I think it was, considering the circumstances, and incidentally made quite a packet of money, as well as brightening things up.'

John Barnwell would later recount the tale of how he was once upbraided by

Longrigg for wearing a scruffy cap, with the suggestion that his county cap would be more appropriate. He responded by informing his skipper that he had never been granted a county cap. When the records were checked, it was in fact found that he had been awarded it in 1937, though no one had thought to inform Barnwell of the fact. He continued to play cricket in his forties in the Liverpool and District League, appearing for Neston. Affluent enough to be a regular for his county as an amateur, he was not so well-off that he could remain entirely a gentleman of leisure. He made a living by breeding silver foxes for their fur, a rather less lucrative business in modern times (and since the end of 2002 entirely illegal).

John Barnwell died on 4 September 1998 at the age of eighty-four in Fivehead, near Taunton, less than a year after his wife, Betty's, death. His nephew, Michael Barnwell, played for Somerset in 1967 and 1968.

330
Ronald Anderson Gerrard
6 July 1935 v. Worcestershire, Dudley

Known as 'Gerry', Ron Gerrard was a popular England rugby international in the 1930s. He was born on 26 January 1912 in Hong Kong, where his father, William George, described as 'brawny but not tall, with huge thighs and a disciplined mind', had risen through the ranks of the police force. The youngest of five children, Gerry showed early prowess as a footballer. When his father died in 1927, the family moved to Somerset, where his mother had been raised. On the advice of W. S. Donne, a family friend and sometime President of the RFU, he was sent to Taunton School, where he encountered rugby for the first time and was soon drafted into the school XV, for whom he would play for three years, initially as a full-back. Under the direction of Alan Marshall, a Somerset cricketer, known to generations of Taunton School pupils as 'Bingy', he added an understanding of the game to his undoubted natural aptitude and became an inside-centre. He also starred for the cricket team, averaging 43.25 in his third and final season at the school.

He in fact excelled at all sports and most athletics events, but it was as a rugby player that Gerry truly shone. In his biography of R. A. Gerrard, entitled *Men of Stout Countenance*, fellow rugby international Donald Crichton-Miller informs us that Gerry combined a sturdy, big-hipped frame with great strength and speed. Able to side-step an opponent or brush off a challenge using his physical attributes, he created many

R. A. Gerrard – 'the inclusion of a rugger international will put up the gate money'.

openings for his team. By 1929 he had been fast-tracked into a Somerset XV for whom he would play on forty-two occasions. He was also soon recommended as a triallist for England by John Daniell, a rather shrewder judge of rugby talent than he was of cricketing ability. Gerry outshone everyone at the trial match and became an automatic choice in the England rugby team. He would in fact gain fourteen caps between 1932 and 1936. In the match against Wales there was controversy when England's star was temporarily blinded in an eye-gouging incident that many believed had been intentional. Gerry was unable to play on and the fourteen men of England lost the game. His form dipped after 1936 when he is reported to have put on weight and lost his lightning turn of speed. Asked to play in the now unfamiliar role of full-back for the trial match, he performed badly.

Demonstrating his all-round abilities, Gerry was runner-up on one occasion in the county's tennis singles championship. He was also invited by John Daniell to play for Somerset CCC on three occasions in 1935, with Daniell remarking that 'the inclusion of a rugger international will put up the gate money'. In the event, Gerry mustered a batting average of 7.20 in his three appearances.

On leaving school in 1930 with little in the way of academic qualifications, we are told by Crichton-Miller that 'his English and Mathematics were sufficient to start him off as a pupil in Civil Engineering'. He was offered a job by Coles & Coles, in Bath, and would later work for the City Surveyor's Department in the city.

A very introverted man, confident in his own abilities but a modest presence, especially so in the company of strangers, he was nevertheless seen as a talismanic figure, particularly in his adoptive city of Bath. His credentials were further enhanced when, on the day before his twenty-third birthday, he saved a drowning boy whilst surveying beside the River Avon, in Bath.

In 1935, he joined the Territorial Army as a second lieutenant, partly through patriotic duty and partly as a means of maintaining his fitness. He duly won the national shot-putting competition for the Territorials. It was an unfashionable organisation at the time and Gerry was used as the poster boy for recruitment.

Late in 1935 he was married to Molly Taylor, the daughter of a local architect. Molly was an entirely different individual to Gerry: hugely creative where he was methodical and an extrovert who was an accomplished public speaker, while he was diffident. Later, this remarkable woman would become President of Bath RFC. She and Gerry would have one son – Duncan, born in 1941 –who, owing to the events that unfolded, would retain no memories of his father. Gerry had begun his contribution to the war by training up recruits to the Territorial Army and building air-raid shelters. Thereafter, he had helped with the construction of defences against a possible invasion, the threat of which was snuffed out by the Battle of Britain. Finally, he was given command of the 7th Field Squadron of the Royal Engineers at Gobel Marejaun, near Isnalia, though there was considerable fluidity to the battle for North Africa as land was lost and regained.

With no transport available, Gerry borrowed a motor cycle and rode to the temporary headquarters, where, caked in sweat and sand, he was greeted by Lance Corporal Littlejohn, a down-to-earth Scotsman who promptly offered the new arrival a beer, gratefully accepted, which was withdrawn, using an attached piece of string, from deep in the sand. The two men would become firm friends with Littlejohn impressed by his introverted major's quiet confidence, sound judgement and fearlessness.

The role of the squadron was to clear mines, invariably under enemy fire, and mark out a clear passage for the Allied tanks to advance. In his first engagement, Gerry was awarded a DSO for his outstanding bravery as he led the task from the front for eleven days. Casualties were heavy. The work continued, with Gerry and his men at the vanguard as the Allies advanced towards Tripoli. On 22 January 1943, days before his thirty-first birthday, Gerry and Lance Corporal Littlejohn had overseen the clearing of mines with Tripoli in view. Sending Littlejohn ahead, Gerry went back to ensure that the tanks following his car were not straying beyond the marked area. Too late. A tank had been driven outside the correct zone and hit a mine. In the ensuing chaos, as Gerry tried to restore order, another mine was set off and some shrapnel hit him in the temple, killing him instantly. A random death after he had taken so much care to preserve the lives of others.

Gerry's loss was felt keenly by family, friends and fans. A colleague, Frank Wills, raised a fund for scholarships to Taunton School as a memorial to a celebrated alumnus. The money poured in.

He may have made little impression on Somerset's cricket fortunes but this quiet, talented sportsman had impacted countless lives for the better.

331
Ernest Dyson Falck
17 July 1935 v. Worcestershire, Wells

E.D. Falck

Ernie Falck was born in Huddersfield on 21 October 1907, the eighth child of John Henry Falck and his wife, Emily (née Brook). His father owned a factory preparing sausage casings from the linings of animal intestines. From a young age, Ernie showed

E. D. Falck of Wells City CC: 'the finest bastman the club has ever had on its books'.

talent as a sportsman and was playing Yorkshire League cricket as a teenager for the Primrose Hill side in Huddersfield. A press report in 1929 of a match versus Honley informs us that 'E. D. Falck, the youthful Primrose Hill player, who has been capturing wickets freely, called attention to himself by making 86 runs without being defeated'.

An accident in his early twenties very nearly put paid to his sporting career. On falling from a ladder, he fractured his skull and although he recovered from his injuries, he suffered alopecia as a result of the trauma and was entirely bald for the remainder of his life. He was married in Huddersfield in 1932 to Margery Gledhill, with whom he would have two sons.

By 1933, Ernie and his father had decided on the need to expand their business into the South West and the son was sent to Wells to set up the offshoot of J. H. Falck & Sons. In December 1933 he placed an advertisement in the *Wells Journal* stating: 'Wanted – Building, with stone floor, drain, water laid: radius eight miles Wells – Falck, Red Lion, Market Place, Wells'. Ernie and Margery did not have to wait long. By the following month, they were in possession of a factory on South Street in the city and had successfully applied for a change of use to the manufacture of sausage casings. Thus began the new phase of their lives. Ernie would remain an integral part of the local sporting scene throughout the rest of his working life.

He began playing immediately for the Wells City football team and the following May, made his debut for Wells City CC, when he scored 42, offering a glimpse of what was to follow. In June he won the Jack Hobbs Bat, a national award for the most outstanding performance each week by a club cricketer, sponsored by the *News Chronicle*. He had scored 156 of his side's 218 versus Purnell's at Paulton. 112 of his runs had come in boundaries and he had demonstrated 'mighty hitting to all parts of the ground'. The *Wells Journal* notes after the final game of his initial season (against the Theological College) that:

> *Ernest Falck was in fine form as usual, and hit up a brilliant 91 not out. Not satisfied with this he took 6 wickets for 14 runs. Falck, without doubt, is the finest batsman the club has ever had on its books; and, I hear he is a clever footballer.*

He was a regular scorer of centuries for his club and often among the wickets. In 1938, he established a new club record of 64 wickets in a season for Wells CC. He was in fact rarely out of the local paper's sporting headlines in the years leading up to the Second World War.

He would, however, only play for Somerset on four occasions, across the 1935 and 1936 seasons. He began brightly on his debut on his home ground in Wells, scoring nearly a quarter of Somerset's runs in a game in which the team mustered little more than 200 runs in total across their two innings and would have made far fewer, but for some hearty and successful slogging by Wellard and Andrews, after the cause was already lost. Thereafter he struggled for first-class runs and came away with a batting average of 10.57. This dented neither his confidence nor his performances for his club side.

The elder of his two sons, Garry, describes his father as a 'strict disciplinarian, with very traditional values'. But sometimes we all fall prey to temptation. During the war, Ernie continued to run the sausage casing business as an essential food supplier but fell foul of the law when fined £50 by the Bath Magistrates' Court in 1942 for illicitly taking receipt on the black market of 'seven sides of bacon and six hams', apparently purloined by his source from a Bath warehouse. His sporting career was, by contrast, more or less unblemished. After he had hung up his cricketing boots, he took to golf with great success, as he did also to snooker and darts, where he was a member of the

A family holiday in Torquay showing (left to right) Garry, Neil, Margery and Ernie Falck.

committee for the Wells and District Darts League.

There was welcome news for the business after the war when the company was approached and asked to produce the anti-coagulant Heparin for Glaxo. This provided an unexpected financial windfall. After retiring from his sausage casing business, the running of which passed on to his sons, Garry and Neil, Ernie moved to Bridport, in Dorset, where he died on 19 February 1982 at the age of seventy-four.

332
Edmund Joe Adams
20 July 1935 v. Essex, Clacton-on-Sea

E. J. Adams – 'a very private man and one of life's gentlemen'.

Known as Ted or Teddy, he was born on 1 February 1915 in Shepton Mallet, the second of two sons of a stonemason-cum-bricklayer, Ernest Robert Adams, and his wife, Mary, a schoolmistress. Their home was in fact built by Ernest who subsequently spent time abroad employed in the construction of skyscrapers on Staten Island, New York, while the boys were growing up. They would later move to Wandsworth in London. Elder brother Tom went on to be a schoolmaster, whereas Ted would spend much of his adult life employed as a travelling salesman.

He made just one appearance for Somerset, scoring 5 runs in his only innings, but it remained a source of quiet satisfaction that he had represented the county he loved and would in fact remain a supporter of throughout his life. His club cricket was played with Roehampton, described as the oldest village cricket team in London, having been founded in 1842. Ted would continue to play for Roehampton and the Club Cricket Conference for many years, generally opening the batting and for some seasons acting as the captain of the Roehampton side. With an insatiable appetite for the game, he would go to Alf Gover's indoor nets in the winter. When he had ceased playing, his knees apparently having 'given way through wear and tear' he umpired both for Roehampton and the Club Cricket Conference.

His 'patch' as a commercial traveller embraced the West Country and parts of London and he was also involved in Roehampton's West Country tours, which were concentrated in South Devon. His regular returns to the area brought Ted into contact with Joan Bruton, whom he was married to in Plymouth in 1942. Joan would for many years act as the scorer for Roehampton. They had no children and she would predecease him.

Never one to open up, Ted Adams was reluctant to describe his war experiences. A lance bombardier in the Royal Artillery, he would not venture beyond describing the war as having been 'too hot and too much sand'. Immediately after the cessation of hostilities he acted as a groundsman at Cheltenham and was awarded a benefit match in 1947 but he then returned full-time to his previous role as a salesman.

He loved cricket and football and his life revolved around the sports, including following the fortunes of Wimbledon FC, whom he watched at Plough Lane over many seasons. With his support for Wimbledon FC and Somerset CCC, Ted clearly had a taste for the plucky underdog. Kathy Hatt, a friend of more than fifty years whose husband played club

Ted Adams – opening batsman and groundsman at Roehampton CC.

cricket with Ted, describes him as 'a very private man and one of life's gentlemen' who was very meticulous, a man of routine whom she describes as having the 'most beautiful handwriting'. Others also describe a kindly man who rarely opened up but was a patient and encouraging coach to inexperienced teammates.

Towards the latter part of his life he considered a return to Somerset, coming close to purchasing a flat beside the County Ground in Taunton, but opted in the end to remain near to his ailing elder brother, Tom.

He died on 24 March 2005 in Kingston-upon-Thames at the age of ninety, leaving generous bequests to his closest club cricketing friends.

1936

"They invariably played bright and interesting cricket."
His Grace the Duke of Somerset, President

Championship Position: 7 of 17

Harold Gimblett led the charge with over 1,500 runs, including five centuries, and was rewarded with an England call-up. Frank Lee also contributed over 1,000 runs but the county batting averages were topped by Mandy Mitchell-Innes and Jack Meyer, both only available on a limited basis. Arthur Wellard entertained as usual with his prodigious six-hitting exploits, most memorably his five sixes in one over off Tommy 'Tosser' Armstrong of Derbyshire, at Wells. Wellard also took 143 wickets, most of them at fast-medium but an increasing number with the off-spin bowling that he was now deploying when the conditions suited it. He was well supported by Horace Hazell and Bill Andrews.

Somerset beat that season's surprise County Champions, Derbyshire, home and away. They were the only team to do so. Among the debutants, Jack Meyer, in Somerset to found Millfield School, was a welcome addition, and Peter McRae shaped up to being a fine player before the Second World War put paid to that.

The gates increased as a result of some scintillating play, and the three victories at the Weston Festival – the first time this had been achieved – added greatly to the cause. It was fortuitous that a balanced core of pros had come together – Gimblett and Lee offering a contrasting opening pair, Andrews and Wellard complementing each other, Hazell maturing into a useful left-arm spinner and Luckes quietly competent behind the stumps. And yet the committee resolutely refused to accept that the age of amateurism was dead.

333
William Newman Bunce
16 May 1936 v. Lancashire, Old Trafford

M.I.Bunce

A booklet detailing the history of Lodway CC informs us that, 'one of Lodway's best ever all-rounders, Newman was a left-handed bat in the Frank Woolley mould and an accurate and hostile right-arm bowler. He invariably topped the batting averages and played a number of games for Somerset.' He in fact played in a combined total of fourteen first-class fixtures in 1936 and 1937, coming away with a batting average of 12.61 and a highest score of 46, and taking 4 wickets at 46.50 apiece.

Newman Bunce was born in Pill, near Bristol, on 17

April 1911, the son of the local master butcher, William Charles Bunce and his wife, Grace (who bore the appropriate maiden name of Bullock). Educated at Cotham Grammar School, Newman was an only child who grew into an impressively-built specimen, 6 ft 4 inches tall and immensely powerful. Perhaps the ready supply of protein had built up his strength. Former Lodway player Mike Lovell reveals that:

You are invited to

"Bunce the Butcher"

for Satisfaction

BALTIC PLACE PILL

Telephone — 2106

W. N. Bunce – played cricket for Somerset CCC and football for Bristol City and Bristol Rovers.

Newman Bunce was the strongest man I've ever met. He always wanted to make the Lodway wicket a batsman's paradise and we had a heavy roller that had been pulled by a horse in the distant past. As young lads it required eight of us to move it, but Mr Bunce, as we called him, could pull it on his own. No one else could shift it.

For a number of years an automatic choice as opening batsman for Bristol & District representative XIs, he was also a fine goalkeeper, combining height, strength and courage. Unusually, given their historical rivalry, he played in goal, as an amateur,

both for Bristol City and Bristol Rovers. His debut for the latter, in January 1935 was particularly memorable for him, given that his side handed out a 7-1 thrashing to Northampton Town.

Newman's father died in 1942 while the son was serving with the RAF but he would return to take the reins at the family's butcher's shop in the village. He was married in 1951 to Margaret Hockridge, with whom he would have two children. A man of many talents, he was an accomplished bass singer and organist. He would run the butcher's shop until his retirement.

Newman Bunce – 'the strongest man I've ever met'.

He died in Pill on 29 May 1981 at the age of seventy. There is a memorial plaque to him on the wall of the Lodway club's new pavilion.

334
Hubert Hunt
23 May 1936 v. Northamptonshire, Kettering

Hubert Hunt, known as Bert, was born in the village of Pill on 18 November 1911, one of nine children of James Henry Hunt and his wife, Eliza (née Thomas). He was the younger brother of George, who also played for Somerset. Their father worked at the Bristol Docks, helping to direct the passage and loading and unloading of ships.

Bert was drafted into the Lodway club side as a teenager and quickly made his mark as an off-spin bowler and aggressive middle-order batsman. By 1933, at the age of twenty-one he was fully into his stride, plundering 1,179 runs and 104 wickets in twenty games. The following year he was offered a professional contract with Kilmarnock CC, replacing brother George, who had spent two seasons there. George had recommended to Kilmarnock that they should consider Bert and – given his striking club form – there was little or no hesitation on their part.

By 1936 he was back in the Bristol area and was selected by Somerset on eleven occasions during that season. His off-spin bowling would yield 15 wickets at 19.00

runs apiece, including a 7 for 49 against Derbyshire at Ilkeston. Bert also averaged a modest 7.69 with the bat. In a less cash-strapped county than Somerset he might have been afforded further opportunities, but by this time, all-rounder Arthur Wellard was turning increasingly to off-spin when conditions favoured it, so that employing Bert was seen as a luxury they could ill afford.

He was married in 1938 to a Bristol girl, Freda Emily Weadon, with whom he would have two sons. When not engaged as a cricketing pro, Bert would contribute to the family coffers by working as a labourer on building sites. He was offered professional terms with Penzance CC for one year before the Second World War and three seasons afterwards. Whilst plying his trade there he was selected regularly for Cornwall in Minor Counties matches. After 1948 he returned to the Lodway side. The brief history of the club informs us that Hubert Hunt was 'the best bowler the club has produced' and 'a splendid, hard-hitting batsman'. Having settled back in Pill, which lies adjacent to Lodway, he became a self-employed painter and decorator.

Bert Hunt – played as a pro in Scotland and Cornwall before returning to the village of Pill in Somerset.

He died in Pill as a result of lung cancer on 28 November 1985 at the age of seventy-four. Although his work as a professional cricketer had taken him to Scotland and Cornwall, the village of Pill in Somerset had always been his true home.

335
Allan Arthur Pearse
6 June 1936 v. Kent, Frome

He was registered as Allan but spelt his Christian name as Alan. An article in the *Western Daily Press* of 1935, mulling over the extraordinary arrival in first-class cricket of Harold Gimblett notes that 'he has a club mate at Watchet of whom great things are expected – Alan Pearse, aged 19, an equally natural bat, whom Somerset hope to try out shortly'. And try him out they did in June 1936, but there was, as they say,

A. A. Pearse - an institution at Watchet CC but a marginal figure in the first-class game.

only one Harold Gimblett. Harold's teammate was a fine club batsman but never hit the heights for his county.

Born in Watchet on 22 April 1915, he was one of twins, the other christened Leslie Lewis. His parents were Arthur Burdon Leontine Pearse and Ellen (née Winn) and his father owned the Exmoor Paper and Bag Company, founded in 1916 in Wansbrough Mill which had been serving as a paper mill in Watchet since the 1750s. One report suggests that it was used as a flour mill for a brief period before the factory was let to Arthur Pearse. Importing wood pulp from Scandinavia, Arthur was soon claiming that his company was the largest producer of paper bags in Britain. Their life was not without incident. Fire proved a regular hazard with piles of wood pulp stored in the yard and there were reports of two men falling to their deaths in the mill in 1937.

Educated at Minehead Grammar School, where he was made head boy, Alan was always destined for a career in the family business and would work his way up, his father determined that the son should prove his worth. By 1939 he was the warehouse foreman.

Not only was he a talented club all-rounder, a fast-medium bowler who was equally capable as a batsman, but he also played at centre-half for Watchet FC. He arrived on the first-class cricketing scene when the Somerset supporters were ever hopeful of another miracle. His champion was William George Penny, known as 'W. G.' a vice-president of Somerset CCC who had done much to promote cricket in Watchet, funding an annual fixture between W.G. Penny's XI and a County XI and doing so by dipping into the wealth he had gleaned from his tailoring business empire. W. G. was himself a player of no great distinction, bowling lob (underarm) deliveries some half a century after they had gone out of fashion, though he apparently took an occasional wicket.

As for his protégé, Alan Pearse would alas never achieve cricketing greatness. In nine games over three seasons he averaged only 5.78 with the bat. He was only asked to bowl two overs.

He was married in 1940 to Ada Marjorie (née Eno), the daughter of a retired police officer. Ada was seven years older than Alan, thirty-two at the time of their wedding. They would have no children. During the Second World War he served in the RAF, primarily in the Middle East. His twin brother, Leslie, was also in the RAF.

On returning to civilian life, Alan continued to indulge his passion for cricket. A report in the *Wells Journal* of 1948 speaks of a 'superlative spell of bowling' for Watchet where he completed twenty consecutive overs at fast-medium pace, taking 6 wickets for 36.

As well as becoming the Managing Director of the family company, Alan threw himself into public service, serving after the war on the Watchet Urban District Council and later on the County Council (Williton Division). He retained a lifelong interest in education, becoming Chairman of the Governors of his alma mater, Minehead Grammar School, and serving as a governor of the West Somerset School and Williton Secondary Modern. He was also a leading light in the British Legion and Rotary Club. In later years, his favoured sports became billiards and snooker, with an obituary claiming that he was a talented exponent of both games.

Sadly, his wife Ada died in 1953. Alan was never remarried and died in Watchet on 14 June 1981, twenty-eight years after the loss of his partner. He was sixty-six at the time.

336
Geoffrey Littlejohn Ogilvy
10 June 1936 v. Sussex, Hove

There is a breathless quality to the business career of Geoffrey Ogilvy: never in one place for long and always ready to try his hand at a new venture. He was born in Lee, to the east of Lewisham, on 25 January 1906. His father, Herbert Charles Ogilvy, was a chartered accountant, married to Catherine (née Brown). Geoffrey was educated at St Bees School in faraway Cumberland and in his final year, the school magazine informs us in its profile of members of the First XI that he was:

a good slow-wicket batsman, combining strong back play with forcing power. A very safe and neat field but not quite quick enough at moving to a ball.

He later claimed to have gone to Oxford University, but this appears to have been an embellishment to what would already be a crowded curriculum vitae. He embarked on a career in the Prison Service, where he would remain for six years. Spells in charge of education at Portland Prison and Wormwood Scrubs were followed by a period at the Feltham Borstal Institute, where he was the games master. He played cricket for

Geoffrey Ogilvy – as a schoolboy he combined 'strong back play with forcing power'.

Dorset and rugby for Blackheath and the Kent Public Schools XV. He was also an accomplished golfer. His life story took on a different trajectory when he left to work for a little under five years for Quellyn Roberts & Co. Ltd. The company owned a number of hotels in Wales and here Geoffrey learned the tricks of the trade as an hotelier. By 1934 he felt ready to purchase his own business and bought the Hare and Hounds Hotel in Shepton Mallet from the Fitch family, this providing his fleeting connection with Somerset. An image of him captaining G. L. Ogilvy's XI at this time shows him to have added considerably to his waistline after the years spent in the hospitality trade.

He was married in 1935 to Marguerite Adams, from Conway, whom he had met whilst working in Wales. They would have three sons but in the meantime they worked together to build the business, although Geoffrey found the time to play cricket for Men O' Mendip and Shepton Mallet. The local paper describes his 'merry knock of 127' for Men O' Mendip versus the Somerset Light Infantry in 1935. He was by now boldly styling the Hare and Hounds as the 'leading commercial hotel in the district'.

In 1936, having established his credentials in club cricket, he was invited to play on two occasions for Somerset. He would begin brightly enough with a score of 29 against Sussex in his first knock, but that would prove the high point. The game against Cambridge University, their first ever visit to the County Ground at Taunton, proved a miserable affair. A newspaper report notes that 'with Gimblett in the test side, attendance was considerably below the average'. The fearless young smiter of the ball was already the main attraction. We are informed in the same article that 'early in the match, G. L. Ogilvy … had the misfortune, while racing for the ball, to pull a thigh muscle. He left the field in obvious pain and was attended by a doctor.' Later, Reggie Ingle was called away on urgent business, so that Somerset required two substitute fielders. With Geoffrey Ogilvy needed at the crease the following day, Horace

Hazel agreed to be his runner, though the innings ended in a run out. Later the rain came down and the match petered out, ending in an uneventful draw. Geoffrey came away with a first-class average of 14.66.

In 1937 he and Marguerite sold the Hare and Hounds and began a similar venture at the Lamb's Hotel in Ely. This was followed by spells in Anglesey, St Leonards-on-Sea and Hastings before a final move to the

THE
LEADING
COMMERCIAL
HOTEL
IN THE DISTRICT.

THE HARE & HOUNDS,
SHEPTON MALLET.
___
Good
Accommodation
for Travellers.

Spacious Dining and
Reception Rooms
NEW LOUNGE.

Full Particulars Apply the Proprietor

G. L. OGILVY.

G. L. Ogilvy – the years spent in the hospitality trade added to his waistline.

Isle of Man. He was now describing himself as a restaurateur rather than an hotelier. When he died at the age of fifty-five in Dreekskerry, Maughold, on the Isle of Man on 20 January 1962, he had left a note in his will, stating that he wished 'to place on record my grateful appreciation of all the loving kindness which my dear wife Marguerite has shown towards me and the way in which she has brought up our children'. It reads not just as a statement of uxorious devotion: more an acknowledgment that his endless round of new ventures was a cross his wife had been obliged to bear and perhaps an admission that he had spent too much time tending to his businesses or enjoying his leisure time engaging in cricket and golf. He was neither the first nor the last man to have done so.

337
Donald Edward Scott
10 June 1936 v. Sussex, Hove

Don Scott was born in Forest Gate, Essex, on 5 June 1898, one of three children of Mark Henry Scott and his wife, Catherine Amy (née Fogg), known as Kate. An early photograph, probably taken in 1907, shows the parents seated in the family car with Don seated in the front and brother Herbert Mark and sister Rona Ethel in the back. In 1911, his father, an engineer, moved his family to Frome in order to start a business, managing a 'motor works and general engineers'. A farsighted venture in the early days of the motor car, it was in fact the first garage in the town. M. H. Scott informed

Pioneering garage owner Mark Henry Scott sits in a motor car with son Don beside him: in the back (left to right) are Kate, daughter Rona and eldest child, Herbert.

Don Scott – a leading figure at Frome CC in the 1930s.

the public that his cars could undertake 'the work of several horses at the cost of one'. As well as selling and repairing cars, Mark Henry used his engineering skills to convert Ford cars into delivery vans. The two sons would inherit Scott's Garage – for so long a familiar landmark in Frome – and would continue to work together until the business was sold in 1969. It subsequently became known as Linwood Motors and is still in existence. The Scotts were a closely-knit family and would live together for some years in a large house in Vallis Way in the town. So closely-knit, in fact that Don had been married in 1922 to his first cousin, Kate Edith Fogg. Whether through choice or circumstances, the couple had no children.

Don and Herbert would both play together for Frome CC, with Don taking over from his brother as captain in the 1930s. Reports of his 'sound' batting suggest that he was possessed of a good technique and not a 'slogger'. He also bowled regularly for the club. He played on only one occasion for Somerset, batting at number six and averaging 12.00. He was also an enthusiastic member of the Frome Operatic and Dramatic Society and a member of its committee. During the 1940s he added the role of Chairman of the

Frome Fancier's Association, overseeing the annual awards for prize specimens of poultry, rabbits and such like.

He died as a result of bronchopneumonia at the age of eighty-two in St Aldhelm's Hospital, Frome, on 9th January 1981. His wife, Kate – who had known him throughout her life as a cousin, friend and then partner – died in the town eleven years later, at the age of ninety-four.

338
Rollo John Oliver Meyer
20 June 1936 v. Northamptonshire, Bath

Known as Jack or Boss, he was a maverick whose restless, enquiring mind, quick speech and animated gesturing left those around him either in awe or utterly bewildered. Born on 15 March 1905 in the rectory at Clophill in Berkshire, he was the son of the canon, Horace Rollo Meyer, and his wife Arabella Crosbie (née Ward). The family soon moved after the father's appointment to Watton-at-Stone in Hertfordshire. His parents encouraged free thinking. Alan Turing, who later established himself as a brilliant code breaker at Bletchley Park, spent much of his youth at the Meyer household, encouraged in his enquiries by Arabella Meyer. Jack's account of his upbringing invites scepticism, as with much that he uttered, sometimes venturing far-fetched stories or unexpected opinions for sheer devilment. His claims that he survived his childhood at times on a diet of potatoes or that his mother killed the family hens by feeding them rhubarb leaves so that he was obliged to shoot sparrows should both be taken with a pinch of salt. As for the facts: at the age of thirteen he won a scholarship to Haileybury, where he revealed a brilliant, innovative mind, an independent spirit and great skill as a cricketer. On arriving at Pembroke College, Cambridge, he made an immediate impact as a quick bowler and became a regular member of the Varsity team throughout his period as an undergraduate, taking a total of 133 wickets in 30 first-class games for Cambridge University. During the vacations he made appearances in Minor Counties matches for Hertfordshire.

After his graduation he was offered employment as a cotton broker in Bombay, but, never one to be tied down by rules and procedure, he hated the job. Cricket and rackets offered a diversion and the man who had been tipped by some as a future England player in fact played for India in 1926, as well as appearing for the Europeans.

279

Jack Meyer – never lost his impish love for the unexpected.

One of the many strokes of good fortune to come his way was that Ranjitsinhji – a brilliant cricketer from cricket's Golden Age – offered Jack a tutoring post in 1929. Word spread of his prowess as an inspirational teacher. Married in 1931 to Joyce Evelyn Symons, with whom he had two daughters, he was offered the opportunity, the following year, to oversee the Palace School in Dhrangadhre, created by the local Maharaja for his own children and those of his ministers and civil servants. With over 100 pupils, most of whom spoke very little English, Jack was obliged to resort to small class sizes, a policy he would later redeploy to great effect. When the Maharaja decided that his three sons required a proper English education, he suggested that Jack Meyer should found a new school within reach of London. Jack's mother, the irrepressible Arabella, then set about finding a large house for rent in the South of England. Doors were closed when she explained that 'coloured pupils' would need to be housed. The Clark family, Quakers based in Street and famous for their shoe-making business, took a more enlightened view and agreed to rent out Mill Field, as it was then called. In June 1935, Millfield school opened its doors to three sons of the Maharaja together with a further four Indian boys from Dhrangadhre. A mere two months later, there was a major setback when the Maharaja visited, only to conclude that five boys would be withdrawn as the school was too far from London. With only two boys to teach, most pioneers would have given up. But Arabella refused to allow her son to bow to ill fortune and by 1937, the numbers had climbed to twelve. In 1939, as much through necessity as an appetite for the unexpected, Jack took in the first girl student. The war would provide a boost, as some parents sought a safe haven, but the true turning point was when the cabinet minister (and future prime minister) Clem Attlee, whose son suffered from dyslexia, known then as 'word blindness', put his trust in Jack and was astonished at the turnaround. The numbers soon swelled. New facilities were needed and Jack used his contacts – having commanded the local Air Training Corps as a flight lieutenant – to take possession of the Nissen huts used by the US troops during the war but now vacated. By 1953, the future of the school looked assured and Millfield was set up as a charitable trust. With places in demand, Jack was able to adopt an unstructured approach to school fees where he set them on a pupil by pupil basis. The wealthy were asked to pay whatever he felt he could get away with charging and the talented poor were welcomed free of charge. Sporting prowess was a key criterion and Millfield is of course famed for the number of brilliant sportsmen among its alumni. Jack Meyer was awarded the OBE in 1967 for his services to education.

From the time of his arrival in Somerset, he would turn out regularly for the county. By then he had slowed as a bowler but had grown in maturity as a batsman, adding defence to his powerful attacking strokes, which included what Raymond Robertson-

R. J. O. Meyer – Millfield was his crowning achievement: a statue at the school acts as a permanent reminder of a man with a flair for the original.

Glasgow termed 'an extraordinarily vicious hook'. He would indeed score a double-century, later claiming – with his usual taste for devilment and invention – that he had proffered game of an unspecified type to bribe some of Lancashire's outfielders into ushering the ball over the boundary. Between 1936 and 1949, in sixty-five first-class matches for Somerset he would take 158 wickets at 28.31 apiece and would average 28.16 with the bat. *Wisden* spoke of:

> *A mercurial forcing batsman and a bowler who delivered just about everything under the sun at a slow-medium to medium pace. He was asked to captain Somerset CCC in 1947 and already afflicted with a chronically bad back and dodgy eyesight, he found his county in a similarly poor condition.*

As a player and as a captain he never lost his impish love for the unorthodox and although his teammates must have at times wondered what to expect, he was popular with the pros and amateurs alike. His generosity was legendary. From the small gesture – such as the time he reached into his back pocket and apologetically handed Arthur Wellard a pound note after dropping a catch in the slips – to the time he enthusiastically set about raising money for Wally Luckes after an outstanding season in which

Somerset's unassuming wicket-keeper had bolstered Jack's captaincy with a record number of dismissals.

A compulsive gambler, Jack's liquidity was subject to wild fluctuations and there were rumours, dismissed as nonsense and another flight of fancy in some quarters, that his light-hearted quip that he had gambled with Millfield funds was the reason for his replacement as headmaster in 1971 by another Somerset captain, Colin Atkinson.

After a spell as warden of the school, Jack was offered a fresh start when he was invited to become the first headmaster of St Lawrence College, near Athens, established along the lines of the English public school system.

Having retired to England, Jack Meyer died at the age of eighty-five at Kingsdown Hospital in Bristol on 9 March 1991.

Somerset's Dennis Silk stated in a tribute that 'Jack Meyer was a genius', adding that Millfield was the crowning achievement of a man with a 'flair for original, unorthodox solutions' who genuinely loved his pupils and wanted them to explore until they found whatever it was that they could excel at, because once they had unlocked the key, life 'ceased to be grey and humdrum'. In the end, no headstone could do justice to this extraordinary man. His ashes were scattered on the wicket at Millfield. Flippant to the last, he had suggested that the ashes of a dead man might add some much-needed life to the track.

339
George Baker Burrough
27 June 1936 v. Cambridge University, Taunton

George Burrough was born into a farming family in Butleigh, near Street, on 8 February 1907. His father, George Baker Burrough Snr and his mother, Sarah Melona (née Jones) were farmers managing Hill Farm in the village and George and his brother, Bob, were destined for a similar life. Educated at Wellington School in West Somerset, he later took to country pursuits, in particular hare coursing, where he owned a succession of fine racing greyhounds, 'Golden Seal' being preeminent among them. As well as participating with his own dogs, George was often called upon to act as the 'slipper' – the man charged with releasing two competing greyhounds simultaneously in pursuit of their quarry, ensuring that no unfair advantage could be gained. He was also a fine shot, skilful enough to win competitions. Cricket may have been a lesser sport in George's eyes, but he was rather good at it, turning out for Street, primarily

G. B. Burrough – 'subtly controlled and varied bowling', but hare coursing was his favoured pursuit.

as a right-arm off-spin bowler but also capable of making runs with the bat. One local press report describes him as 'an extremely talented if engagingly modest cricketer who took innumerable wickets with his clever spin bowling'. In his only appearance for Somerset he took 1 wicket for a total of 38 runs and, batting at number eleven, contributed 27 runs in a tenth-wicket partnership of 57 with Horace Hazell. It was a creditable performance and his lack of further first-class games owed everything to his commitments as a farmer.

The Burrough family were immersed in village life. Newspaper reports reveal George regularly among the honours at the annual village shows, winning prizes for his cheeses, roses and other exhibits. At the inaugural Glastonbury Horticultural, Arts & Crafts Society Show, for example, we read that:

> *Amongst the horticultural successes, Mr G Burrough of Butleigh took first prizes for everything he exhibited. His collection of fruit puzzled some folk, who knew plums, apples and redcurrants well enough but not mulberries.*

We should perhaps consider the presence of mulberries as akin to the occasional unexpected googly that had yielded positive results, taking Street CC's opponents by surprise.

He was married in 1939 to Eileen Linda (née Holloway), a Glastonbury girl, with whom he would have three children. The newly-weds took possession of Higher Rocks Farm in Butleigh, while George's brother, Bob, increasingly oversaw the running of Hill Farm, in time inheriting the place on the death of their father.

After the war, George was instrumental in reviving the Butleigh village cricket team. His performances were often noteworthy, his name appearing with some regularity in the *Wells Journal* Honours List. In the 1950 season alone, his off-spin delivered match-winning hauls of 7 wickets for 8 runs, 6 for 5, 5 for 12 and 5 for 13. Whilst the wickets may have offered some assistance and perhaps not all the teams they played were up to scratch, we are informed that 'his opponents in club cricket often found themselves hopelessly at sea when facing his subtly controlled and varied bowling', always accompanied by 'his disarming smile'. When he retired from the game, the side was disbanded for a while but reappeared with George as their President. He was also made an honorary life member.

His father, George Snr, had died in 1952. George Snr had been a no-nonsense employer who in 1922 was fined for having assaulted a labourer whom he suspected of having stolen some of his poultry. George Jnr on the other hand is invariably described as a benign character. By now a pillar of the local community and for many years Chairman of the Parish Council, he continued to manage his farm until his death in Butleigh on 9 May 1965 at the age of fifty-eight. There was genuine sadness among the people of the village for the loss of a kindly soul who had loved both the place where he farmed and the country pursuits he engaged in. Higher Rocks Farm was inherited by his son, Ray, who has continued the family tradition as a farmer and a club cricketer.

George Baker Burrough might well have had the ability to have made a successful career for himself in the first-class game, but he had neither the time nor the inclination to do so.

340
Arthur James Ricketts
1 July 1936 v. Surrey, Taunton

Arthur Ricketts must surely have endured among the most miserable of first-class cricketing careers. In damp conditions he fielded for 71 overs without being asked to bowl, while Surrey were winkled out for 196 runs. And then, scheduled to come in as the last batsman, he never got his chance, with the match being abandoned owing to rain with Somerset reeling on 38 for 8. If he had harboured any illusions about being anything other than a makeweight, then the events that had unfolded would have disabused him of the notion. The Somerset committee would have been unconcerned by Arthur's plight but more preoccupied with the fact that the match incurred a thumping financial loss. Later in the 1936 season he was invited at the eleventh hour to play against

Arthur Ricketts – neither batted nor bowled during his only appearance for Somerset.

Lancashire on the basis that R. J. O. Meyer had withdrawn, only for the decision to be reversed the following morning. In the event, Jack Meyer scored 202 not out in Somerset's second innings and Arthur bore no grudge.

The *Taunton Courier* noted in its report of the earlier fixture that 'Somerset gave a

*A. J. Ricketts– a slow left-arm
bowler who played for Watchet CC.*

trial as a professional to Arthur Ricketts of
Watchet, who has been recommended to them. He
is the third member of the Watchet club to play for
Somerset this season.' The others were Harold
Gimblett and Alan Pearse. In fact, Arthur would
have needed no introduction. In 1932 he had
played for W. G. Penny's XIV versus a Somerset
XIV along with an eighteen-year-old Harold
Gimblett. Opening the bowling, Arthur took six
wickets. In the same fixture the following year he
batted at number four while Gimblett, deployed as
a bowler, took five wickets. Both were considered
all-rounders at club level, with Arthur a left-handed
batsman and a slow left-arm bowler in the mould
of Somerset regulars Jack White and Horace Hazell
– which inevitably limited any opportunities.

He was born in Farmborough, a village near Bath, on 27 August 1913. His father,
Henry James Ricketts, was a bricklayer, married to Alice Maud (née Brooks). Arthur
would become a carpenter and joiner by trade but also attempted to supplement this
with income as a cricketer.

Having established his reputation at Watchet CC, Arthur moved for a while to
Chewton Mendip, and while based there was invited regularly to the indoor cricket
school at Cutlers Green in Essex, run by 'a Yorkshire gent named Captain R. Wilson'.
He would bowl at a number of batsmen, including first-class cricketers such as Colonel
Percy Robinson, formerly of Gloucestershire. In the time-honoured manner, half a
crown would be placed on the stumps and given to any bowler who dislodged it.
Arthur would reminisce that:

> I was a carpenter by trade and during the winter the County Ground pavilion was
> a carpenter's shop. I made a lot of slat seats for the members in front of the pavilion. I
> had no official contract – a little under £3 a week – and I lodged with Bill Hobbs, the
> Somerset scorer at the time. I used to bowl to visiting county sides having some batting
> practice in the nets. I think Taunton in the old days was a poor place to be for a young
> cricketer… Still, I'm lucky. I survived World War Two, did four years.

Such a sunny outlook on life must surely have been a necessity for the pros on the
margins of Somerset cricket. Even those who enjoyed notable success found the atti-
tudes they encountered a hard cross to bear. Former housemate and Somerset scorer,
Bill Hobbs, less robust than Arthur, took his own life not long after the county side

had parted company with him.

Arthur became a regular in club cricketing circles in Watchet and Williton, continuing to play for many years. Former teammates describe him as a quiet, gentle-natured man who was never a great one for socialising. He was never married and when he died at the age of eighty-six on 12 April 2000 in Williton Hospital, his estate was bequeathed to his older sister, Edna, and her three sons.

341
George Henry Rowdon
8 July 1936 v. Essex, Colchester

George Henry Rowdon.

George Rowdon was born on 6 October 1914 in Midsomer Norton, the son of Arthur James Rowdon, who ran the family's plumbing, decorating and building business and was married to Lily (née Gregory).

He played his club cricket for Midsomer Norton and captained the side for a number of seasons. An off-break bowler, he proved a regular wicket taker. He was also a very agile fielder and, when occasion demanded it, a competent wicket-keeper. His greatest triumphs, though, were as a technically correct opening batsman, consistently among the runs and compiling many centuries over the years. He attributed his success in part to the specially-made bats he was provided with by his good friend Harold Gimblett. Heavily weighted at the bottom and with a short handle, the bats suited the game of both players and Harold was always happy to pass on his spares. There was, however, a gulf in the runs accumulated by the two men. George played in only one first-class game for Somerset and averaged 5.50.

G. H. Rowdon – enjoyed a long and successful club career with Midsomer Norton CC.

Married in 1939 to a local girl, Mildred Rose Edgell, known informally as Millie, he would have two sons. Neil and Hugh Rowdon agree that he was an amiable man but 'a pretty strict disciplinarian' when it came to their upbringing. This extended to his coaching sessions in the local club nets where 'he was a stickler for playing the game 'the right way', with a straight bat'. Possessed of a competitive

George Rowdon is presented with the Somerset Knock-Out Cup by Bill Greswell (Somerset President and former player) in 1964.

spirit, George was always ready to ensure an advantage for his side. He would note, for example, when the visiting team had a pacey attack and would turn to the tin bath of slurry he kept at the ground, utilising the contents to slow the wicket. He also retained an encyclopaedic knowledge of opponents' strengths and weaknesses.

George continued in the family tradition and learned the plumbing trade. His grandfather, Arthur, who was a longstanding member of Somerset CCC, had begun the business operating from his home on Midsomer Norton High Street. There is still a transom window above the door of Number 31 bearing the legend 'A. J. Rowdon & Son'. It is now the subject of a preservation order, ensuring that a connection with the town's past remains in place for posterity. Although George volunteered for the Second World War, he was turned down after a blood test revealed that he was suffering from anaemia. The recruiting officer jokingly informed him that he should have been receiving rather than giving blood. George therefore worked for the duration of the war in a nearby factory, involved in the assembly of batteries for military equipment.

Once he had taken over the family business, he offered his services as a plumber on a 24-hour-call-out basis throughout the 1950s and 1960s, gaining a reputation for his cheery, efficient service in all weathers. He continued to play cricket for his town until the age of fifty-five and went on to coach the youth team until he was approaching seventy years old. A high point in a successful club career was winning the twenty-over Somerset Knock-Out Cup in 1964. Captaining a Midsomer Norton side that included his two sons, he led them to victory at the County Ground in Taunton. He was later made President of the club he had served so well as a player.

His other great love was badminton. He played the game to a high standard and became Secretary and President of the Avon and Somerset Badminton Association. The George Rowdon & Sid Moxon Tournament is still held in North East Somerset.

Sport remained his overriding passion, as a participant, coach, administrator and spectator, although he was also a keen birdwatcher, spending time pursuing the hobby with his wife, Millie, while they walked the Mendip Hills. After his retirement from cricket and badminton, they were able to spend more time together in this way. Indeed, it was after one such trip that, closing the garage doors of their home in Midsomer Norton, he collapsed and died of a heart attack while Millie was in the house, brewing a cup of tea. His death occurred on 14 February 1987. He was seventy-two at the time.

342
Richard Southcombe
11 July 1936 v. Worcestershire, Yeovil

Richard Southcombe, known as Dick, was born in Taunton on 22 November 1909, the second of three sons of Sidney Lincoln Southcombe and his wife Sarah Florence (née Camby), known as Florence. Dick's paternal grandfather had set up a glove manufacturing business at Stoke-sub-Hamdon, near Yeovil, in 1847. The glove-making industry was concentrated around Yeovil on the basis of the water there, ideal for the tanning of leather. At one time there were approximately fifty separate manufacturers in the region, and Richard Snr had had the sense to start his enterprise in the village that acted as a staging post on the London to Bath road, with a ready supply of customers. The business thrived, soon employing nearly two hundred members of staff and extending into the manufacture of shirts and spats.

Educated privately in Weston-super-Mare, Dick was sent on leaving school to work in Manchester in the offices of Horrocks, a well-known manufacturer of cotton goods, while older brother Douglas was groomed to take over the family business in the full-

Dick Southcombe – a stylish batsman and a talented rugby player.

ness of time. While living in the North West, Dick played on the wing for Sale RFC. A naturally gifted ball player, he was a tall, powerfully built man with a good turn of speed. He was spoken of at the time as a possible England player. Then in 1928 the death of his father meant that Dick would return to the Yeovil area to help manage the business (now renamed as Southcombe Brothers Ltd) along with brothers Douglas and Wilfred (always known as 'Bunny'). Dick oversaw the setting up of a new venture when he brought the tanning process in-house. The brothers must have made a success of things because, despite the rise of global competition and the collapse of the vast majority of glove manufacturing in the UK, the company is still extant, offering luxury and specialist leather gloves. In truth, although Dick worked hard to develop the business, it was never an obsession. Sport, on the other hand, was something he turned to at every available opportunity. He was married in 1934 to Betty Strange, daughter of a farmer from Spetisbury in Dorset. Betty, too, was a sportswoman, a county hockey player who later took up golf. Their only son, Peter, would be handed the reins of the tanning business at the earliest opportunity.

Back in 1928, having returned from Lancashire, Dick had thrown himself wholeheartedly into the local sporting scene, captaining the Yeovil rugby and cricket teams for a number of years. A stylish batsman, his orthodox stroke-making was a joy to behold and he also bowled off-breaks as and when required and was a fine slip fielder. He was called up to play cricket for Somerset on two occasions – once in each of the 1936 and 1937 seasons – but mustered a batting average of only 5.00.

During the Second World War he was commissioned as a flight controller in the RAF. In the latter stages of the war he was on the first flight into Kastrup Airport (Copenhagen) when Denmark was liberated and subsequently he helped to oversee flights in and out of the region by Allied aircraft.

On returning to Somerset, Dick decided that he had been too long out of the game to take up cricket again in any serious way and turned his attention to golf. He soon outgrew the Windwhistle golf course, near Chard, and he and Betty became regulars at the Yeovil Golf Club, which he would serve with distinction for many years. He captained the Dorset team from 1960 until 1962 and later became Honorary Secretary and Chairman. He was also Chairman and President of Yeovil Golf Club. Such was the debt of gratitude felt by the Yeovil club that a memorial to him stands at the fifteenth tee.

His son, Peter, reveals that Dick was effective as a leader because of his charm and ability to persuade others to help the cause. He also has vivid memories of playing for his school versus the team's fathers and fielding while Dick, obliged to play with a bat sawn at half width, was still able repeatedly to stroke the ball beautifully to the boundary. Peter's wife, Frances, adds that her father-in-law was 'a lovely man, a real gentleman' who showed her how to play golf with infinite patience. She modestly adds that he failed in his mission though through no fault of his.

After suffering a stroke in 1988, Dick Southcombe died at the age of eighty-five at a nursing home in Yeovil on 3 August 1995.

R. Southcombe – after a brief first-class cricketing career he became a leading figure in Yeovil golfing circles.

343
Foster Moverley McRae
22 August 1936 v. Worcestershire, Kidderminster

Peter McRae, as he was known, was born on 12 February 1916 in Buenos Aires. His father, Sydney Spencer Redgrave McRae was something of an adventurer, married to Sophie (née Moverley). Sydney spent much of his working life in South America,

F. M. McRae – 'these boys who have gone were the flower of our race'.

describing himself at various times as an engineer, merchant, courier and traveller. He would be married for a second time in 1939, outliving his new wife – twenty-three years his junior – and dying at the age of ninety-six.

Peter and his sister, Sheila, were adopted at a young age by Rev. Percy Shattock, vicar of Kingston St Mary, near Taunton, and his wife Ethel, and this is perhaps the time when he took on his new name. Percy and Ethel had been married in 1907, while both in their thirties, and had no children of their own. Percy Shattock had been an excellent sportsman, winning a blue at tennis while at Keble College, Oxford, although in later life he was dogged by ill health. He died in 1937 after twenty-one years at Kingston St Mary and is described as 'a tall, spare figure and a kindly presence'. Perhaps he had seen a kindred spirit when adopting Peter who was a bright and sporty but sickly child.

Sent to Christ's Hospital in Sussex, Peter then went on to study Medicine at the University of London. He played rugby as a three-quarter for St Mary's Hospital while he worked there and for Taunton on his visits home. He also played for the Barbarians and was selected for an England trial in 1937 but was forced to withdraw, owing to a leg injury. He also overcame his lack of robust health to become an excellent cricketer. Stanley Nelson, writing in *The People* in 1945 refers to 'F. McRae, whose brilliant fielding and adventurous batting could make even Bramall-lane [sic] attractive'. Elsewhere, it is reported that 'he was worth 30 or 40 runs before he ever took guard, being a superb fielder at cover or extra-cover'. Having made his debut in 1936 as a twenty-year-old undergraduate, he would play on 25 occasions for Somerset, averaging 24.30 with the bat. By 1939 he was maturing as a player and was second only to Harold Gimblett in the county's averages. He scored one century in that year, against Hampshire at Taunton.

After qualifying as doctor he volunteered for the Royal Navy as a lieutenant surgeon where it was his misfortune to be aboard HMS *Mahratta* when it was sunk by a U-Boat on 25 February 1944 in the Barents Sea. The ship was part of a convoy to Russia and the first torpedo had struck at dusk, leading to the order to abandon ship.

While the lifeboats were being lowered, a second torpedo hit midships, according to a report 'smashing all the boats and killing most of the crew.' The report adds that 'seventeen survivors scrambled onto a crowded Carley Float with their doctor'. Aware that the float was inadequate to deal with so heavy a cargo, Peter McRae quietly announced that he appeared to be in the way, let go of the inflatable craft and was never seen again. He was only twenty-eight when he died and it was a mercy that he left no wife or children. He is commemorated on the Portsmouth Naval Memorial.

Raymond Robertson-Glasgow said of Peter McRae that 'none who knew him could resist him, with his charm, his modesty, and the gentle humour that goes with the bravest hearts'. Speaking after the war, Lord Moran, at the time President of the Royal College of Physicians cited the example of Peter McRae, observing that 'he came to us ... a frail boy and became one of the great athletes of his time. But what endeared him to us all was the 'kick' he got out of everything in life – his quiet gusto ... These boys who have gone were the flower of our race ... If they did this for us surely, surely we shall do this for them – we shall go forward into the future without bitterness and without faction.'

Peter McRae – 'a superb fielder at cover or extra-cover'.

1937

"It was really Andrews's season. He bowled beautifully,
always full length, always noisily expressive."
David Foot in Sunshine, Sixes and Cider

Championship Position: 13 of 17

Bill Andrews became only the fourth Somerset player to complete the double. Andrews and Arthur Wellard took nearly 280 wickets between them. At The Oval, in June, Andrews took 8 for 12 in Surrey's second innings, setting up an unexpected chance of victory. Wellard was at his brilliant, brutal best with the bat and had steered his side to within 11 runs of victory when his partner, the amateur Seymour Molyneux, was run out, leaving Arthur high and dry on 91 not out.

Frank Lee had a fine season with the bat, accumulating well over 1,800 runs, including four centuries, though, as David Foot notes in his history of the club, 'there were few innings that you could recall a decade later'. Harold Gimblett provided more excitement but less consistency and might have matched Lee's haul had he not missed six matches owing to a thigh strain.

In July, Arthur Wellard won the first of his two England caps. During the Weston Festival, Jack White announced his intention to retire at the end of the season. J. C. White's contribution to Somerset's cause had been immense. Already a major force before the First World War, he had taken more than 100 wickets in thirteen consecutive seasons from 1919 and had twice achieved the double. As for the debutants, their contributions proved marginal.

The new President, Dick Palairet – a former Somerset player who had proved his credentials as an administrator at Surrey and on the Bodyline Tour of Australia – announced that Reggie Ingle had resigned. Many believed that the captain had been given little choice but to do so. It would lead in time to a self-imposed exile on the part of Ingle, who perhaps had reasons to feel aggrieved. Fellow Bath solicitor Bunty Longrigg was announced as the new captain.

344
Paul Seymour Morthier Molyneux
22 May 1937 v. Leicestershire, Leicester

P.S.M.Molyneux

Seymour Molyneux was born in Wells on 12 January 1906. His mother was Clara Tilton (née Conner). His father, Edward Paul Molyneux, a schoolmaster, would later move the family to Streatham Hill, where he ran a small private school. He was sent to Allhallows School in Devon, a county where both parents had roots, and here he excelled at cricket, rugby and athletics, winning the Victor Ludorum for two years in succession. Rugby was perhaps his best sport and he went on to play for Exeter RFC. Entries in the school magazine about Seymour the cricketer are muted. We are told in one report that 'Molyneux very foolishly threw his wicket away attempting an impossible run'. A scan through the scorecards confirms that 'run out' was Seymour's dismissal of choice. In his final year, his coach concedes that he is 'a very good bat of the aggressive type who scores very quickly … [and] a good field'.

He chose to pursue a career in Ceylon's (Sri Lanka's) thriving tea industry, moving there in 1925. Initially, he was Assistant Manager at the Talawakelle Tea Group in Dimbula, Nuwara Eliya. Here he found time to indulge his passion for cricket, whilst also representing Ceylon at rugby and hockey, the latter against the Indian Olympic Hockey Team.

He was married in 1929 to Audrey Helen Worth, the daughter of Harold Lindsay Worth, a successful tea and rubber planter. The couple returned to the UK on leave in 1930, staying with Audrey's parents, who had recently retired to Exmouth. Six months later, Seymour and Audrey returned to Nuwara Eliya in Ceylon. The sporting and social facilities for the colonial tea planters of the hill country were exceptional. Seymour played for and captained the Dimbula Athletic and Cricket Club throughout his time there, acquiring the moniker 'Moly'. His club combined with others in the area to form an Up-Country side once a year to play Colombo CC. Playing alongside or against him were fellow Somerset cricketers W. T. Greswell and F. A. Waldock.

Seymour and Audrey returned to Exmouth in April 1937. It afforded an opportunity for him to play English cricket that summer, including six games for Somerset. His appearances for the county probably resulted from his connection with Bill Greswell, although his efforts were less noteworthy than Bill's. His highest score in ten innings was 25 and his batting average was 9.40. Despite being a competent off-

Seymour Molyneux was included in the Somerset XI who played Leicestershire at Leicester in 1937.
STANDING: H. L. Hazell, C. K. Linney, W. H. R. Andrews, A. W. Wellard, W. N. Bunce,
H. F. T. Buse. SEATED: W. T. Luckes, R. Southcombe, G. M. Bennett, P. S. M. Molyneux, F. S. Lee.

spin bowler, he was not asked to bowl. His was the last wicket to fall in a thrilling finish against Surrey at The Oval. Forgetting all the lessons his school coach had drummed into him, he was run out attempting to give Arthur Wellard the strike with one over remaining. Wellard was on 91 not out and is said to have turned to Alf Gover, who was to bowl the final over, and muttered darkly about the blight of amateurs in first-class cricket. Seymour's failure to make any further appearances was not a judgement on his skills as a runner between the wickets but a result of the injury that had had him put down the batting order. He returned shortly thereafter to Ceylon.

During the Second World War, he served with the Indian Army and in the latter stages of the conflict was a major, second in command of the 6th Battalion of the 15th Punjab Regiment, engaged in fighting the Japanese in the Far East. The Allhallows school magazine has an entry for October 1944, stating that 'the first swallow has arrived. The first Christmas card of the year from Seymour Molyneux. He hopes to be demobilised early in December when he returns to Ceylon.'

Prior to the war, Seymour and Audrey had been friends of a fellow tea planter, Robert Burnaby, and his wife Daphne Lesley Madeleine (née Parmenter) but the enforced separation during the war had placed a strain on both marriages and Seymour and Daphne would later be drawn together while their partners were out of the country. By 1949, they were visiting the UK, with Daphne travelling under the surname of Molyneux. Divorce followed for both couples and Seymour married Daphne Burnaby in Ceylon in April 1953. His first wife, Audrey, was never remarried and died in Honiton, Devon, in October 1991.

Seymour and Daphne continued to live in Ceylon until 1956 when he went to work for Matterson & Bosanquet, in Coonoor, Tamil Nadu, India, where Nilgiri tea is produced. Ten years later they retired to Hove in East Sussex. Seymour and Daphne had no children together. Following a stroke, he died at the age of seventy-four in the Brighton General Hospital on the 13 March 1980. Daphne died in Eastbourne in 1998.

345
Edward John Hack
12 June 1937 v. Lancashire, Old Trafford

Edward John Hack.

Edward Hack was referred to in all bar the most formal of situations as Son, a name bestowed on him at a young age by his sister, Lucy. He was born in Clevedon on 1 October 1913. His parents, William Henry and Ruth, resided at the Excelsior Club in the town. The institution had been built for the young men of St Andrew's Church following a donation of land by a Miss Woodward, using some of her inheritance as a member of the Stuckey Bank dynasty. William and Ruth acted as the caretaker managers of the club and lived in residence with their offspring. Son was the youngest of six children.

He was for many years the opening batsman of Clevedon CC and consistently among the runs, with local press reports suggesting that he was an accumulator of runs rather than an aggressive batsman. Although he also kept wicket on occasions and bowled for the club, it was primarily for his success as a batsman that the county called on him. He was also a talented footballer, selected in 1939 by Somerset, whose captain at the time was fellow county cricketer Brian Gomm of West Bromwich Albion.

In his only game for the Somerset cricket team, Son scored 6 runs in his one innings in a drawn game. Although he was mentioned as a possible player immediately after the Second World War, he was never chosen again. During the war he served as a lance corporal with the 7th Battalion of the Somerset Light Infantry. The *Shepton Mallet Journal* paints an interesting cameo of life for the battalion immediately after the war. Under the direction of Major Durie, a *sportplatz* was converted into a cricket ground, in his words 'to establish a corner of England where men could relax and enjoy cricket

Son Hack – represented Somerset at both cricket and football .

played in surroundings as similar to the home club grounds as possible'. It was perhaps deemed a higher priority than establishing shelter for any of the defeated Germans whose homes had been bombed. The ground came complete with heavy and light rollers and a pavilion adorned with the crest of the Somerset Light Infantry. The report concludes with a note that the efforts at creating this paradise were hampered by the lack of equipment:

During the tea interval of a match last week in which he had made 61 runs, Lance Corporal E. J. Hack of The Excelsior Club, Clevedon, Somerset, referring to this lack of equipment, said that the shortage of cricket bats and balls had become so acute that unless some were forthcoming in the near future it would be impossible to play further matches.

Son would in fact go on to enjoy a hugely successful time playing for the Somerset Light Infantry. Some bats were clearly found. Indeed the battalion newsletter notes in October 1945 that 'it has been L/Cpl Hack's year. The stamina of this remarkably consistent all-rounder is quite amazing … He has been the very backbone of the side and our many victories are largely due to his great efforts with bat and ball.'

A wartime marriage in 1942 to Jean Ethel (née Thompson) ended in divorce and was followed in 1951 by his marriage to Joan (née Pallent), which proved happy and long lasting. He and Joan had four children – three sons and a daughter. From 1955, Son worked in the role of Senior Clerk for the South Western Gas Board, based in Bath. He retired in 1977. Rev. Arthur Hack says of his father:

A modest man, dad reluctantly gave into my pleading and turned out to make up the numbers for the Parents XI in 1964 in my first year at City of Bath Boys' School. Despite no longer playing regularly and being tossed the ball by the skipper as a last resort, dad promptly demolished the School First XI with a heady mixture of swing, cutters and even leg-breaks, all delivered with scarcely a change in his action.

Having remained in Bath after his retirement, Son Hack died in the city on 20 September 1987 at the age of seventy-three.

1938

"With Mr M. D. Lyon's regular attendance and with
the addition of Buse to the professional strength, the
captain had nine regular players, leaving only two
places to be filled."

Richard Palairet (President and Former Player)

Championship Position: 7 of 17

At last Somerset had a settled team with a strong core of players available through-out the season. Bertie Buse proved a useful addition to the roster of contracted pros with in excess of 1,000 runs and over sixty wickets. Although Harold Gimblett's progress had faltered, he still managed to score more than 1,300 runs. He was upstaged by Frank Lee, with over 2,000 runs and seven centuries, a county record. Bill Andrews completed another double, although his bowling partner, Arthur Wellard, was outstanding with a record 169 wickets for Somerset. Wally Luckes had another excellent season, playing his part in seventy-four dismissals. Their captain, Bunty Longrigg, had been fortunate to inherit a well-balanced team, but he made the pros feel valued and proved an ebullient leader.

Some close finishes added to the excitement as the season progressed. Three tight games were won with minutes to spare. The pick of the bunch was arguably the game against Gloucestershire at Taunton in front of a packed crowd. Wally Hammond had set up a declaration with a magisterial 140 not out before Arthur Wellard had bludg-eoned Somerset to within sight of the target with a knock of 68. With only four deliveries left to play, one wicket remaining and four runs required, Wally Luckes had lofted an attempted boundary. Clapp had charged forward and dived to take the catch. The ball had fallen just short of him and had carried for four, sparking wild celebrations.

With a satisfactory seventh place in the Championship after a record-breaking ten wins and the bank balance a heady £2,835 in credit, surely the facts were staring the committee in the face. The age of amateurism had passed. Professionals represented a sound investment and not a drain on costs. Only the staunchest of traditionalists would have been blind to the evidence.

The season's only debutant, Trevor Jones, became the youngest player to have registered a century for the county. He let it be known that he was seeking a professional contract. The traditionalists of course rebuffed him.

A representative Somerset XI (including eight county players) who played North Warwickshire at Coventry in 1938: the three men annotated 'WsM' were members of Weston-super-Mare CC. STANDING: H. L. Hazell, S. Hayward (WsM), A. W. Wellard, P. Bridges (WsM), J. A. Rigby (WsM). SEATED: H. F. T. Buse, H. Gimblett, W. T. Luckes, W. H. R. Andrews, W. F. Baldock, F. S. Lee

346
Archibald Trevor Maxwell Jones
11 June 1938 v. Nottinghamshire, Taunton

Trevor Jones was born on 9 April 1920 in Wells, the son of Archibald George Jones, a motor engineer who was regarded as a fine club cricketer for Wells City CC and was married to Muriel (née Webb). A pupil at Wells Cathedral School, Trevor was introduced into the Wells City CC team as a thirteen-year-old, already showing rich promise. He was recommended to Somerset by, among others, Sam Weaver, a well-known international footballer who would also go on to play for the county. At the time of his introduction to the Somerset side, Trevor was eighteen and had just left school. The *Wells Journal* describes him as 'a batsman of exceptional merit, a useful spin bowler, and likely to develop into a first-class all-rounder'. Excitement reached fever pitch when, at the age of 18 years and 104 days he came in at number 9 in a match at Leicestershire and, sharing a partnership of 146 with Wally Luckes, went on to become the county's youngest century maker. According to the writer David Foot, most of the team had already changed and packed their bags, wrongly anticipating an innings defeat.

Trevor Jones – established a record as Somerset's youngest century-maker.

Trevor had by now been offered a job with Imperial Tobacco, who always had an eye to strengthening their cricket team. He made polite overtures to Somerset, letting it be known that he would rather develop his skills as a pro than be trapped in an office. His promise was noted in *Wisden* who felt that he could, with 'greater experience'

develop into a fine player, but Somerset prevaricated. Playing as and when he could, he never quite managed to repeat his heroics. After another season the Second World War intervened.

He served with the North Somerset Yeomanry in the Middle East before returning to an administrative role at Imperial, where he would remain until 1958. Between 1938 and 1948 he was available for only twenty-one first-class matches and came away with a disappointing batting average of 11.40 and 3 wickets at 44.00 apiece. There is a sense of an opportunity missed. As if to emphasise the point he scored runs freely for Imperial and Bristol Optimists and in 1949, the year after he and Somerset parted company, he went on to score more than 1,000 runs in Saturday matches for Imperial. There was no animosity and he retained his connections with the county, regularly attending dinners for the Somerset Former Players' Association and chairing the group in the last years of his life.

A. T. M. Jones – cricket, gardening and bridge were his abiding passions.

He was married in 1946 to Inez Le Patourel, who hailed from St Austell in Cornwall and was known as Pat, and they would have two sons and a daughter. After leaving Imperial Tobacco, he ran a mushroom farm in North Somerset for twenty years before managing The George Hotel in Frome with his brother, Derek, between 1979 and 1982. He then moved with Pat to St Merryn, near Padstow in Cornwall, where he found time to indulge his passions for gardening and the game of bridge, at which he was exceptional and said to be close to international standard. He was the leading light in the Cornish bridge scene until he was obliged to undergo a triple heart bypass operation.

He died at Truro Hospital on 17 June 2005 at the age of eighty-five.

1939

"And so to 1939 which was rather a nightmare."
Bill Andrews in The Hand that bowled Bradman

Championship Position: 14 of 17

An experimental eight-ball over was introduced to the County Championship. Whether or not this contributed to niggling injury problems for quicker bowlers is unclear but both of Somerset's strike bowlers – Andrews and Wellard – were absent at times owing to injury, though this failed to stop them claiming 261 wickets between them. Bertie Buse and Horace Hazell offered useful support. Harold Gimblett was in scintillating form and might have topped 2,000 runs had the season not been curtailed. Frank Lee again accumulated runs – over 1,400 of them – and Bertie Buse also scored more than 1,000. In a year notable for injuries to the pros, Wally Luckes chipped a bone in his hand and was replaced for a number of games by Frank Lee.

Somerset's professionals (from left to right): W. T. Luckes, H. Gimblett, F. S. Lee, W. H. R. Andrews, A. W. Wellard, H. F. T. Buse.

COURTESY OF BARRY PHILLIPS

The Somerset XI who played Worcestershire in a tied match at Kidderminster in 1939.
STANDING: H. L. Hazell, H. Gimblett, A. W. Wellard, H. F. T. Buse, F. S. Lee, W. T. Luckes.
SEATED: S. Weaver, G. M. Bennett, E. F. Longrigg, F. M. McRae, J. Priddy.

This was Arthur Wellard's benefit year and a record sum was raised for the hugely popular and lion-hearted entertainer. Among the debutants, Geoffrey Fletcher and Hugh Watts had both shown signs of rich promise. Of the two, only Watts would survive the Second World War.

There was much excitement at Kidderminster, where a low-scoring game against Worcestershire ended in a tie. Horace Hazell had clawed Somerset back into contention with a bowling analysis of 5 for 6 in the second innings. The scores were level as Hazell, instead of nudging the winning single, for some unaccountable reason had a rush of blood, went for glory and was clean bowled. There had only been three County Championship ties in the inter-war years. Somerset had been a participant in all three.

The fixture list was foreshortened for reasons unrelated to cricket.

347
Anthony John Patrick Ling
5 July 1939 v. Essex, Westcliff-on-Sea

A J Ling

With a sense of irony, *The People* notes in 1939 that 'for their match with Essex at Westcliff-on-Sea, Somerset introduced a newcomer to first-class cricket in A. J. P. Ling, of Limpley Stoke – that well-known Zummerzet village.' Pat Ling was not the first man to have been poached from Wiltshire. He was born on 10 August 1910 in Skewen, near Neath, in Glamorgan and was the son of a civil engineer, John Richardson Ling, and his wife, Mabel.

Pat attended Stowe School, joining the institution in September 1923, six months after its foundation. He was appointed captain of the cricket First XI in 1928 and also played for the rugby XV and was made head boy. Press reports of 1929 show him as

head boy, greeting the future King of England, Prince George, on his visit to the school. He was also captain of Wiltshire Colts that year and is described as 'an attractive left-handed batsman'. Between 1930 and 1934 he played for Carlisle while he was based there, working in business, and was said to be 'a prolific run-maker', performing well enough to be selected for the Border League XI versus a Scotland XI. His parents had hailed from Cumberland and he was perhaps staying with family members as he alternated between playing for Carlisle and, on occasions, for Wiltshire. Between 1934 and 1936 he would make nine appearances for Glamorgan, averaging 19.20 with the bat. An enthusiastic local press reporter informs us that 'a former Carlisle player, who was always a favourite at Philiphaugh, is hitting the high spots down Glamorgan way. He is A.

A. J. P. Ling – 'an attractive left-handed batsman' and a poultry and pig farmer.

J. P. Ling, the noted batsman and bowler. A 37 not out on Saturday against Leicester[shire] looks good to me.' Glamorgan declined to utilise his skills as a bowler to any significant degree. He took no wickets in his two overs for them.

In 1937, by now establishing a business as a pig and poultry farmer at Stoke Limpley, he was married to Kathleen Marjorie Greaves, known as Maisie, daughter of a Wiltshire JP. Still a keen cricketer and playing a number of times for Somerset Stragglers, he was presuaded to turn out for Somerset in five first-class fixtures during the 1939 season, but averaged only10.66. The *Somerset County Gazette* describes him at the time as 'a good defensive bat who can force the pace on occasions'.

Exempted from serving in the Second World War owing to the need to manage his farm, he acted as an ARP warden for the duration. Having retired from the farming business with no children to pass the entrreprise on to, he moved to Eastbourne, where he died on 12 January 1987 at the age of seventy-six.

348
Samuel Weaver
5 July 1939 v. Essex, Westcliff-on-Sea

Sam Weaver was the seventh child of a miner, Eli Weaver and his wife, Martha. He was born in Pilsley, Derbyshire, on 8 February 1909 and, had it not been for his talent as a sportsman, was destined for a similar life. Indeed, despite showing rich promise as a schoolboy footballer, Sam spent two years down the mines while playing football for local teams in Derbyshire. Spotted by Hull City at the age of nineteen, he was offered what he regarded as the princely sum of £6 a week during the season and £4 during the summer months, with a bonus of £2 per win. Sam would retain the wiry strength and determination to succeed characteristic of so many young men from the Midland or Northern coalfields, driven by their desire never to return to working in the pits.

In 1929, Newcastle United came knocking on his door and he would remain with them from 1929 until 1936, becoming something of a cult hero in those parts and latterly captaining the side. An FA Cup winner in 1932, Sam would suffer the bitter taste of failure the following season, when, perhaps typically, Newcastle fell away and conspired to embrace relegation. 5 ft 10 inches tall and an uncompromising but stylish left-half, he is credited with being the inventor of the long throw-in. Regularly able to project the ball upwards of 35 yards, on one occasion at St James's Park in a game

Sam Weaver – England footballer and pioneer of the long throw-in.

against Huddersfield, he surprised everyone by clearing attackers and defenders alike with the ball sailing immediately into touch. His astonished colleagues were allowed to mark the spot and measured the distance after the game as fully 48 yards. Writing in an article, he explained the technique:

The length obtained does not depend primarily upon sheer physical force, but upon skilful use of the back muscles. Actually, you use your back as a kind of lever.

He could equally well have been talking about pace bowling, which was his forte as a cricketer.

Sam was awarded three England football caps over the 1932 and 1933 seasons. The last of the three (when Scotland defeated England 2-1 at Hampden Park) was witnessed by a crowd of 134,710.

In 1936 he was transferred to Chelsea whom he would captain from 1938 until the outbreak of war. During the war years he made guest appearances for Leeds United and Derby County and afterwards appeared for two seasons with Stockport County before learning the ropes of management in supporting roles firstly at Leeds and then at Millwall. In 1954 he threw in his lot with Mansfield Town and something akin to a love affair blossomed. For twenty-five years he was associated with the club as coach, manager, trainer, physiotherapist and chief scout. Over many of the summers he was hired by the Derbyshire cricket team as their physiotherapist. He was awarded a testimonial in 1981with a fixture against Wolves.

Sam Weaver – an F. A. Cup winner with Newcastle United.

What of his cricket and his connection with Somerset? He was married in 1936 to Nora Louise Lyons who hailed from Midsomer Norton in Somerset and with whom he would have four children. The burgeoning family would decamp each summer to his mother-in-law's house in the Somerset town. A left-arm seam bowler, Sam had already played for Derbyshire Second XI and enjoyed regular success as a club player in Somerset. He would play twice for the county in 1939, generating much excitement but enjoying rather less success than he had done in his other sporting career. He averaged 12.50 with the bat and conceded 63 runs without taking a wicket. He was 3 not out in his second and final match, against Worcestershire and standing at the non-striker's end, watching events unfold as the amiable and normally dependable Horace Hazell lost his head with only one run required for victory and was clean bowled, with the result that the match was tied.

Such excitement was a distant memory when Sam died at the age of seventy-six on 15 April 1985 at Basford on the outskirts of Nottingham. His ashes were scattered on his beloved Mansfield Town's pitch at Field Mill.

349
Brian Arthur Gomm
26 July 1939 v. Essex, Wells

Brian Gomm was born in Castle Cary on 24 June 1918, the only child of Arthur and Lucy. His father was headmaster of the local primary school, having followed his own mother, Florence, into the teaching profession. Educated at Sexey's Grammar School in Bruton, where he proved an outstanding footballer, cricketer and athlete, Brian left school at the age of eighteen, having already attracted the attention of at least one football scout. A letter addressed to his headmaster reads:

I am led to understand that there is a lad at your school named Gomm who is rather above the average in ability as a soccer player ... I may be able to do the lad some good permanently, but of course would consult and interview his parents first of all

He is described at the time as being 6 feet tall and 12 stone in weight. His career as a footballer began at Shepton Mallet but he was soon playing for Yeovil & Petters United as an inside-right and on occasions as a centre forward. He also played for Corinthians and became captain of the Somerset football team.

Brian would in fact decline the opportunity to become a professional footballer and opt to train at Dudley College to be a History teacher. While studying at Dudley he played regularly for West Bromwich Albion Reserves and would return in the 1945-6 season to appear four times in the First XI, still playing as an amateur.

In 1939 he was offered a teaching post not as a History master but as a Physical Training instructor in Smethwick. He was first required to complete his training at Carnegie College (part of Leeds University). His career then took an unexpected turn when he began a period of military training at Catterick at the outset of the Second World War. Within a week, he was granted leave to play cricket for Somerset in two fixtures. A report in the *Western Morning News* informs us that the twenty-one-year-

Brian Gomm of West Bromwich Albion FC.

old was 'a good batsman, he has made some substantial scores for the Somerset Second Team'. He had also appeared on a number of occasions for the West Midlands club side West Bromwich Dartmouth CC.

A right-handed batsman and medium-pace left-arm bowler, he made little impression in the first-class game, averaging 2.33 with the bat and taking no wickets at a cost of 21 runs in his two appearances for Somerset.

In 1941 he was appointed a second lieutenant in the Indian Armoured Corps. His superior officer, Lt A. Singh would later recount that on being informed of Brian's prowess as a bowler, he delegated the task of aiming grenades at the enemy, noting that 'thanks to the bowling of Brian Gomm, the Italians were on the run and there was no sign of them within half an hour'. He was subsequently transferred to the Royal Corps of Signals as a captain in 1942, though in November of that year, having already been mentioned in despatches, he was taken as a prisoner of war, captured by the Italians near Tobruk. There would be no more pitching of grenades with a persistently accurate line and length.

Brian would represent the Army in a number of fixtures after the war, playing alongside the likes of Herbert Sutcliffe and Wally Hammond, jokingly describing the latter as 'henpecked'. Married in 1947 to Elsie Jeanette (née Brewer), known as Jeanette – although her husband and the family always referred to her as 'Johnny' – the couple would have a son and two daughters. Brian would remain in the forces until 1955, obtaining the rank of major and serving as a careers officer before

B. A. Gomm – continued his cricketing career with the Army.

becoming an instructor at Sandhurst.

After returning to civilian life in 1955 he joined Perkins Engines in Peterborough. Friends and family considered it a brave decision to resign his commission and endure the company's management trainee programme. Jeanette would describe it as 'the worst year of my life'. Her husband was, however, soon enjoying a hugely successful career with Perkins, becoming a company director. After an initial posting as Deputy Managing Director of the Indian subsidiary, he had spells overseeing the subsidiaries in Johannesburg and then Melbourne. There followed a period as Global Sales Manager, based in Peterborough, and then European Manager, when, interestingly, he was approached by British Intelligence and invited to put his military and business acumen to the test by spying on the Russians – an offer he immediately declined. Tight-lipped secrecy was never likely to appeal to so gregarious and open a man. Later he was appointed Managing Director of the German operation. He remained with Perkins until his retirement.

Brian Gomm liked to win at sport and in life but was easy in his own skin and able to rub along with everyone, whatever their station in life. His daughter, Jackie, confirms that 'he was an amusing and sometimes deliberately provocative raconteur, who saw the best in people and had tremendous enthusiasm and energy, but also had a calm and steely resolve'.

A major project in later life was the building of a holiday home on the Greek Island of Paros. His son, Robin, an architect, designed and oversaw the building of what became a much-loved retreat for friends and family.

He died in hospital in Peterborough on 23 April 1995 at the age of seventy-six. His wife, Jeanette, died in 2016 at the age of ninety-four.

350
Geoffrey Everingham Fletcher
29 July 1939 v. Northamptonshire, Northampton

Geoffrey Fletcher was born on 20 July 1919, at Charterhouse School in Godalming. His father, Major Philip Cawthorne Fletcher, married to Edith Maud (née Okell), was a teacher there and Geoffrey one of four children. Philip Fletcher would become something of an institution at Charterhouse, teaching at the school until 1945 and elected Mayor of Godalming on three occasions. He was a man of great energy and for many years a member of the Godalming Operatic Society. His son Geoffrey was sent to Marlborough College, where he proved a fine sportsman, in the hockey and cricket First

Geoffrey Everingham Fletcher – a fine sportsman whose life was cut short in the Second World War.

BY KIND PERMISSION OF MARLBOROUGH COLLEGE

XIs for three years and captain of both in his final year. He was also intellectually outstanding, winning an Exhibition to New College, Oxford. In 1939 he was awarded a hockey blue, having already appeared for the Wiltshire team as a teenager. Described by *Wisden* in its summary of the 1938 season as 'one of the best school cricketers of the year', it is almost certain that he would have gained a blue, but for the war. A right-handed batsman, although he had played in four first-class games for Oxford in 1939, with a top score of 65, he had not been selected for the Varsity match. He would play in only one match for Somerset, scoring 34 runs while being once dismissed. We are left to ponder what this talented young man could have brought to Somerset cricket, had the Second World War not cut short his university education, his sporting career and indeed his life.

Commissioned as a second lieutenant in the Prince Consort's Own Rifle Brigade in March 1940, he had risen to the rank of captain by the time of his involvement in the so-called Battle of the Mareth Line in March 1943. The objective was to wrest control of strategic positions in Tunisia. The mission would succeed but with the loss of approximately 4,000 Allied lives and substantial though less numerous losses for the Italians and Germans who retreated in good order.

The summary of the events that led to Geoffrey Fletcher's demise, written by Lt Col F. Stephens of the 1st Battalion of the Rifle Brigade, is unsentimental and precise, confirming that, having been given orders the previous evening for a dawn attack, the battalion arrived at the start line at 04:45. At 05:00 the twenty-minute barrage had commenced and the troops had assaulted the enemy position, capturing it in less than an hour with 'news of success sent to Battalion HQ by wireless'. Among the casualties, two officers are listed: Major Kelly (commander of C Company) and Captain Fletcher (commander of I Company).

A bright young man with the world at his feet had had his life snuffed out on 27 March 1943 at the age of twenty-three at Djebel Saikra, Matmata in Tunisia. He lies buried in the nearby Sfax War Cemetery in Tunisia.

After the war his parents retained their ties with Somerset. Major Philip Fletcher had purchased Hinton Priory near Bath in 1932 and set about restoring it after retiring from Charterhouse in 1945. In 2010, his grandson, a nephew of Geoffrey, Rt Rev. Colin Fletcher, Bishop of Dorcheseter, opened a new day house for sixth formers at Charterhouse, known as *Fletcherites*. It was named neither after Geoffrey nor his father, Philip, but after the latter's cousin, Sir Frank Fletcher, a former headmaster of Charterhouse. A talented family, then, who had earlier been robbed by the war of one of their own – a young man who had shown immense promise.

351
Hugh Edmund Watts
19 August 1939 v. Hampshire, Bournemouth

Hugh Watts

Hugh Watts was born on 4 March 1922 in Stratton-on-the-Fosse, Somerset. His father, Nevile Hunter Watts had earlier been a schoolmaster at Downside School. Nevile's sister, Helen, was a prominent suffragette who was twice imprisoned for her beliefs, first at Holloway Prison and then at Leicester Prison, from whence she was released following a hunger strike. After ninety hours, her protest had begun to stir too much public animosity against the authorities for their comfort. She was feted in the Nottingham area, where her father – Hugh's paternal grandfather – was at the time the vicar of Lenton, on the outskirts of the city. Her friend and fellow-suffragette, Emily Blathwayt, would write that 'she is a nice girl, but difficult to talk with because besides being very deaf ... she speaks so that it is difficult to under-. stand her'. The affliction had not stopped Helen from bravely standing up and making a number of public speeches on the injustices of the voting system. She was also prepared to speak up against some of the tactics deployed by fellow suffragettes, in particular the campaign of arson attacks on bastions of male chauvinism, including cricket pavilions.

Prominent suffragette Helen Watts (top) and her nephew, Hugh (above), who opted for calmer waters as a teacher at Downside.

Nevile and his wife, Clare, would have six children, all boys. The subsequent electoral changes would therefore have little or no impact on the voting rights of Hugh or his brothers. Hugh attended Downside School, where he was a successful left-handed batsman and leg-break bowler. Indeed, such was his reputation as a schoolboy cricketer that he was invited to a trial with Somerset. He would later recount the tale of how in that match Arthur Wellard had him plumb LBW but failed to appeal. When Hugh later politely admitted to Arthur that he had been expecting an appeal, Arthur revealed that he had been under strict instructions that the committee should have a good look at the schoolboy and an early dismissal was therefore to be avoided. He was drafted

Hugh Edmund Watts in the Peterhouse College cricket XI.

into the county side while still at Downside and before going on to Peterhouse College, Cambridge. He would win his cricketing blue, although not until he resumed his studies after the Second World War, where he served in the Greenjackets (the Rifle Brigade). Commissioned as a second lieutenant, he would finally leave the military in 1947 with the honorary rank of major. While serving in Italy he had been seriously wounded when a bullet narrowly missed a lung and lodged in his right shoulder. It was never removed.

After completing his degree he came back to Downside to teach History and act as cricket coach. Known to his teammates as 'The Abbot' on account of the black Benedictine habit many at the school wore, he would play for Somerset sixty-one times between 1939 and 1952, as and when scholastic duties allowed. On some days, his headmaster was persuaded to release Hugh during term time, such as the occasion in 1948 when Somerset, having appointed three captains to share the duty, were unable to call on any of them so that Hugh was asked to step into the breach. According to an obituary by David Foot, Hugh undertook his captaincy duties 'with quiet charm and a classless manner that pleased the professionals'. During his career with Somerset he made one century and fifteen half-centuries, coming away with a batting average of 25.11. He took no wickets in the few overs he bowled.

He was married in 1953 to Ursula Mary (née Dodson) with whom he would have three sons and a daughter.

In 1963 he left Downside to found a Roman Catholic prep school with Dereck Henderson, a teacher at St Edward's School, Oxford, and a fellow cricketing blue. Moor Park is based near Ludlow and opened its gates in 1964 with 10 boys. By the time of Hugh Watts's departure in the 1980s, it housed 160 boarders and 50 day pupils.

After retiring to Trebetherick in Cornwall, Hugh was frequently to be seen on the golf course and was Captain and Secretary of the St Enodoc Golf Club. He died in Trebetherick on 21 December 1993 at the age of seventy-one.

Born in the county and Oxbridge educated, a very good cricketer but not a great one, Hugh Watts is perhaps the quintessential Somerset cricketer. It is therefore fitting that he was the final man to make his debut before the onset of the Second World War. During the match against Derbyshire at the County Ground, at the end of August 1939, his captain, Bunty Longrigg, remarked to Hugh that this was likely to be the last time they would play together. He was wrong. Both men would appear after the war. Six men would lose their lives in the conflict, the greatest losses in cricketing terms being Peter McRae and Geoffrey Fletcher, neither of whom would have the opportunity to fulfil their potential.

And, just as they had done in 1919, Somerset would surprise everyone in 1946. This time they would reach the dizzyingly high position of fourth in the County Championship, Harold Gimblett delighting the crowds with nearly 2,000 runs and Arthur Wellard, undimmed by his advancing years, picking up 119 wickets.

That, though, was as good as it would get for a number of years.

Index of Somerset Cricketers 1919-1939

Order of debut appearance shown in brackets.
Page reference for each player's biography is also given.

Sanders, A. T. (230) 17
Scott, D. E. (337) 277
Seamer, J. W. (316) 223
Smith, C. F. See Fairbanks-Smith, C.
Southcombe, R. (342) 289
Spurway, F. E. (241) 42
Spurway, M. V. (302) 189
Stanbury, R. V. M. (327) 256

Thomas, W. R. (292) 166
Thomson, A. E. (264) 98

Waldock, F. A. (244) 48
Watson, A. M. (314) 219
Watson, J. R. (318) 229
Watts, H. E. (351) 315
Weaver, S. (348) 306
Wellard, A. W. (288) 156
Wharton, L. E. (250) 65
Whiting, W. S. (255) 79
Wilde, W. S. (298) 183
Wilkins, D. A. (286) 153
Winter, C. A. (260) 87
Woodcock, G. (253) 73

ERRATA

The following errors were included in **Somerset Cricketers 1882-1914**:

Pg 71 – J.J.A. Parfitt d. *15.05.1926* should read *17.05.1926*

Pg 84 – J. E. Trask b. *27.11.1861* should read *27.10.1861*

Pg 96 – T. Crump d. *18.01.1907* should read *08.01.1907*

Pg 119 – L. C. H. Palairet b. *25.07.1870* should read *27.05.1870*

Pg 196 – G. R. Hunt d. *Old Burleston* should read *Old Burlesdon*

Pg 231 – F. P. Hardy b. *26.06.1881* should read *26.06.1880*

Pg 339 – J. Bridges d.*29.09.1966* should read *26.09.1966*

Pg 364 – H. F. Garrett b. *13.11.1894* should read *21.12.1893*